Belonging to Others

Cultural Construction of Womanhood Among
Muslims in a Village in Bangladesh

By
Jitka Kotalová

UPPSALA 1993

Doctoral thesis at Uppsala University 1993

Abstract

Kotalová J., 1993. Belonging to Others. Cultural Construction of Womanhood Among Muslims in a Village in Bangladesh. Acta Universitatis Upsaliensis. *Uppsala Studies in Cultural Anthropology* 19. 252 pp. Uppsala. ISBN 91-554-3105-4.

This study is about womanhood. It addresses the discourse within anthropology of experience and anthropology of gender. A Bangladeshi Muslim community provides its ethnographic focus.

Bangladesh society is structured through two distinct yet mutually dependent systems. One is based on lineal succession and age seniority of men, the other on exchange of women in marriage.

Muslims in Bangladesh assume that a woman is detachable in two senses: from her birthgroup, and from one husband to another. Marriage thus means spatial and social continuity for a man, but transformation for a woman. Because a woman is rendered transformable, she is considered to be in need of protection and control. In Bangladesh this entails institutionalised restraint on her spatial mobility and social visibility.

At marriage a woman's sense of belonging is divided between father's and husband's home. She thus retains double membership, and a degree of distance from both. In this, married women epitomize outsideness much like that of the anthropologist in the field. Both share the experience of attachment-and-distance in their common concern to understand a new world. Both must interpret their experience of double belonging in order to know how to go on.

My aim is to describe the social organisation, to specify the context on which my understanding of life in Bangladesh is grounded, and to comment on the process by which ethnographic knowledge is produced.

A prime ethnographic concern is to explicate: moral order and categories of distinction within which a person in South Asia operates; agnatic ethos within which concepts of gender are embedded among Muslims.

The normative order is discussed first in the whole-part relation at the conceptual level, and then as the process through which it is upheld in daily life in disciplinary procedures and a systematic corporal-verbal didactics. Further I demonstrate how the agnatic constructs—patriline and community—are constituted: patriline through lexical, moral, biogenetic and botanical metaphors of belonging; community through the way it is recreated in prayers, funerals and food exchanges.

Womanhood is portrayed as a series of transformations on and with a woman's body; attainment of her social completeness is conveyed through symbolic analysis of wedding; the sense of double belonging which wifehood implies becomes apparent through analysis of post-marital journeying to the natal home.

The epistemological focus of this study is: cultural learning and management of otherness; incorporation of metaphor in the process of learning, and its strategic power; ludic features in rituals of transformation.

Throughout the study emphasis is placed on: transformational nature of cultural categories; the uses people make of cultural stereotypes; the means through which the dominant imagery may be reversed or alternative views to dominant ethos expressed.

I argue that the actors use the social structure imaginatively, and that the restraints actually provide opportunities for a critical view. In fact, muslim women in Bangladesh achieve dissent from authoritative discourse by resorting to the very means that are meant to silence them.

Jitka Kotalová, Uppsala University, Department of Cultural Anthropology, Trädgårdsgatan 18, S-752 20 Uppsala, Sweden.

ISBN 91-554-3105-4
ISSN 0348-5099

Distributor: Almqvist & Wiksell International, Stockholm, Sweden

Printed in Sweden
Textgruppen i Uppsala AB, 1993

ACTA UNIVERSITATIS UPSALIENSIS
Uppsala Studies in Cultural Anthropology 19
Distributor: Almqvist & Wiksell International, Box 4627,
S-116 91 Stockholm, Sweden

Jitka Kotalová
Belonging to Others
Cultural Construction of Womanhood Among Muslims in a Village in
Bangladesh

Doctoral dissertation to be publicly examined in room 1025, Kulturantropolo-
giska institutionen, Trädgårdsgatan 18, on Friday 28th of May, at 10.15 a.m.,
for the degree of Doctor of Philosophy

Abstract
Kotalová J., 1993. Belonging to Others. Cultural Construction of Womanhood Among Muslims
in a Village in Bangladesh. Acta Universitatis Upsaliensis. *Uppsala Studies in Cultural Anthropology* 19. 252 pp. Uppsala. ISBN 91-554-3105-4.

This study is about womanhood. It addresses the discourse within anthropology of experience and
anthropology of gender. A Bangladeshi Muslim community provides its ethnographic focus.
   Bangladesh society is structured through two distinct yet mutually dependent systems. One is
based on lineal succession and age seniority of men, the other on exchange of women in marriage.
   Muslims in Bangladesh assume that a woman is detachable in two senses: from her birthgroup,
and from one husband to another. Marriage thus means spatial and social continuity for a man, but
transformation for a woman. Because a woman is rendered transformable, she is considered to be
in need of protection and control. In Bangladesh this entails institutionalised restraint on her spatial mobility and social visibility.
   At marriage a woman's sense of belonging is divided between father's and husband's home.
She thus retains double membership, and a degree of distance from both. In this, married women
epitomize outsideness much like that of the anthropologist in the field. Both share the experience
of attachment-and-distance in their common concern to understand a new world. Both must interpret their experience of double belonging in order to know how to go on.
   My aim is to describe the social organisation, to specify the context on which my understanding of life in Bangladesh is grounded, and to comment on the process by which ethnographic
knowledge is produced.
   A prime ethnographic concern is to explicate: moral order and categories of distinction within
which a person in South Asia operates; agnatic ethos within which concepts of gender are embedded among Muslims.
   The normative order is discussed first in the whole-part relation at the conceptual level, and
then as the process through which it is upheld in daily life in disciplinary procedures and a systematic corporal-verbal didactics. Further I demonstrate how the agnatic constructs—patriline and
community—are constituted: patriline through lexical, moral, biogenetic and botanical metaphors
of belonging; community through the way it is recreated in prayers, funerals and food exchanges.
   Womanhood is portrayed as a series of transformations on and with a woman's body; attainment of her social completeness is conveyed through symbolic analysis of wedding; the sense of
double belonging which wifehood implies becomes apparent through analysis of post-marital
journeying to the natal home.
   The epistemological focus of this study is: cultural learning and management of otherness; incorporation of metaphor in the process of learning, and its strategic power; ludic features in rituals
of transformation.
   Throughout the study emphasis is placed on: transformational nature of cultural categories; the
uses people make of cultural stereotypes; the means through which the dominant imagery may be
reversed or alternative views to dominant ethos expressed.
   I argue that the actors use the social structure imaginatively, and that the restraints actually provide opportunities for a critical view. In fact, muslim women in Bangladesh achieve dissent from
authoritative discourse by resorting to the very means that are meant to silence them.

*Jitka Kotalová, Uppsala University, Department of Cultural Anthropology, Trädgårdsgatan 18,
S-752 20 Uppsala, Sweden.*

Uppsala 1993   252 pp.
ISBN 91-554-3105-4

Acta Universitatis Upsaliensis
Uppsala Studies in Cultural Anthropology
19

Contents

Acknowledgements

I would like to thank the agencies whose grants made my research possible. The fieldwork research was sponsored by the Swedish Council for Research in the Humanities and Social Sciences and the Swedish International Development Authority. A four-year post-graduate study scholarship was provided by Uppsala University. The Wallenberg Foundation sponsored my research at the India Office Library and Records in London in 1986 as well as my participation in the European Conference of the Bangladesh Studies Group in Bath 1988. The Swedish Institute supported me financially at the time of my affiliation with the School of Oriental and African Studies in London in 1988/89. Additional aid was received from Uppsala University—Schwartz stipend grant and twice a travel grant for post-graduate researchers. I am grateful to the Axelsson Johnsson Foundation for providing access to their premises—the study room at Craven Street—during my study visits to London.

SIDA's Training Center in Uppsala offered opportunities to earn money which made it possible to survive the lean periods.

I am grateful to Professor Anita Jacobson-Widding for her efforts to secure financial aid while still letting me write in my own way.

My thanks to The Royal Society of the Humanities at Uppsala for a generous printing grant.

The discussions with anthropologist Michael Jackson, during the workshop he held at the Department of Cultural Anthropology in Uppsala in the Autumn of 1987, provided an intellectual life-line at a time when I did not know how to go on with this project. The epistemology he propounded as a writer and lecturer were an example to me of anthropological scholarship.

I also profited from discussions with Birgitta Holm, Mona Eliasson and Birgitta Paget through the seminar they organised at the Centre for Women's Studies at Uppsala University in the Spring of 1988; not only on problems of gender but also on a wide range of theoretical topics.

I would like to thank Enid Nelson for her hospitality, and her patient and amused listening to the bewildered accounts of my fieldwork and Asian Odyssey on my return, and for converting my first attempts to textualise it into readable English. And to Monica Udvardy for introducing me to the mysteries of word-processing as well as for her willingness to dispute, at any time, any topic of anthropology, feminism or life. I thank all those colleagues at the Department who helped to recover the pieces of my text which in the course of writing were recurrently lost to the memory of the computer.

I am especially grateful to my archeological friends, Helena Sofkova-Knutsson and Kjel Knutsson, who made the loneliness of writing bearable; I thank their colleague at the Department of Archeology in Uppsala Jackeline Taffinder for editing a couple of initial drafts. For working on final drafts I thank Margareth Sykes and Gordon Evans who attacked my over-long sentences and searched in vain for the words I had invented.

Again, I gratefuly acknolwedge the support of the Swedish Institute which enabled me to stay in London in the Autumn of 1988 and the Spring of 1989. While affiliated to SOAS I had the opportunity of attending lectures by David Parkin, post-graduate seminars at the Department of Anthropology and Sociology as well as inter-collegial anthropological seminars at the University of London; all provided a great source of intellectual excitement and inspiration. I am particularly indebted to Audrey Cantlie and Nancy Tapper, who at the beginning of my stay at SOAS jointly supervised my work and who, from a very different critical perspective have, through their qeustions and suggestions, forced me to rethink my own position on many problems. Throughout my stay and up to the present Audrey Cantlie has read, commented and edited various drafts of each chapter. I owe a great debt to her for her guidance and good humour. She gave me confidence to pursue my own ideas. Because of her experience and knowledge of the South Asian world and her insight into other worlds as well, she succeeded in persuading me that I could actually make it. For this I shall remain in her debt.

The creativity of my London period was also due to the violoncellist Asa Jacobsson with whom I shared the flat at Craven Street; her rehearsals of Arpeggione sonata aleviated the unbearable heaviness of writing a doctoral dissertation and made my stay there most pleasant.

For taking the time to answer my letters requesting ethnographic advice I wish to thank Peter J. Bertocci, Therese Blanchet, Erik af Edholm, Alf Hornborg, Clarence Maloney, Eva Pettigrew, Aminur Rahman (Tipu), Eva Rosen-Hockersmith, and Willem van Schendell. I also gratefully remember the Bangladesh-related talks with Alia and Giazzudin Ahmad in Lund, Therese Blanchet in Dhaka, Oxford and London, Shafiqur (Jewel) Rahman and Farouk Faisel in Uppsala, Meghna Guhathakurta in York and Sarah White in Bath and Oxford, which in the course of writing provided new insights and made the Bengali culture vividly present even after fieldwork.

I would like to thank the following people for providing shelter, food, hot showers, medicine and words of encouragement during my fieldwork—anthropologist Therese Blanchet in Dhaka, Professor Shahanara Hussain at Rajshahi University, Dr. and Mrs. Aktarul Zaman, my ex-colleagues stationed at SIDA's Development Co-operation Office in Dhaka 1982–83, my friends among the Southern Baptist Mission, 7th Day Adventist, HEED and the Roman Catholic Mission—particularly Thom and Gloria Thurman, Dr.Tamara Sleeter, Linda Mitchell, Eva Pettigrew and Padre Decembrino. A special note of thanks goes to Sheik Belayet Hussain, who in spite of his conviction that no European ever could understand Bengali society, helped me to an understanding of life in Gameranga from the male point of view.

My deepest appreciation goes to the villagers of Gameranga for tolerating my intrusion into their private lives and their patience in answering my questions which they certainly found strange. They gave me food, protection, laughter and a different life: a life of Belonging to Others.

Uppsala, December 1990

Preface

Late one night, on December 22nd 1988 in York, thinking of a motto for my dissertation, I asked my friend and host Meghna Guhathakurta: "Do you know of a Bengali metaphor that depicts the unpredictable nature of women? Something that would do as a motto for my book?"

"Many! I cannot remember one right now, but let me sleep on it; if worst comes to worst I'll compose one for you myself".

When I entered the kitchen the next morning a tape recorder was on and emitting the familiar tones of a *desher gan*.

"Here is the song for you ... do you like *Bangla cha* or English? ... It is Farida Parvin singing, likening your female informants to the shiftiness of deltaic landscape".

It went:

Ei Padma, ei Meghna, ei Jomuna, Shurma nodi tote amar rakhal mon gan geye jae.
The Padma, The Meghna, The Jomuna, The Shuroma, my wondering heart sings along the riverbank.
Ei amar desh, amar prem, anondo-bedonae, milano, biroho-shonkote.
This is my land, my love in joy and sorrow, union and separation—in times of crisis.
Ei Padma, ei Meghna, hajar nodir obobahike.
The Padma, the Meghna in the delta of a thousand rivers.
Ekhane romonigulo nodir moto, nari-o nodir moto kotha koe ...
Women here are like rivers, like rivers women speak ...

Bangla cha—tea prepared Bengali fashion
desher gan—patriotic song
rakhal mon—distracted mind, soul, heart
shonkote—breakdown, crisis, trouble

Encompassment of the Fieldworker

CHAPTER 1
Aim of study

This is a study of social organisation, focusing on the symbolic construction of womanhood in a Muslim peasant community in Bangladesh. My aim is twofold: ethnographic and epistemological. By a thorough explication of how the two levels of social organisation—agnation and affinity—are imagined, spoken and lived on the ground as interpenetrating categories and arrangements of belonging, I shall explore the way gender, womanhood in particular, is constructed among Bangladeshi Muslims.

Aside from ethnography I shall specify some of the contexts on which my understanding of life in Bangladesh is grounded. As a result this text also provides a commentary on the process by which ethnographic knowledge is produced.

Bangladesh society is structured through at least two distinct but overlapping systems: one based on agnatic lineality (lineal succession and age seniority of males); the other on exchange of women in marriages by which the continuity of patrilines is secured. Gender conceptions are thus embedded in a wider ethos of agnation which constitutes the principal locus of objectification in Bangladesh.

The most striking characteristic of the agnatic emphasis in Bengali Muslim culture is that half of its population—those who retain an eminent role as life-sustainers—are defined by their absence. Unless thoroughly concealed, women are not to be seen at public events, in the street or on public transport. In public discourse women are explicitly denied any value. On specifying the attributes of "people of this land" when providing self-definitions, or stating the "number of children in the family" informants, even female, provide definitions from which one-half of the population—themselves—is persistently excluded. The invisibility of women in the public sphere which initially prompted my interest in gender thus proved to be refracted through and embedded in many different social spaces and symbolic systems.

Another feature of agnation in Bangladesh is that marriage (as the principal form of gender relatedness and the mark of adulthood i.e. completeness), means spatial and social continuity for a man but transformation for a woman. Because a woman is rendered transformable, and hence in need of protection and control (which in Bangladesh entails restraint on her spatial mobility and visibility), her experience of social structure leads her into an ambiguous position. At marriage a woman's sense of belonging is divided between father's and husband's home. She retains a double membership in, and hence a degree of distance from both. She does not quite belong to either the father's or the husband's patriline. En route in between these two points of orientation she views the world from behind the veil and the world views her as one without an independent position. In this sense of domestic belonging, married women epitomize outsideness analogous to that of the anthropologist in the field. The shared element is the experience of tension between similarity and difference (attachment–distance) implied in their common concern to understand a hitherto unknown world. The fervor to adjust without getting dissolved (Kondo 1986), to recover meaning from the experience of double belonging, and to know how to go on, are central to both situations.

While agnation preserves the unbreakable unity of patrilineally related males, marriage gives rise within each patriline to a category of outsiders (albeit putative): the imported wives. Thus marriage opens the patriline to the possibility of otherness and the danger of dissent while also securing patrilineal continuity and integration across agnatic ties. This means that alongside the discourse and imagery of lineal continuity (vertical ordering of reality), which is of indisputable ideological primacy, there exists a way of thinking about the self and a way of relating to the social world which is more diffuse and circuitous. Structurally, the institution aimed at sealing patrilineal integrity is also the main locus of dissent.

In this ethnographic context, I take relations of visibility/invisibility (actual and symbolic, physical and social) and continuity/ discontinuity (in relation to space and life stages) to be the main factors differentiating women's and men's perspectives on belonging. My basic contention is that Bengali Muslim women's sense of self and belonging is profoundly affected by the shift in space they undergo at marriage and by their position as a muted, invisible category vis à vis men. It is also my contention that all non-dominant groups— women in this case—are to a greater extent than the dominant groups, aware of this double perspective on social structure; the physical move Bengali Muslim women undertake on marriage makes the tension between belonging and distance, with its ensuing double vision, particularly pronounced.

These contexts invite the central questions of my inquiry:

How does a society that sustains the invisibility and muteness of women, construct womanhood from birth to marriage?

If women constitute a separate category from men, as suggested by their veiling and ritual exclusion on the public scene, how is their sense of belonging (or separateness) organised, articulated and reproduced in various cultural domains?

If the dominant structure and ethos are articulated in terms of male position and orientation, what are the cultural provisions for articulation of muted, non-dominant views?

How do women assimilate themselves into the structure that subordinates them?

These questions relate to the the grounds of human actions and ideas about the self (Marcus 1986:45). I posit "belonging" rather than "identity" as the focus of investigation. While identity suggests an objectified, frozen self in fusion with society, belonging points to the fluidity of the cultural setting and the relational dynamics within which the self in Bangladesh is produced. In other words it emphasizes the interactional and contextual grounding of cultural meaning and the embeddedness of social organization in human relations.

Dealing with social organisation as an organisation of belonging invites a distinction between conceptualisation of human beings as persons belonging to a society and human being as a self experiencing that belonging. This distinction between 'outer' and 'inner' aspects of being was introduced to anthropological discourse by Mauss (1968[1938]). Other earlier contribution was Freud's work on the relation between "conscious understanding and unconscious dynamics embedded in social relations and cultural forms" (Marcus 1986:46; see Crapanzano 1980, Kakar 1978,1984, Obeyesekere 1981)[1]. Ethnographic studies of reflexive awareness[2] owe much to Mead (1934), who pioneered the theory of self. Kapferer (1984) is one of Mead's followers in assuming that "self is a product of social experience". Singer (1984:81,83) presents a similar line in his exegesis of Peirce's semiotic theory.

An analytical distinction between the concepts of individual, self, and person is proposed by Harris (1989, see also Leach 1982:149). Harris stresses the need for such a distinction to avoid the confusion prevalent in many ethnographies. While I take her critical review as a useful starting point, to apply the concepts consistently to my data poses some problems which I discuss below. The main difficulty lies in the plural, indeterminate nature of the culture studied (Marriott 1976, Ramanujan, Tambiah 1974, chapter 2 and 7 below) and also in the nature of fieldwork (chapter 3) upon which my knowledge is mainly grounded.

[1] The current interest in cultural critique makes the list of ethnographic literature concerned with self far too voluminous to be listed here. It includes some of the authors quoted in this text. Schwartzman (1978) interpreting play and Handelman (1979) re-reading Naven, gained from the theoretical insights of Bateson (1956). Others acknowledge the influence from the social linguistics of Bakhtin (Karp 1987) and Benveniste (Fernandez 1985). Those approaches to self which appear in the most recent studies in the anthropology of experience derive their insights from the hermeneutics of Gadamer (Bellah 1979, Kondo 1986) and the phenomenology of Merleau-Ponty (Csordas 1989, Jackson 1983a,b) and Dilthey (Turner 1982, 1984).

Studies concerned with concepts of the person include but are not limited to Cohen (1985), Dumont (1980), Fortes (1983), Goffman (1975), Jacobson-Widding (1983), Marriott (1976), Roy (1975), Singer (1984) and Östör (1982).

[2] Concerned with ritual performance, Kapferer (1984) voices his theoretical filiation with Mead as he writes: "Individuals have a self and an awareness of conscioussness of it; in other words they reflect upon it if they take the attitude of the 'other' and respond in accordance with a set of social and cultural typifications, that Mead called the 'generalised other'".

Belonging to a kind of specie

Harris suggests that the concept of the individual be used for a member of hu-man-kind, i.e. a "normal" human being. In her view, the command of lan-guage is the most important attribute as it enables humans to develop a self and to participate in "social interaction as discourse". The second major fea-ture is body composition and structure. (I shall return to this bodily aspect in the discussion of self).

To equate a "normal" human being with the individual poses a problem. The very core of the South Asian monistic world-view is a belief that "every dif-ferential set of substances and beings"—rocks, animals, humans, spirits, non-Muslims, men, women—is conceptualised as *jat*. The *jat*s differ not only by capacity to speak or by physical shape but also through particular codes of moral order (*dhormo*)[3]. The code of moral order for humans is inherent in their physical substance, yet it is subject to modification by actions (Marriott 1976). For example an anthropologist conceptualised as one of a different *jat* at the beginning of fieldwork was partially absorbed in exchange for giving out "from [herself] particles of [her] own ... [essence]" (Marriott ibid). As Harris acknowledges, the differentiation of agentive capacities that character-ise personhood (below) is culturally specific. In the Bengali concept of agency, the supernatural species (*bhut*, Lokhi) are endowed with a capacity to induce auspiciousness or misfortune. In this way even non-humans possess the attribute of personhood.

A forceful critique of the universal applicability of the concept 'individual' has been raised by Dumont (1980). He asserts that an autonomous, "indivis-ible" individual is a product of Western political ideology and is incompatible with societies affirming explicit cultural premises of inequality.

Whereas Dumont's argument rests on examination of the Indian holistic system of caste hierarchy[4], Marriott derives his insights from the monistic premise of inseparability of moral code and substance. In view of the permea-bility of humans discussed above, I follow Marriott (ibid.) who suggests that

---

[3] The Sanskrit word *dharma*, pronounced in Bengali as "*dhormo*", refers to three categories of Hindu ethics: "the eternal ... principle of harmony pervading the entire universe; the caste *dharma*, relativistic ethical system varying from caste to caste; and the personal moral conduct of the individual ...". In orthodox Hinduism *dharma* thus subsumes "the totality of social, ethical, and spiritual harmony" (Lannoy 1975:217) and "is only possible, and valuable, when [its oppo-site] *adharma* also exists to balance and contrast with it" (O'Flaherty 1976:13, see also Khare 1982, Selwyn 1981). Following the Bengali Muslim peasants I use the word whenever I refer to 1) the moral code or normative principle which guides but not entirely determines a person's ac-tion, 2) the actions directed to sustain a particular lifestyle, 3) the features defining that lifestyle and 4) appropriateness of a person's action according to her social position (i.e agency). For fur-ther discussion of the use of *dhormo* by my informants see chapter 6, 7 and 8.

[4] In contrast with the explicit moral discourse in the West, which stresses equality of all humans, Indian social organisation appears as a "Social whole informed by hierarchical opposition of pure and impure, where human beings are regarded as possessing different and unequal attributes of humanity" (Carter 1982).

the term "dividual" fits better than "individual" with the South Asian way of thinking[5]. In this view "transactions between dividual actors are at the same time transformations within such actors, while transformations of the actor are simultaneously transactions within the actor" (Carter 1982). The transformational styles of Bangladeshi Muslims, with respect to belonging in a wider sense (to a *jat*, unit of social structure, piece of land, or to another person) are focused on in chapters 3, 7, and 11.

Being a person

Personhood, as Harris points out, entails agency. To be a person means being publically considered an agent, i.e. "somebody who authors" his action. The focus on cultural agent directs attention to standing or "belonging" in the sociomoral order of society, an object to be studied in relation to culture[6]. Conceptualising human beings as agents does not mean that personhood is always fully attained or even ascribed to all. Agency presupposes public recognition. There is an ongoing "process of analysing, interpreting, and labeling of conduct so as to generate a stream of public discourse about agency and nonagency" (Harris ibid.). Not all the doings of humans pass as purposefully directed actions. Harris claims that agentive capacities may be declared or denied: "Imputing to people the absence of agentive capacities renders them as lesser persons, non-persons, or former persons". Personhood thus, like belonging, is a dynamic concept; both have a temporal dimension and are situationally contextualised. The range of these capacities is critically related to the construction of gender (chapter 10, 11). While competing discourses co-exist with respect to most domains of knowledge, there was a concensus in the area of my study as to the location of women's agentive capacities. Accordingly, women's agency is critically bound to their reproductive ability (i.e. biology) and their adjustment to the affinal group (management of self). As there is no alternative moral career for a woman (female *jat*) beyond wifehood and motherhood the range of these capacities is narrower for women than for men and, because rooted in biology, also liable to circumstances which are beyond the total control of the authors (wives not husbands are accountable for a couple's reproductive failure). Declarations like "women lack any value", "do not listen to them", a tendency to discount female children in interviews point clearly to the curtailment on agency and thus of personhood.

---

[5] While I agree with Marriott's idea of "dividual", in the text I usually prefer to use the term "person".

[6] This is not to claim that there exists a mechanical causality between a person and the environment (Singer 1984:158). As Goffman (1975) and others (Bettelheim 1987) show, "some measure of freedom to choose among possible lines of action" (Harris ibid.) is universally assigned to the person even in the most totalitarian of social institutions or organisations.

Diminution of personhood and constitution of self

Self constitutes the existential locus of a person. To focus on selves is to direct observation on the experiencing, self-aware human beings. Selfhood entails reflexive awareness, i.e. recognition of oneself as an "object in a world of objects" (Csordas 1989, Harris ibid., see also note 2). Person and self are related but different concepts. While agentive capacities constituting a person are liable to public confirmation and may therefore be denied to some, the workings of a self—the capacity to experience and interpret—is not. Self develops in an interaction with others and is thus continuously refracted by external factors. Therefore it relates to personhood in an indirect, opaque way.

While disclaiming the possibility of knowing the precise nature of my self or the selves of others I admit that the question of "How is it to be like a Bengali Muslim woman" has engaged my imagination since my first encounter with Bangladesh. One must ask how people declared to be lesser persons or non-persons at times, manage to reconstitute their selves? I first became aware of women in Bangladesh in their absence. The actual encounter took place after I arrived as an investigating anthropologist in their households. The nature of that dialogue[7] is condensed in the episodes in chapters 3 and 12.

Rather than intrapsychic structures and processes, I limit my concern with self to questions regarding the possibilities of social order which permit partial-persons to develop self-awareness. Perhaps diminution of agency correlates with a range of cultural devices which permit liberation and resistance in everyday life. It seems that the very means employed to restrict movement and speech may possess properties counteractive of the goals they are aimed to achieve (see chapter 9).

I maintain that veiling and silencing restrict womanhood among Muslims in Bangladesh, but at the same time constitute sanctioned ways in which society paradoxically institutionalizes doubt and questioning. Both, are also forms of concealment and distancing that provide opportunities for assuming a critical stance. The tight link between ludic and didactiv features in rituals in which women achieve personhood-wedding (chapter 18) and post-marital journeying (chapter 12), enables women to produce their own version of the two worlds (natal and affinal) and so to perform critical interpretations. Thus the rituals through which a women attains adulthood make her "the student of herself" (Babcock 1984).

---

[7] I rely on Marcus' (1986:30) explication of the concept: "Dialogue has become the imagery for expressing the way anthropologists (and by extension, their readers) must engage in an active communicative process with another culture. It is a two-way and two-dimensional exchange, interpretive processes being necessary both for communication internally within a cultural system and externally between systems of meaning." I would add that the quotations of informants as well as other cultural interpreters which appear in the text are an extension of this dialogue—an attempt to transform "a monological performance into a dialogue" (Babcock 1984). My concept of dialogue also covers thinking that "takes the form of an inner dialogue structurally similar to and continuous with the outer dialogue of conversation with others" (Singer 1984:81).

Emphasising language as a factor differentiating homo sapiens from other species, Harris points to its subversive potential: "In the public world of mutual construal, people use and manipulate the structure and generative capacities of their own language and culture to create, re-create, and alter their institutions". In contrast, the body—as another criterion in distinguishing humans—is referred to by its external characteristic—shape, composition, growth (Harris ibid.). While these signs are of extreme importance in the Bengali discourse on *jat*[8], personal well-being[9] as well as agentive capacities[10], I hold that there is more to the human body than that[11].

As demonstrated in chapter 8, the earliest cultural learning of gender is accomplished through embodiment. An important consequence of this is that knowledge acquired corporally survives in an embodied state and hence the meaningful statements and acts (particularly of non-literate people) will not necessarily be conveyed verbally. Neither is the self-image or world-image of those people necessarily construed conceptually or through intellectual speculation. More than words, the movement and posture of the human body provide women (chapter 18) and men (chapter 10) with means of conveying a wide range of meanings. By extension, recognition that the knowing body is the speaking body (Jackson 1983) permits us to see the self-evident movements which are denied the status of action, (draping a sari around the body, tending a fire or pouring water) as meaningful operations of semantic creativity (Bourdieu 1986:115, Parkin 1982). The centrality of the human body as a means of self-expression is of particular importance to those categories of people whose discoursive capacities or physical access to the areas where the dominant discourse takes place is restricted[12].

Lastly and most importantly, I see the properties of social order and its cultural forms (focused on in chapters 9–16) as the central aims of my investiga-

---

[8] I had to re-compose my body and what pertains to it (see chapter 18) before any interaction with my informants could start yet the difference between mine and their bodies never ceased to engage their interest (Kotalová 1986).

[9] E.g. unoiled hair is attributed to maldisposition.

[10] For instance, as my body was deemed too "soft" for the performance of domestic tasks like cooking, laundry, making fire or carrying things, I had been denied the agency imputed to my gender in Bengali Muslim society. Also my real pursuit—walking around and writing down my observations—was by villagers construed as non-action.

[11] Recent work on child development (Trevarthen 1989) provides evidence that pre-linguistic self-awareness in human infants is developed long before acquisition of language and personhood (knowing how to behave and what to do). This means that emotional evaluation of relationships and social roles starts before the child learns language (ibid.).

[12] That human experience and knowledge is not necessarily expressed linguistically, is forcefully raised by Csordas (1989) who writes of "gestural constitution of self" and invokes Merleau-Ponty's notion of "language as a bodily act" or verbal gesture as a root of speech. Vygotsky (1986) writes of "inner speech", Jackson (1983 a,b) points out the centrality of bodily metaphor while Bakhtin (1986) links the lower order of carnival culture with the unrestricted use of the body that deals "a blow to the epistemological megalomania of the official culture" (Clark 1984:313, see also Bakhtin 1991:256,266). Bourdieu (1986) posits the body as the locus of cultural learning in his discusion of the concept of habitus.

tion, because these are constitutive of human agency (Harris ibid.). However, I would like to stress that the relationship between order and agents is in constant dialogue with other features that come into play in particular forms of communication. As shown in chapters 3, 12 and 18, apart from structural embeddedness, a person's belonging is something that is negotiated and produced in social interaction and is therefore fragmented through acts of interpretation and self-reflection.

CHAPTER 2

Theory, method and ethnographic writing

The pervasive problem of how to understand, analyse and describe the culture of the Muslim community in Bangladesh, is its inherent plurality[1]. Social units are overlapping, political loyalties rapidly shifting, statements of informants seem contradictory, always inconclusive. The scholars concerned with Bengali culture point to the "categorical and highly structured manner of regarding phenomena and of viewing a person's place in the society" (Lindenbaum 1968) on the one hand and to "hazy, unprecise overlapping of cultural categories" (Fruzzetti 1976b) on the other. The analyses of the social structure in the communities of the world's largest delta, are replete with attributes like "elusive", "fluid" (Bertocci 1970) and "resilient" (van Schendell 1981).

Both aspects—disposition for rigid categorization and hierarchical thinking as well as marked fluidity—were alternately experienced during my fieldwork. To a large extent, the refractions from the dominant ethos (agnatic hegemony) are embodied in various sub-cultures (sects, religions—which nevertheless constitute a critical component in construction of self and gender among Muslims) and in personal selves (men and women in various life-stages and moods). The existence of competing discourses is further embedded in a variety of cultural domains (e.g. the legal system in *bichar*, police station, *madrassa* or medical theories as propounded by local healers, midwives, Red-Cross hospital in the area). As will be demonstrated below, this plurality is highlighted in the confrontation with outsideness, such as an anthropologist's entry to the community. This is because encounter itself is an event "in which everyday order is challenged" (Bourdieu 1986) and because the ensuing dialogues vary with the perceived nature (substance) of the listener, the context and, most importantly, over time. As will be shown, mutual understanding is grounded on the interlocutors' position and expressive style as well as their previous experience of similar encounters; it has a temporal dimension. The time-span between my entry and departure from the field affected the local view of my outsideness and so the way my informants asserted themselves and emphasised accordingly various domains of belonging. Informants' experience with people like myself—a white, urban European

[1] By this I mean not the existence of different cultural groups within a single society, but the different viewpoints and shifting perspectives within a common culture. Ramanujan (1989) writes of "multiple diglossia" when he characterizes equally context-sensitive Indian culture.

Christian speaking the language of ex-colonialists undoubtedly influenced their expectations of myself.

Thus, aside from the cultural and interactional context, the progressive history of encounters weighs as an important factor diversifying the stereotypic dichotomy of self/other.

As a new guest I was presented with and socialized into a simple, typical model of womanhood. The instructions as to the proper ways for a decent woman, were given by way of powerful exaggeration of differences between them and myself, between women and men and also by way of a strong hierarchization of dichotomies. The gradual acquisition of an "old guest" status uncovered a chain of refractions of the objectified consensual views. As the tension between attachment/distance decreased, and the villagers re-positioned me inwards to the backstage, I was also exposed to a more heretic discourse of power and was then able to look outwards, across the boundaries they strove to maintain intact. This increased insideness made me aware of the contextual and situational nature of emphasis in local exegeses. What I had tended to experience as a split between exterior and private and between theory and practice gradually became blurred and undivided in my informants' conceptualization of life. The shift of my status and point of view (that affected my understanding), from relative strangeness to relative familiarity, can be paralleled by the situation of a new wife (*notun bou*) in a patrilocal culture like Bengali. *Notun bou* is a category that marks the most critical stage of a Bengali woman's life, denoting the marginality of a woman newly married, newly arrived and settled into a household which consists of virtual strangers. The association of wives with outsiders was re-affirmed when mobs of children drew attention to my presence by shouting "*notun bou* is here". Like foreigners, the wives and mothers come from somewhere else and "the basic dilemma of the agnatic group is to deal with the anomalous presence of those people who are in the group but not of it" (Whyte 1981). The *notun bou* as well views her husband's household and community with the shifting perspective of an outsider-and-an-insider, constantly interpreting, negotiating and consolidating between these two intellectual and emotional positions and between two sorts of belonging, agnation and affinity. To avoid repudiation, both *notun bou* and anthropologist balance the need to appear to conform to the rules and image of a woman at a particular life-stage against the need to maintain some degree of integrity. In terms of efficacy both have to provide tangible evidence in their respective spheres of practice that they contribute to the prosperity of the group to which they belong: a wife must objectify herself as a mother in the household into which she is married; for the anthropologist "fieldwork must culminate in the construction of ethnographic text" (Kondo 1986) in the academic community[2].

---

[2] See description of *nayor* in chapter 12 and chapter 18 n.39 for further discussion of the parallel between anthropologist and a new wife.

By way of introduction to cultural plurality, I have chosen the way my presence was seen at the point of entry as compared with subsequent perceptions. Here I would like to stress, that the dialogical nature of fieldwork is only one factor which gives to encounters their two-edged quality (i.e. self-image intended for others versus personal experience). As will be demonstrated throughout the volume, in Bengali Muslim culture itself there are domains which consists of values and orientations different from those that are propounded by the dominant ideology—agnatic hegemony and Islamic monotheism (cf. Ramanujan 1989). And it is even more important to consider that villagers, irrespective of their degree of subordination and poverty, are not passive recipients and followers of rules but active agents, using cultural tenets imaginatively and strategically as points for orientation. My exploration into cultural/gender identity among Bengali Muslims was initially guided by methodological concerns of academic anthropology which was then dominated by a search for synchronically operating structure according to which each culture was supposed to operate. An implicit intention was to find a kind of model for comparison. Fieldwork experience, however, shattered any attempt to "fix them" into such a model. It was not for lack of categorical statments of the dominant ideologies by informants and their insistence on rules. On the contrary, my field-notes are replete with such evidence. What intrigued me, however, was the ease with which my informants were ready to deconstruct the fixity of the universe they had so emphatically asserted. The means of expressing dissent available to people I studied are subtle. Apart from metaphors (and other tropes) they may resort to performative devices and various labile aspects of personal expression—such as furtive gestures and strategies, minute details in style of speech and dress or gaps like silence; or laughter or weeping filling these gaps. Body gestures and movements are such means per excellence. These fleeting, fugitive indices of social interaction, as Erving Goffman has shown, may prove the most decisive aspects of social existence (Bourdieu 1983, see also Csordas 1989, Karp 1987).

In verbal discourse deconstruction usually took the form of inserting sentences which immediately modified any generalised evaluation laden with a binary contrast. As if any assertion had to be qualified by a counterclaim: "to some extent", "maybe", "sometimes", "it depends", "everyone sees it differently", "not all people" were the provisions by which most explanations were introduced or concluded.

These reservations to the englobing generalizations were most poignantly expressed by a young landless farmer's daughter who refused to be my "assistant" when I approached her, but was eager to be my maid (*kajer lok*). On one occasion when she refused to accompany me to the post office on the grounds of decency ("mature girls like myself do not walk so far"), I wondered, "But your cousin Hosnara is also mature and unmarried, also poor, and I see her always on the road". In reply my companion extended my palm for scrutiny and retorted, "Are the five fingers on one hand alike?" (*Hater pach angul ki, ek-shomoy?*)

My informant seemed to recognize the subversive potential of figurative speech and resorted to metaphor to challenge my attempt to read her motives in simple structural terms. So, while I shall attempt to "fix" behaviour and actions in a structural model, I wish also to maintain the correspondence between the incongruities, contradictions and fluidity embedded in Bengali culture and my mode of presentation. This will also replicate the manner my informants presented themselves and the fragmentary, ambiguous, fleeting nature of fieldwork itself.

A note on transcription

Like most of my informants in Gameranga I am illiterate in Bengali. Given the domestic style of communication with my informants (i.e. discontinuous speech permeated with bodily gestures) and my learning through shared experience I have chosen to present Bengali terms as I perceived them being pronounced. Thus I avoid standard phonetic transcription which would make reading of the text unnecessarily tiresome. My transcription more or less conforms to Murshid's (1988) Dictionary but I have tried to preserve the peculiarities of the local dialect[3].

---

[3] I am grateful to Dr. Radeci from SOAS and Professor Maniruzzaman from Chittagong University for suggestions regarding the transcription but any mistakes are mine.

CHAPTER 3

Fieldwork:
implications for epistemology

It has been argued that the sense of belonging is heightened in encounter with outsiders (Cohen 1985:110–113, Boon 1982:6,25,213) particularly those of visibly non-domestic origin.

Accommodating an unescorted woman on uncertain business is not a daily event in village Bangladesh. For people of the community such an intrusion presents first of all the problem of confrontation with the possibility of otherness, even the existence of conceptual anomaly. In male-oriented cultures, gender becomes a salient point of comparison if the outsider is a woman. The questions regarding her identity centre around the topics which have precedence in the villagers' classificatory paradigm—they are comprised by a single theme—marital status and reproduction: anything of interest beyond this is asked about her husband. Her individual credentials are not deemed sufficient for status estimation in a culture where belonging is the prime criterion for establishing identity. There is a gender difference in the focus and style of communication. While men employ a verbal lineal style of interrogation, women—to whom I appeared as looking like a woman but not as being one—are specifically interested in physique. Not only did their questions centre on bodily matters and attributes but the verbal communication was substituted by physical scrutiny of my body, appearance and dress. To women, it seemed, the ambiguity I embodied posed a serious challenge to their assumptions about their own identities (Kondo 1986). Their response in the face of gender anomaly was to make me as Bengali as possible in accordance with their conception of womanhood (ibid.). To lessen the difference between them and myself, they made my body the target of transformation (into something more Bengali and likeable).

Their unsolicited comments on my own body and the body management of others like me (the foreigners they had heard about) thus provided the most vital clues for understanding the women's ways in the village.

As Douglas (1966:52) pointed out, in every culture we find "various provisions for dealing with ambiguous or anomalous events". Elsewhere I have described the process for a Bangladeshi community:

"In order to communicate with the hitherto unknown, the community's immediate concern is to obtain as many clues as possible regarding the identity of the stranger then to locate her within the existing pattern. The ultimate concern is absorption" (Kotalová 1986).

To illustrate the dialogical context framing my understanding of life in Gameranga, I shall narrate some of the key episodes retrieved from my field-notes and memory. This narrative also touches on some of the points made so far regarding plurality of meaning, plural embeddedness of womanhood in cultural codes, the context of the communicative event and the interlocutors' positions.

Fieldwork: play of identities

In the household where I settled in Gameranga, the permanent household members were a female servant—a widow of fifty from the same *para* (ham-let) and the landlord's adopted son—a boy of fifteen of Bede origin. At that stage they were the main personages responsible for my nurture, protection and socialization into the niche appropriate for a woman. The network of socializing agents was gradually extended to include other women in the community.

My stay entailed many conflicts. These, rather than hampering my work to any great extent, were productive of understanding as they provided insights into what *we* are not[1].

Preludium—February 1981

On my reconnaissance trip, long before my fieldwork started, I wore pyjama and kurta of domestic manufacture, my hair was short and I spoke only a few sentences of Bangla. Being the first woman of my *jat* (race) to come to the village I was received with unreserved curiosity and inquisitiveness. On the second day a woman lured me from the crowd of children into her yard. There I was encircled by a group of women who insisted in words and gestures that I reveal my sexual identity, "What are you, a girl or what?" Unconvinced by my answer they asked to inspect my chest. The oldest one lifted up my shirt. What was revealed seemed to satisfy their doubts, but the check-up did not end at

[1] I spent four and a half years in Bangladesh. I arrived in November 1979 to take up a job with the Swedish International Development Authority. Three years later I left my Dhaka residence to conduct fieldwork in a rural area. Part of my understanding of rural life in Bangladesh is grounded on this experience of a village on the southern edge of Faridpur district between November 1982 and December 1983. The last two months of that period were spent in a small *thana* hospital where I commuted every day. This increased my informants and enlarged the perspective. I now met medical professionals, people from adjacent communities, and experienced encounters with my neighbours in a new setting and new roles. At the end of December 1983 I moved from Gameranga to the subdivisional town to procede with my investigation on a larger and different scale. I divided my time between a missionary hospital and a government hospital. These two constituted the "area and scope of research" for three months. Finally I returned to Dhaka. There I spent three months indexing field-notes and talking to people from the southern Faridpur district. Physically I left Bangladesh for Europe in April 1984.

this. The same old woman squeezed my nipple and commented, "Empty, no milk? No children?" To ridicule my "emptiness" she grasped her own bare, pendulous breasts, shook them ostentatiously and declared triumphantly, "I have got six."

Inauguration and settlement—7th November 1982, 5 pm

A girl of about twelve (later I learnt that her name was Kulsum) was delegated to see how I was settling into my residence in one of the attic rooms of my landlord's *doutala* (two-storied dwelling). She entered shyly when I was in the process of sweeping the floor. I gave her an encouraging look, she took the broom from my hand and continued vigorously what I had started as if to correct my clumsiness. "Will you wear a sari now, as you are staying with us?" she asked abruptly, impatient to bring up the actual point of her visit. "Yes, I have brought two, but do not know how to wrap it …". The broom fell out of her hand as I opened the metal trunk and took out the simpler of my brand new saris. "Not that one", she protested and pointed to the bright orange cloth which showed underneath. In a few seconds, still shy but moving her hands expertly as she had done with the broom, Kulsum tied a piece of rope round my waist, very tightly, took one end of the sari, tucked its edge behind the middle of the front waistband and continued by wrapping the rectangular piece of gauze cloth around my body. When the other decorated end was left, she halted, asking "Are you married?". "Yes, but …" made her stand on tip-toe as she attempted to reach the top of my head with the embroidered end of the cloth. "It is too hot", I protested vehemently and threw the "tail" over my shoulder. In the meantime, a crowd of older women had surrounded the house as if perfectly aware of what went on inside. Their murmur crystalized into clear persuasive "*Ashun, dhekaen, nishe jan …*" (Come, show us, come down …). Descending from the attic I was met by critical looks and the silence of the female audience on the stage. Encouraged by Kulsum's firm grip of my hand, I followed her, decided to give in and succumb to the will of a twelve-year old.

As she led me in the direction of her *bari* (homestead), women and children from the courtyards along the path and canal screamed, "*Notun bou … memsaheb, dekhen … ei dike ashun … amar bari ashben na? … Singapuri mem …!?!* (New wife … look at memsaheb … come here … will you not come to our house? … Singapuri memsaheb), drowning Kulsum's instructions as to how fast I should walk. Suddenly, as we entered someone's courtyard, a group of older women obstructed our way and pulled me inside to the enclosure. One of them put on a reprimanding, aggressive tone to tell me "You … people like you, here in our village, if you want to stay, you have to please God and therefore ought to cover your head, we are Muslims here … It is your duty." To my resolute "But I am not one" (Muslim) they retorted "Christian, *napit* (a Hindu neighbouring caste), all women who come here to our *para* cover their head ... don't you see that *madrasa* (Islamic school) is near ... it is sinful". Not paying any attention to my defensive allusion to Koran ("your book speaks of covered bosom, not head") an anonymous voice from the angered crowd added, "Soon the men will be returning from the field and her head is bare." A few depreciatory comments were made by a visiting relative of urbanized outlook as to the length of my sari which left my ankles bare.

Morning after

As I entered the porch attached to my attic room, I noticed two women whom my landlord engaged at harvest time working in the yard. One walked clockwise treading out the rice grain on the ground, while her companion smeared the corner of the yard with cowdung paste. I recognized them as the main actors of yesterday's confrontation. With bare heads, their breasts half covered, they shrieked loudly at something I did not hear. My amazement over the casual style of their attire and licentious laughter gave rise to the first emphatic question marks in the fieldnotes on observed inconsistencies. (These were mainly directed at the disjunctions between the Islam I experienced in print and Islam as locally interpreted and, even more acutely, between these two and Islam as lived.)

Nevertheless, I went on covering my head dutifully. My efforts to look adjusted flagged by the month of May when the heat felt unbearable; I even dispensed with a petticoat, my sari being held up by a single jute string round my waist. Some of my neighbours (whose example I followed) noticed, but no overt reprimands were forthcoming. "I am encompassed. Amn't I?" reads a fieldnote of May 15th.

As time went by ... (Fourth episode)

One evening in the quarrelsome month of May screams of ubiquitous *jhogra* (brawl), drove me out of bed to see what was happening. I was confronted with the usual gestures, loud agitated voices, everything pertaining to the scenario of *mara-mari* (row). It started abruptly, developed rapidly and finally dissolved into threats of a police case. As I joined the departing audience, trying to figure out who was the villain and who the victim in the fight, a young woman who walked behind me through "jungle" addressed me worriedly, "Sister, how do you dare to walk around with your hair loose, uncovered and so late in the evening? Do you not know that in the gardens *bhut* (evil spirit) is on the lookout, lusting for human blood?". With her left hand holding her child astride her hip, she used her right hand to point to the tops of the trees— the assumed domicile of spirits. Her caring, concerned expression and tone of voice brought to my mind the very different style in which my first bareheaded appearance in a sari had been so severely criticized seven months before. On the earlier occasion the reason given for covering the head was different, and so too seemed to be the speaker's intentions.

Commentary

The experiences left me with several questions:
– Why did informants enforce a norm on a visitor they themselves did not care to follow consistently?[2]
– Why did my later negligence escape their reprobations?
– What was the reason for re-invoking the norm after a period of tolerating non-conformity ?

Clearly, the ethnography presented in the narrative displays contradictions on several levels[3].

Ethnographically, the events relate to the draping of a sari by village women; analytically to three themes: the application of a cultural code (covering the head by married women), the locus of symbolic meaning and the nature of social knowledge. Before attempting an interpretation I shall explicate the normative aspects of veiling and from this viewpoint recapitulate the events.

Structurally, veiling by women married into a community is related to the community boundary; from an individual woman's perspective, veiling relates to a particular life-stage. Considering a woman's life in structural terms, *achol* (decorated end of sari) thrown over the head denotes marriedness; this life-stage commences when a new wife is brought into the household of her in-laws. At the same time the control over her is transferred from her father to her husband. This multiple transformation is effected on the wedding whereby the new wife, after arrival at her new home, is objectified as immobile and invisible. In a ritual I describe in the final chapter, she herself stages the objectified view of herself.

In view of this, the above series of interactions can be summarized as follows:

Bodily appearance (*achol*—a physical extension of a woman's self) is the issue in question here. The dispute regarding the propriety of covering the head reveals a contradiction between textual enunciation as followed by the ethnographer and local interpretation as emphasised by the informants.

The daily routine work of informants, observed from a distance, reveals a total disregard of the norm they had attempted to enforce upon a newcomer at a previous—the initiatory—encounter. In spite of this, the bewildered, embar-

---

[2] I had similar experiences with respect to forms of greeting.

[3] The first is the contradiction regarding the norm of covering the female body in the Book (Islamic texts, on which informants ground their justifications in many other contexts) and its emic interpretation; second is the inconsistency between the norm as stated (norm locally interpreted) and as lived by insiders; a third discrepancy is between the initial vigour of enforcement and the subsequent tolerance of my lapses.

The last is the difference in justification of the norm given to a newcomer and the reason later given to an accommodated (though incomplete) guest absorbed into the community (thus the ideological matrix from which the justification of the norm on each occasion derives is different).

rassed and angered ethnographer responds by doing her best to conform to their expectations, at least with respect to her personal attire; for a time she follows their guidance on the proper wearing of a sari, untill one day she ceased covering her head. Thus the first seven months were characterized by her enthusiastic attempts to reduce the ambiguity she embodied ("... so as to resemble a woman I wore only a sari, covered my head, a pair of glass bangles and stopped cutting my hair ..." Kotalová 1986). Later her eagerness to conform subsided.

As fieldwork progressed, and her language and cultural skills improved, she was able to move with more ease (even bare-headed) without her every step awaking startled reactions; unexpectedly at that time, the issue of covering the head emerged again. By then not as a straightforward injunction, but in a concerned, coaxing, voice to persuade "a sister" to protect herself against evil forces.

Now, taking the assumed inconsistencies as evidence of contextual variation (rather than confusing or contradictory data), the sequence of events becomes meaningful in a different way.

Common to each narrative sequence is an effort by the informants to interpret and to make meaning of the ethnographer, to control her behaviour and to recreate her in their own image of womanhood. This I have previously interpreted in terms of management of ambiguity and identity. That I collaborated willingly not only attested to their success (Kondo 1986), but proved to them my awareness of the rules. If we consider Bourdieu's (1986:114–124) claim that there is no meaning in symbolic representations (codes, norms, rules, generative schemes, language) other than practical, the emphatic insistence on normative orthodoxy in the first encounter can be read as a sincerely meant concern to make an outside woman aware of the norms in the first place so as to speed up her ability to use them strategically (i.e. contextually). Social efficiency depends first of all on grasping the official rules; only then can various connotative associations of veiling be manipulated (covered–uncovered head, loose–tight hair in various places and times of day) and alternative practices effectively used.

Apart from the stereotypic use, reserved mainly for an audience, *achol* is a piece of female attire with a large potential of strategic uses. This latter function blurs the boundaries between inner–outer self and allows shifts between these two aspects of personhood (a woman may conceal or reveal oneself, her child, even stolen objects). It also has a wide range of utility for mundane purposes—hiding stolen objects, carrying forbidden food.

It seems that once I developed a sensitivity to body-concealment and demonstrated a practical mastery of conventional usage of the sari, informants left me to my own devices. As if then the rules remained implicit in the acts of breaking them or emerged in their defiance.

The considerable attention I give in this study to official representations and

discourse (within which womanhood is located), follows the same logic: in order for the alternative views and visions to be exposed, the cultural setting
within which they are expressed has to be outlined in detail. What I seek to
understand about symbolic representations is how they structure perception
and emotion and how they are invoked in the concrete situations of daily practice.

Now, it is time to turn to the last encounter in which the issue of veiling
arose. The reference to my bare head was re-introduced unexpectedly. The
place and time of day, and the stage of fieldwork, in combination, led to concern of a different kind. It seems that, as the fieldwork progressed the guest
was being re-positioned inside. Henceforward, the villagers assumed a different kind of responsibility for her well-being than at the beginning. My appearance on that nighttime outing was commented upon on the same metaphysical
grounds as would have been the case with a member of the community. I was
introduced to a discourse that operates with explanatory paradigms of harm
and danger different from those of official monotheistic Islam. It revealed a
metaphysical realm populated with ghosts who are particularly dangerous to
unescorted, unprotected, dishevelled women encountered at dusk in the
jungle. This realm of discourse is only revealed to those belonging to the community.

In the first case the injunction on veiling was based on the assumption that
without such knowledge, social efficacy and skill are hampered; informants
aimed to speed up my ability to use these rules strategically (i.e. to fulfill their
meaning); in the second, the woman translated the norm into a new context. In
combination, the first and the last event of interaction reveal most poignantly
the changing uses people make of stereotypes (cultural categories expressed in
signs and messages) with the passage of time. In short, the events epitomize
the local practice "official with strangers"—"practical with insiders". Epistemologically it is a case of the point of vision on the continuum between the
state of initial strangeness and the state of encompassed otherness.

The question remains whether what the narratives convey is evidence of
contradiction or rather of predilection of Bengali Muslims for an eclectic position in respect of doctrinal truths—a perspective which I myself intend to
adopt in my writing about them. This means that instead of pursuing a single
theory I will be picking up whatever is available within current anthropological discourse that can be matched with my field experience.

PART ONE

Social World

To facilitate the vision of the structure of the social world that shapes the experience of people in Gameranga, I shall start by invoking the circular concentricity and encompassment of a botanical species and a daily item in the local diet—the onion. The movement housewives pursue everyday to convert onions into an edible substance parallels my own way of learning, interpreting and writing about the world I shared with them. The metaphoric allusion (to the realm of transformatory method) will be followed by a brief overview of social, spatial and moral categories deployed in people's speech; this constitutes at the same time a lexicon of local terms. Thereafter I shall delve into the concept *dhormo* which is a system of representations, classifications and norms as complex as a "culture". The organisation of divisions within *dhormo* is elaborated by reference to the Dumontian notion hierarchic encompassment where each larger category encompasses all the earlier ones. Thereby I link the local concepts to the anthropological discourse on the modes of domination and of subversion. One way of presenting the working of a system of divisions as "encompassment" in daily interaction is to show how it is revealed through a group's self-definitions provided for outsiders. Gender division is given particular attention. As I will show in chapter seven and twelve, the alternation between encompassing and encompassed position is attainable through subtle forms of expression. The encompassed category—women in that case—can simultaneously reproduce the structure of domination and resist it by among other things articulating the definitions of Bengaliness in an exaggeratedly self-depreciatory mood.

CHAPTER 4

Metaphor of relatedness

Siblingship, marriage and filiation are the aspects of kinship by which society in Bangladesh is organized. Its units and their relatedness can be visualized as "the circles of an onion with the center circle being the family, which for a male means the household in which he grows up and to which his bride comes when he is married" (Cohn 1971:115). This botanical metaphor, which Cohn applies to Indian social and spacial organization, indicates as well the concentric, atomistic character, agnatic orientation and patrilocal residence which pervade the domestic scene where most Bengalis spend their formative years. I shall borrow myself the image applied to Indian society and address myself the task of peeling of the layers of the onion, which I take as corresponding to the boundaries which encircle social units as well as categories of social knowledge.

A reference to concentric circularity and containments of a botanical species points to a particular form of socio-spacial relatedness, as well as the tendency in South Asian thinking to regard units, substances and categories, which in a Western mode of thinking are considered functionally of a highly diverse nature,[1] as mutually transformable and permeable (Madan 1972, Marriott 1976). It suggests the substantialism that pervades the Bengali view of the universe, person and action, according to which the worlds of humans, plants and animals are imaginable as analogy of each other[2]. From this perspective then, "every entity in the world is involved in a complex and shifting concatenation of qualities and actions, both seen as 'substances'" (Appadurai 1986).

To invoke onion as a metaphor of social life is to acknowledge the simultaneity and circularity in which social life is enacted, whereby "each part exists simultaneously by and for itself, and in relation to other parts, as part of a larger whole" (Weil 1987). Or, as Jackson (1983b) puts it in his theorizing the function of a poetic metaphor (an onion in case of my argument), it "accomplishes the link between ... world through a scale reduction in which social, natural and personal worlds correspond evenly, so allowing us to feel equal to the wider world ...".

---

[1] Such as for example material substances (land, botanic species) and humans or a person's emotion and intellect.

[2] For example in weddings of prostitutes where the groom may be substituted by a tree or a cat if no man is available.

By claiming that the social system can be visualised in terms of spheres, domains and sub-domains, whether of activity, exchange or meaning, I do not attempt to invoke an image of an ideologically self-contained and self-sustaining cosmos that "stands perfectly for the whole" (Appadurai 1986). I have chosen the above analogy of circles as a starting point from which to look at social organisation in a Bengali Muslim community. The metaphor originally imputed to Indian social organisation conveys only one aspect of structural fluidity. It does not exhaust the open-endedness and shifting perspective the social actors surmise across the the various boundaries that encircle them. What the botanical symbol ignores is the dynamism of the units and the fuzziness of social life. This I shall attempt to redress by pointing to the choices available to people for trespassing boundaries[3].

[3] See chapter 3 above and chapters 9,10,11 (n.21),13.

CHAPTER 5

Social units—
overview and vocabulary

Here I shall outline the basic categories (circles) constituting the social world of Gameranga. As each term will re-appear in different contexts in the course of reading I shall confine this chapter to a brief description.

In the context of social organization, the minimal kinship and settlement unit in Gameranga is a household (*ghor, chula, shongshar*) which usually accommodates a conjugal couple with their offspring, i.e. family (*poribar*). An unmarried or widowed person, agnatically or affinally related to the family head (*malik*) may be temporarily or permanently attached.

Households are defined with respect to their male head[1] and it is through him that a family is agnatically related to co-resident households in the courtyard. This link, through a common male ancestor and co-residence, provides the physical, political and emotional basis of the wider unit homestead (*bari*) and also the basis of agnatic ethos. *Bari* has some resemblance to the localized patriline (*gushti*) although it may also include households without an agnatic link to the founding families or households lacking genealogical depth which is necessary for constituting a *gushti*. The ancestral memory does not exceed three or four generations and no written genealogical records are kept. Therefore, spatial proximity is as important a factor for the quality of social interaction as is the blood link. Households which represent a more distant branch (*shiri*) of a founding line may reside within the precincts of a *bari* or may be localized in a different neighbourhood (*para*).

The existence of *gushti* is frequently revealed in daily language by reference to "brothers" (*bhaiera*), thus emphasising the aspect of fraternal solidarity, including exchange of food on certain ritual occasions, and defence of honour (*ijjat*) in combats (*mara mari, golmal*). As I shall explain later (chapter 11), even non-blood brothers may be included.

Gushti is also recalled when the members themselves talk of relations of blood (*rokter attio*) or of being of the same womb (*ek peter bhai*), usually to point to strong or failing loyalties. There does not exist any prescription with respect to *gushti* endo- or exogamy, nor are links systematically recorded. It is important to stress that *gushti*s in Gameranga are not the units of appropriation of landed property or livestock, nor are they labour or consumption groups.

---

[1] Households are doubly identified either by reference to the householder's name or the cooking hearth, depending on what purposes the definition serves.

The notion of property is family-centered. There is no jointly owned ancestral land as reported from West Bengal (Davis 1983:67), and work is carried out by individual households. Apart from rhetoric, the extended family form in terms of economic unity is uncommon in Gameranga. Family property and space are divided upon the death of the father between his sons who establish separate households and henceforward pursue their autonomous economic interests. A portion of family wealth is distributed among daughters at the time of their marriage. Extra-household co-operation is limited to occasional reciprocity, like money-lending, helping with house or hearth construction or borrowing a draught animal for ploughing. This occurs, however, between households of equal status and resources; an agnatic link is not a sufficient motive for co-operation and patron–clientship often operates across the kinship units.

The lineal collectivity is formalized in the patrilineal inheritance of names and pedigrees (*bongsho*). It is further embodied in the office of *matubor*, who is a *gushti* spokesman and leader. Through the *matubor*, a *gushti* is represented in community "council" (*shomaj*) or "society", which is activated at times of emergency, usually in moral–legal matters. *Gushti* is further substantiated and felt in the image of bamboo, blood and the ideal of fraternal cohesion. I shall return to these representations.

The office of *matubor*, as most leadership appointments in Bangladesh, is bound to agnation and seniority (birth order). It is semi-hereditary; when the eldest son's abilities and behaviour do not correspond to the requirements of a leader, the rule of inheritance may be redefined and a more suitable member appointed. Ability to mobilize male members of the *gushti* for combat or consensus of opinion in matters of political action, good judgement and superior powers of communication are the paramount qualities of a leader. A *matubor* asserts his power as an advisor to his own kinsmen and kinswomen. Settlements of disputes, conflict solutions and evaluation of marriage proposals are the main topics on a *matubor*'s agenda. He is a spokesman for his *gushti* when one of the members gets involved in a conflict outside and it is his duty to secure access of *gushti* members to external resources such as relief goods and job opportunities. A *matubor* should have the time necessary to keep himself informed about the social and political affairs of the region and the wealth necessary to maintain as clients people from other neighbourhood and villages as clients (Jensen 1984). A certain religious orthodoxy and the ability to read and write are assets. The strongest *matubor* (or *member saheb*) in Uttor Para lacked formal education and wealth but was an eloquent speaker, able to understand and explain to the villagers matters and concepts produced by the urbanite decision makers. He commuted frequently between Gameranga, *thana* (the lowest government administrative unit) and a subdivisional town and was extremely adept at shifting between village and urban codes—sartorial as well as verbal. "He knows the words of officers", people used to say.

Para

Para is a territorial–cum–moral[2] boundary surrounding a community. In capital letters—Uttor Para—denotes North(ern) Para, one of several *para*s that constitute a *gram* ("village").

Though, for a visiting outsider and local children, the beginning and the end of a *para* are hardly noticeable, for village women a *para* boundary divides the world into home (*bari*) and abroad (*bidesh*). For the unmarried it surrounds the home (of their fathers); for the imported wives it encircles one of their homes (*shashur bari*). For both latter categories it is a boundary of their self-control, as their transgressions have implications for community's reputation.

For its population *para* provides a frame of reference for social and political activities such as exchanges of food in connection with life-cycle ceremonies and Islamic feasts. Physically unnoticeable, the moral dimension of the *para* boundary shows clearly in the manner villagers direct allegations of anti-*dhormic* behaviour. Instances of infanticide, laxness about fasting, illicit sex, blasphemy, litigiousness are admitted at times but always relegated to one of neighbouring *para*s. For a visiting anthropologist, the information about moral status of "her" host *para* ("area of study") could best be obtained beyond its boundaries. Particularly in neighbouring *para*s, accusations directed against the *para* I lived in came unsolicited; I myself used to be pressed to reciprocate with information about my domicile that would affirm the stereotypic allegations, whenever I moved beyond its bounds. In spite of a centric bias in these inter-*para* hearsay moral competitions, there exists a consensus in Gameranga about each *para*'s place in the moral hierarchy.

Shomaj[3]

Structurally, inter-*gushti* grouping within a *para* is achieved through *shomaj*, which is rooted in the notion "going together" (Bertocci 1984) but covers quite a range of meanings. In daily usage, *shomaj* translates as "society" or "association", the former referring to the basic and the only institution through which "community" beyond one's family and patriline is created. Reflection on *shomaj*'s collective sanction is implicit in expressions of affirmation like "everybody says ..." (*shobai bole*), "everybody does so ..." (*shobai kore*) or disapproval (rejection)—"people will speak badly" (*manshi mondo koy*). Perhaps the commonest mode of judging individual actions is anticipation of

---

[2] Prestige of a *para* is gained, apart from occupational and economic status, by frequency of disputes and violence, strictness of adherence to purda and other *dhorm*ic tenets like the practice of fasting.

[3] See chapter 10 where the concept is developed with reference to the activities that sustain it.

what people will say. A grave misdeed may lead to a temporary exclusion from *shomaj* of the offender and his family[4].

As an "association" *shomaj* refers to a link between the leading *matubors*, who may be referred to by the Anglicized term "*member*" and who constitute the authoritative "body through which *para* is further linked to wider world" (Jensen 1984), as well as to the judicial authority that the council of *matubors* represents. For each householder, *shomaj* is most dramatically invoked as a group of men not to be forgotten as guests at commensal feasts and in this sense it refers to the most influential men or political supporters, not all of them necessarily *matubors*. The physical composition of *shomaj* can best be seen at funerals, circumcision ceremonies and weddings and it does not necessarily correspond to the category of *shomaj* hearings (*bichar*) where members sit together in the role of judges. In the *para* where I lived, *shomaj* comprised ten *gushtis*, each represented by one or more *matubors* depending on a *gushti*'s size and the relationship between its sub-divisions. As the *shomaj* boundary overlaps with the *para*'s, the *gushti* members settled beyond the territory of the founding line may belong to different *shomaj* than their brothers.

In Gameranga, *shomaj* constitutes the supreme authority regulating extra-household exchange and competition. Both are effected by instrumental, as well as symbolic means. The maintenance of the proper, natural and moral order of society—*dhormo*—is the ultimate justification of the *shomaj*'s intervention in the individual and household sphere. In its executive role, *shomaj* acts as a judicial council of the *para*. *Matubors* assemble occasionally at village courts (*bichar* or *shalish*) to resolve disputes or to decide matters relating to the moral code and conduct (*dhormo*) of those who live within its bounds.

In women's vernacular *shomaj* is used instead of "people" (*manshi*) or "men" (*betara*). Both equations are apparent in dialogues which followed my various suggestions related to the solution of my female informants' health, legal or livelihood problems. Whenever the remedy involved violation of purda, e.g. medical consultations in a nearby hospital, legal consultation with a lawyer or a loan request in a bank, women would object, saying:
"If people see me, they will beat me."—(*Manshi dekhle marbe*)
"Which people are you talking about?"—(*Kishir manshi?*)
"Men."—(*Betara*)

In another common saying "people will speak badly" (*manshi mondo koy*), women warn of the consequences of certain inappropriate actions or at least of their public visibility. There *manshi* embodies a coercive social sanction, the society of men—*shomaj*.

---

[4] Locally it is expressed in an idiom of misfortune—"*shomaj* is closed"—*shomaj bondho*. Unfortunately I failed to pay attention to whether a family may take the initiative and abstain temporarily from membership in *shomaj* (the praxis reported by Dr. Cantlie from Assam), while in the field. To subsequent inquiries among Bengali friends most answered "It can be imagined" though nobody could recall a concrete example from their native villages. Such a practice, Dr.Cantlie pointed out to me, would add to the structural flexibility inbuilt in the praxis of *dhormo*.

PART TWO

Dominant Structure and Categories

CHAPTER 6

Dhormo—lifestyle: texts and praxis

The word *dhormo* is derived from the Sanscrit root *dhr*, meaning "to sustain" or "nourish" (Inden 1976:19) which is suggestive of the attributes of what makes the life of a community persist. In Khare's interpretation (1982:147, 159), it points to "that which is firm". The first two local meanings thus point to the domain of livelihood, the latter to its objective regularities—the normative system. However, in Gameranga as elsewhere in Bengal (Greenough 1983), the natural state of being is not visualized as a mere persistence neither is a norm fixed for ever and for all situations.

In a broader way *dhormo* is related to order in society—the domain of commonsensical truths, the schematic, emblematic aspect of social knowledge. Most commonly it is used to point to the social norm or behaviour "oriented towards what is expected in the specific contexts of a variety of hierarchical relationships" (Roland 1987:215), though in no way to an "unchanging norm for all situations" (ibid.) nor an asynchronic way of being (Inden ibid.)[1].

As a model *dhormo* enters the life of villagers in many different ways—as daily prayer, sacrifice, knowledge of good and evil, as liturgical incantations, etiquette or medicine. In all its forms and facets, it is internalized, instrumentalized, negotiated and manipulated. Being illiterate, most villagers are unaware of Hindu–Muslim syncreticism that has been pervasive in Bengal in the past and is still alive in daily praxis (Prindle 1988, Ahmed 1981, Blanchet 1984). When I used to point out to my informants how some of their beliefs contradict basic assumptions of Koranic doctrine, some would shift the reference to the "habits of this land" (*ei desher achar, riti-niti, jibon jatra*) or say "it is Bengali", "Bengalis are like that", thus pointing to regional identity.

However, I abstain from systematic exploration of syncretic traits in local belief and practices, even from using the adjective in my text, because my informants always referred to Islam whenever they invoked *dhormic* authority. Frequently, the fact that Islam is a religion of the Book, is invoked as a proof of religious superiority and some men, aware of the existence of the Bible, would see this as a point of comparability and a mitigating circumstance when estimating my nature and substance (*jat*). When the situation called for de-

---

[1] The word *dhormo* carries the same polysemic meaning as the word "rule" as posited by Bourdieu (1986:27). My informants used the term when they refered to Islam, i.e. morally superior lifestyle or appropriateness, but also in a morally neutral sense when talking of lifestyles in general. See also chapter 1 (n. 3).

fending the rightness of a particular statement, people would invoke *madrasa* or the Koran. Only a few could cite all five pillars of Islam. Women usually referred to confession, prayers and fasting[2]. In their initial attempt to convert me to Islam they would recite the faith in Allah as "the only God and Moham- mad his Prophet" and compel me to say after. Very occasionally alms were given to beggars on their Friday rounds and great prestige was conferred on those who made pilgrimage to Mecca (*haj*); but women were not explicit about these two doctrines[3].

In any case foreign origin of some of the local concepts would not discredit the claim that their understanding, explanations, practices and rituals are a part of Bengali Muslim culture, even if it nowadays does not fit the sharp Islamic/ non-Islamic boundary promulgated by fundamentalists.

To reiterate: for the peasants in Uttor Para, the moral–legal–economic cat- egory *dhormo* is sustained by Islamic tenets which constitute the dominant ideology[4]. Allah's will is inescapable—each person's destiny is inscribed on the forehead at time of birth. Salvation is attained by gaining merit through the practice of the five pillars (to outweight the penalty of sin). These are inter- preted and revealed to the villagers through local *madrasa*—the Islamic school, and a mosque (*mosjid*) attached to it. Women have no access to any of these but some of their sons attend the classes and the householders them- selves attend Friday prayers. During the slack season, in winter, public reli- gious meetings (*shoba*) are held at which a prominent Islamic functionary from outside may be invited. His exegesis and Koranic recitations are emitted via a loudspeaker (*mayk*) uninterruptedly for a few days and nights, which is the way the word of God also reaches the female population.

The villagers themselves use the term *dhormo* in a pragmatic, rather than transcendenental sense. For instance, whenever they refer to or inquire about a non-Bengali or non-Islamic life style. In my presence, they would first ask one another and then the controlling question addressed to me would come as "What is your *dhormo*?" (*Apnar dhormo ki?*). In this dialogical context, the term corresponds most closely to "religion", but further questioning reveals an interest in the Christian way of doing things, acting, co-habiting and feeling rather than believing, which indicates that *dhormo* includes a broader scope of human concerns than "religion" does in Western parlance. Often *dhormo* is used to convey the features defining a *jat*[5], its rank in a hierarchy and behav- iour appropriate to this, i.e. a lifestyle. In this latter sense, the notion of *dhormo* comes close to Bourdieu's (1986) non-dualistic, body-grounded con- cept of habitus, which is defined as a system of a person's lasting dispositions

---

[2] See chapter 17.
[3] See chapter 15.
[4] In contrast, the dominant ideology—*dhormo*—of peasants in Napit Para is constituted by Hin- duism.
[5] See "People of this land ..." and note 10 and 11 below. The concept is further developed in Kotalová 1986.

that integrates also past experiences ("inscribed in the body"), and is therefore "the result of an organizing action"[6]. Like *dhormo*, habitus designates a "way of being", a "habitual state [especially of the body]" and in particular a "predisposition, tendency, propensity, or inclination" (ibid.,72,82–83,214)—an important resource in "playing social game" (i.e. structuring power and authority) apart from any reference to conditions of a social structure (Foster 1986)[7].

According to Inden (ibid.,18), in the "monistically conceived order of Hinduism [where the pan-Bengali concept originates], the word *dhormo* was applied not only to divine or human *jatis* and *kulas* but to virtually every differentiated set of substances and beings. Everything ranging from a metal rock to a human *jati* or king was said to have its own particular *dhormo*"[8]. Davis (1983:3) recognizes this non-dualistic relationship between self and world in a West Bengal community where "physical nature and behavioural code are not distinct and separate but cognitively non-dualistic features". It seems then, that *dhormo* enjoys the same semantic expandability as the vernacular use of *jat*. Accordingly, the universe is divided into a variety of classes—*jat*s, which are distinguished by their substance and behaviour—*dhormo*. In Marriott's view (1976), South Asians, in order to exist, "absorb heterogenous material influences [and] they must also give out from themselves particles of their own ... essence"[9].

A particular *dhormo* is believed to inhere in this substance, i.e. in something that people of a *jat* share. In the essentialist notion of *jat* moral, corporal and spiritual condition of each genera are collapsed[10]. It is not surprising that the Bengali concern with class-essences confines itself also to the consideration of gender. With respect to humans, a mediaeval Bengali text suggests that male and female constitute a distinct *jat* on the basis of the different location

---

[6] Inden (1976:19) speaks of "interconnected attributes and powers and potential actions thought of as inherent in *jatis* ...".

[7] Subsequently Bourdieu suggested other formulations of habitus—"an interpretative device", "rules for association (in marriage as well as epistemological affiliations)", "socially constructed disposition to perceive social reality" (Bourdieu 1987), "tendency to generate regulated behaviours apart from any reference to rules" (Foster 1986) to mention a few. For an exhaustive discussion of Bourdieu's use of the concept see Broady 1990:228–269.

[8] My insertion.

[9] This dividuality as an essence of monism is not a feature unique in the Indian way of being. The process whereby a habitus is acquired elsewhere is characterized by the same dialectical movement between self and a collective ideology of self. Jackson (1983b) characterizes the dialectical process whereby habitus is acquired by stressing that

"... active realization of correlations between self and habitus presupposes an externalization which has already occurred, in which the self ... in concrete situations has discovered for itself an identity ..." and goes on saying that "... defining feature of habitus is internalized by individuals, and become thereby a part of a collective ideology of self, a common knowledge" (ibid.).

[10] *Jat* which I have in chapter 3 rendered as "race" is but one of the taxonomies that Bengalis use. Not only humans but animals, seasons, times and regions are divided into hierarchically encompassed classes that define "a structure of relevance, a rule of premissible combinations, a frame of reference, a metacommunication of what is and can be done" (Ramanujan 1989).

of *dhormo* in their bodies[11]. Maleness within the human *jat* is generalised by the attribute of precedence as supported by the chronology of creation represented in the Bengali–Hindu as well as Muslim myth of origin (Inden ibid.,24, Thorp 1982). These views persist nowadays in further assumptions as to gender distinction but do not totally determinate the way women and men actually act.

---

[11] "... the code for conduct of the human jati, manushya-dhormo, inhered in its distinctive bodily parts, its mind (manas), while the code for conduct of the female jati inhered in its distinctly bodily substances" (Inden 1976:20).

CHAPTER 7

Person, distinction, rank—organisation of distinction in South Asia

Gender-related *dhormo* brings us from the correspondence between substances and their respective behaviour to the relationship between diverse entities. The Bengali understanding of proper relationship between various categories of people (*jats*), assumes ranking. In official discourse where the objective, schematic aspect of collective reality is explicitly recognized and voiced, Bangladeshis display a remarkable preoccupation with rank. In the appraisals of persons or events in the most casual conversation, official questionnaires, medical journals, police protocols there is a predilection for keeping categories apart and in a straightforwardly hierarchical way.

However, it should be stressed, that like all *dhormic* concepts the ideas of rank, linked to those of effective dominance, rest on the monistic premise of ultimate transformability (or non-separability) between highly diverse substances (Marriott 1976). According to this axiom, "dividuality" does not only make people absorb properties of heterogenous material (biological and physical), influences (like land, food, water, climate, season, "wind") but also assimilate the attributes of humans who pertain to a different *jat* or social rank[1]. Through sharing food, space, work, bodies, exchange of gifts, women may absorb essences of men, servants those of their masters, anthropologists those of the peasants etc. The boundaries of the person in Gameranga are differently drawn from in the West. Dividuality thus renders a person fluid, open to and affected by a variety of social, moral and material forces, which are overlapping or merged into each other[2]. Similarly, a person's belongingness or placement in a rank (ascribed or achieved) is never entirely defining or permanent, as major studies of peasant mobility in Bangladesh show (van Schendel 1981, Bertocci 1970, 1974).

Marriott (ibid.) lists some of the processes in which such transformation may be attained: "Persons, like beings of all other categories, may preserve their particular composite natures and powers by stabilizing (typically by "cooling," removing heat from) their constitutents, and by admitting into themselves only what is homogenous and compatible; or they may transform their bodies with their inherent codes by mixing and/or separating their par-

---

[1] There is for example a widespread belief that the wind (*batash*), as it blows through different species of trees absorbs their respective substances and thus affects a person's bodily well-being.
[2] Cf. chapter 17.

ticulate constituents, sometimes with the help of catalytic heat, or by hetero-geneous inputs". On the following pages I shall detail the process people in Gameranga work through when confronted with aliens; throughout the book I shall give evidence in support of the argument that a potential for trasforma-tion of a person's identity (or any other cultural category) is inbuilt in such events as dialogue[3], ritual[4], play[5], in fact any act of social interaction.

Dumont (1980:239–245) admits to this non-dualistic stance when he speaks of rank relationship as "encompassment of opposites" in the Postface to Homo Hierarchicus. I rely partially on his proposition as it seems to come close to my informants a view of gender, age and status hierarchy[6].

Dumont's notion—the encompassment of the contrary—which he claims is intrinsic to the Indian conceptions—is a premis based on a structuralist ab-straction, whereby in a "relation ... between a whole (or a set) and an element of this whole (or set): the element belongs to the set and is in this sense con-substantial or identical with it; at the same time, the element is distinct from the set or stands in opposition to it" (ibid.,240). Stated simply, the whole is founded upon the co-existence of opposed parts. As with the onion metaphor introduced earlier, what is contained reflects the container; the encompassed (part) is both *within* (i.e. different) and *like* the encompassing, and paradoxi-cally, also contains it (cf. Ramanujan 1989). Bengali categorical assertions re-semble such concentric containments: the informants start with opposed dual categories, which they re-work in the course of conversation, and confuse them so that the initial opposition is cancelled. In the end one cannot tell the difference. As Ramanujan shows in essay from which I have borrowed some terminology, most Indian literary texts are modelled on this container-con-tained scheme: "Every story is encased in a metastory. And, within the text, one tale is the context for another ... Not only does the outer frame-story mo-tivate the inner sub-story; the inner story illuminates the outer as well". Rele-vant for my concern with gender is his observation of the grammatical struc-ture of Kamasutra "which declines and conjugates men and women as one would nouns and verbs in different gender, voices, moods and aspects. Gen-ders are genres" (ibid.).

Pointing to matters of gender, Dumont exemplifies "encompassment" by reference to the biblical story of creation and to the linguistic categories pro-vided for gender distinction in European languages[7].

---

[3] See "People of this land" in this chapter.

[4] See chapter 17 and 18.

[5] See chapter 17.

[6] Dumont (1980) approaches hierarchy from various perspectives: as ranking, disjunction be-tween status and power, as a comparison of value frames. Out of these, it is the relationship be-tween "that which encompasses and that which is encompassed" that informs my point of view, as it seems to retain the dynamism and transformability of the units that is so essential to the un-derstanding of the way Bangladeshis relate to each other and the world.

[7] While some languages use the identical word to denote "mankind" (human race) as well as "man" (as opposite to "woman"), thus rendering a woman inferior, others use two different words, thus fusing the two levels and referring directly to encompassing. Similarly, E. Ardener (1977a,b) focusses on differential modes of linguistic expression as he discusses the gender-biased models of mankind in societies we study and as replicated in our ethhnographic narratives.

In summary, what Dumont seems to posit is that societies operate by way of divisions, that all divisions are complementary oppositions providing the context and motivation for one another and that there is no complementarity without hierarchy. Hierarchy he defines as a propensity to attribute rank to each element in relation to the whole (ibid.,91). This would appear to contradict the Marriott's (and others') contention regarding the monistic nature of South Asian perceptions, but Dumont, aware of the inflexibility of structuralist schemes, adds:

"The same hierarchical principle that in some way subordinates one level to another at the same time introduces a multiplicity of levels, letting the situation reverse itself",

and (celebrating further contingency), insisting on the logical coexistence of both hierarchy and equality, Dumont stresses that

"a social hierarchy is only bearable by these reversals …. :that which at a superior level was superior may become inferior at an inferior level. The left can become the right in what might be called a "left situation", and again, in the complex complementariness that unites them, each of two moieties may appear alternately superior and inferior" (ibid:241, 244),

thus recognizing the transformational ("dividual") potential later documented in the South Asian context by Marriott (1976)[8].

The same kind of contextual emphasis is evident in the ways Bengali Muslims visualise the world and create the system of meaning.

The notion of encompassment thus constitutes the generative scheme invoked in the way people in Gameranga tend to think of difference, and to cope with what is unfamiliar and unforeseen. Conceptually, the abstraction "encompassment" informs the sense of self; practically it foregrounds the "quality of interaction, i.e. the interpersonal means by which issues of influence and domination are carried out" (Underwood 1982:70) or the "struggle for social reality" in Bourdieu's (1987) words.

The functions of the various structural models (which in Bangladesh co-exist and are subsumed under *dhormo*) lie in their capacity to organize the order of the world, the experience of that world (emotion, attitude) and to legitimate that order, so that *dhormo* appears homogenous and self-contained (Herzfeld 1987:95, Moore 1986:167). The strength of these models is that their invocation alerts awareness of location, required for the shift of boundaries—which is a basic premise for playing strategically (Bourdieu 1986, Lamaison 1986). In daily life, any reversal of the norm (e.g. of expected gender behaviour) presupposes the application of the knowledge of the scheme or model, that generates that norm. Symbolic representations of an embodied model also give people a sense of belonging, hence exaggerated claims to impeccability and the extolling of the emblematic traits when the "whole" of the community is

---

[8] Similarly, E.Ardener (1977b) stresses the contextual aspect of dominance-mutedness alternations, depending on the levels of communication—"The englobed structure is totally 'muted' in terms of the englobing one".

threatened (Cohen 1985:110–111). As shown in the previous chapter an anthropologist's entry to the community compelled the women to insist on the proper and correct wearing of a sari. It may also be that a model provides the users with a certain satisfaction that may be derived from its symmetry ("purity") and apparent consistency. As a result anatomical (and moral) division into upper and right part of the body encompassing its lower and left side (replicated in non-bodily spheres) is picked up metaphorically in sayings, songs and other aesthetic pleasures.

I shall at this point revert to the working of the model proposed by Dumont. To invoke and implement asymmetry on the basis of encompassment also means that the larger, encompassing entity is valued positively and represents therefore a preferential, generalized view. This is no mere abstraction. In social relationships those pertaining to this category, also possess the power to name, define, evaluate, animate or deanimate what or whom it encompasses. Encompassing implies a preferential access to semantic creativity, to use Parkin's terms (1982:xlvi) or semantic space to take Bourdieu's (1987) view[9]. More concretely, such a position anticipates the ability to impose on someone a particular interpretation of events and doctrines which constitute the social reality shared by both the encompassing and the encompassed groups. Moore (1986:171) drawing on E. Ardener (1977), writes of the ability of the dominant model "to retain control over the principle of the construction of reality and to frame all competing constructions within its own definitions". This is in sharp contrast to the associations attached to the smaller (i.e. contained) entity: the characteristics of the encompassed tend to retain negative connotations and are rendered marginal, invisible or otherwise regulated.

The idea of encompassment recalls some of the anthropological rendering of gender asymmetry in cultures beyond Asia. Instead of encompassing/encompassed, Hastrup (1978) writes of generalized and specified gender respectively. E. Ardener (1977), addressing the organisation of asymmetry, writes of dominant structures englobing the muted. Like Dumont (1980) he looks for an analogy in differential modes of linguistic expressions when domination (or englobing) is marked by articulateness, the subordination by mutedness; accordingly, "women are rendered inarticulate" by the male structure while the "dominant structure is articulated in terms of a male-world position". Those who are not in the male world position are "muted". As E. Ardener argues, "the muted structures are 'there' but cannot be 'realized' in the language of the dominant structure" (ibid.).

---

[9] Semantic creativity I take as a social actor's ability to impose meaning on or create definitions of social contexts.

Bourdieu (1987) speaks of the "struggle for social space" that imbues social relations with a meaning. This is not necessarily attained by verbal or literate means. In Gameranga, where most people are illiterate and women restrained even verbally, meaningful acts could have been materialized in ephemeral means that parody or affirm the social status quo: silent gesture, laugh, weaving a mat are some of the examples.

Taking all these views into account, the Dumontian hierarchy can thus further be rendered as a capacity and a persistent attempt of the encompassing categories to ensure their dominance by blocking the expressiveness of those they encompass. Hastrup (ibid.), following the line of S. Ardener et al. (1978), is cautious in stressing the transformability of the position (in similar manner to Dumont) as she writes on the semantics of biology—"the relationship between these terms is asymmetric in the sense that men include women at a certain level of comprehension. When the category of man is opposed to the category of animal, that is when we are talking of mankind, women are included. At a lower taxonomic level man opposes woman, ... but the first inclusive relationship remains important ... if we want to understand how it is that men again and again talk on behalf of humanity, as it were".

It should be remembered that apart from women, there are other encompassed groups in Bangladesh, muted in some sense by the dominant, Islamic, male orientation and view of the world. The Hindus, Islamic sects, syncretic sects (*shahadjia*), non-sedentary groups (Bede, Badia) transvestites (*hijri*), tribal populations—to give only a few examples[10]. All of them are to be seen in public occasionally and non of them seem to seclude their womenfolk as markedly as the Muslims do. A Muslim housewife in Gameranga is only a relatively prominent example of muting, where the biological, spatial, verbal, sartorial symbolism join together in the elaborated idiom and practice of purda. Also here, in the case of other non-dominant groups, mutedness is relative to its position vis à vis the dominant discourse. In conversation with Muslims in the community I studied, a model of Bengali society is consistently promoted whereby the features which do not fit this model are devalued or disregarded. "The Hindus", "the city-dwellers", "the ministers" were the focus of disrespect. Yet, in the presentations by Muslim towns-people, peasants themselves are obscured and marginalized. Thus any structure, group or individual is encompassed and muted from the point of view of those who create the definition. As E. Ardener (1977) stresses, what makes the non-dominant group muted is its position apart from the discourse which is conducted in terms of the dominant ideology.

An important point which E. Ardener (ibid.) adds to the Dumontian idea of englobing is his recognition of voidness—more specifically, mutedness and invisibility in the Bangladesh case—as a meaningful way of speaking, and his suggestion that an analysis of discourse based exclusively on written or spoken text and visual presentation is insufficient. Implicit in such a claim is the recognition that the structural meaning is created not merely by the relationship between constitutent elements but also by the gaps between them. That what has been said and seen is only meaningful in relationship to what remains unspoken and hidden. In addition, silence, absence, depletion, impasse and various other expressions of voidness are not necessarily signs of subordi-

---

[10] For a committed account of experience with these groups see Rolt 1991.

nation, powerlessness; on the contrary people in Gameranga resorted to them frequently as strategic resources[11].

"People of this land": self-ascription and problem of interpretation

A prominent example of how gaps constitute meaningful categories and how the domination by encompassment and semantic creativity operates in Gameranga are the commonsensical self-ascribing definitions people create in order to present their *dhormo*.

As mentioned in the Introduction, the opinion that "women have no value" (itself a statement of voidness par excellence) is recurrently voiced by men as well as women (for example as a response to my explicitly stated interest in "writing a book about women"). A more comprehensive definition of Bengali identity was supplied by an elderly woman when I first appeared as a casual visitor in her affinal village. It was during the monsoon, a time of the year when most villagers abstain from travelling by foot. Caught by surprise she greeted me disagreeably saying, "Why are you coming here, there is nothing for a *memshaheb* in this place but mud, hunger and thieves". Later that day, as she sensed my appreciation of her outspokeness and straightforward manner, she toned down her voice and in a more moderate idiom developed the theme of who people of her *jat* were (still convinced that I had come to the wrong place). She said "A Bengali is one, who tucks up the lungi to cut paddy which he then eats with hands [i.e. he eats what he cultivates]" (*Bengali, kapor kasa dia, dhan nare kamkoria hatie khae*)[12].

Both statements, one regarding women, the other Bengalis, were in modified forms replicated by male as well as female informants throughout my stay. The self-depreciatory notions, equating Bengalis with the poor, the thieves, the cheats, the greedy were as common forms of self-representations as assertions revealing feelings of ethnic superiority; however, I have not come across any explicit counterstatement to the assertion that women lack value.

---

[11] As a metaphysical category however, people in Gameranga equal "emptiness" to social death (see chapter 17). Voidness is also revealed in people's preoccupations with acts, events and persons they may remember from the past (sadness or fear invoked by memory of a dead person) as well as those which it is anticipated will take place in future. In fact, most strategic behaviour is aimed at the future. Socialization of daughters for marriage, daily moral choices evaluated with the Day of Judgement in mind, hiding of rice against hard times are a few examples.

[12] *Kapor*—garment, can refer to both sari and lungi (sarong); the verb *kasa dia* meaning "roll up and tuck up" is gendered because this mode of arrangement is never applied to sari. Women may lift their sari to the water level when they are to cross a canal by foot.

In Bengali, the third person pronoun *she* is genderless. The sex of the person referred to appears from the context. Interestingly, in English textbooks employed in the local school, *she* is always translated as "he". Therefore, those village youth who knew some basic English referred to all persons in the narrative as "he".

I shall look at the richer self-definition as it provides a great deal of information about the "Bengali" who is presented as a cultivator and subsistence peasant. It also speaks of the style of dress of those who cultivate the land, their level of agricultural technology and eating manners. A Bengali is presented via bodily involvement with "the culture", as one who cultivates the land. This is consistent with the view of habitus as generated in practice. The most curious feature, however, in the context of my argument is that half the Bangladeshi population—women—are excluded from a definition provided by a woman. This is clear from the reference to dress and involvement of hands with the earth in an area of Bangladesh where no woman ever works in the fields, grows vegetables or wears the lungi. The question remains to ask why women, even those who are not muted in a linguistic sense, choose to present their *jat* in terms that exclude themselves. What makes the definitions of the generalized category "Bengali" shift from self-derogation to self-flattery?

In answering these questions I propose to supplement the structuralist–positional stance by an interactionist approach. S. Ardener's (1978) contention that domination is a function of a group's position in relation to the encompassing ideology and that any attempt at self-expression, unless muted, necessarily assumes the position of the dominant (i.e. male) point of view, may help us to understand the exclusion of self from the englobing definition, but hardly the contradictory attributes which informants attach to predications of themselves[13].

For all its advantages, an interpretation made entirely in terms of the structural position of the interlocutors (from which each has a particular scope of vision, Rosaldo 1983) remains inadequate, as it neglects the process of shifting, the temporary nature of each person's vision. It is the problem with the "dominant structures" perspective (like with generative schemes, models or definitions of any sort), that it does not explain refractions—inconsistencies, contradictions, disjunctions. Notably, it ignores personal idiosyncrasies.

A complementary perspective whereby the working of dominance is viewed as a relationship created and re-created in social interaction, is suggested in the quotation above from Underwood's (1982) study. Focusing on intimacy and power relations between women in a Tamil household, Underwood argues for the shift of emphasis from the essentialist notion of power (as accrued in structures available to persons), to the view of power as a quality of interaction. In the same vein, the main proponent of interactionist analysis,

[13] E. Ardener (1977b) is rather concerned to explain how the ethnographer's focus on the "articulated"-key informant's interpretations during fieldwork foregrounds the replication of the mutedness of the "muted" groups in anthropological texts. Doing this, Ardener elucidates the link between the conventions of fieldwork and the gender bias in the constitution of anthropological knowledge. One of the consequences, for South Asian ethnography, is that in the recent past most research has centered on the caste system, viewed from the point of view of one of the privileged groups. This trend is now being reversed as shown by the profusion of publications concerned with "the muted" or "subaltern" groups. See Appadurai 1986, Hanlon 1988, who see the bias in anthropological presentations of India from yet a wider perspective.

Erving Goffman (1979:6), writes, "The expression of subordination and dominance through … situational means is more than a mere tracing of symbol or ritualistic affirmation of the social hierarchy, they are the shadow *and* the substance" (my emphasis). Cohen (1985:115), who is specifically concerned with the interpretation of self-ascriptive collective definitions (what people say about themselves) emphasises the embeddedness of these definitions in the process of mutual interpretation between "other tribes and other scribes". He maintains that the very need to define self is prompted by the confrontation with non-self and asserts that it is the situation of encounter (with otherness)[14] and not the position in their home-structure that makes people project the image of themselves as identical with the norm, the typical. At the same time it is there that the self-reflection—refraction of the coherent whole—takes place and the meaning lies. Alluding to Boon (1987), Cohen (ibid.) writes, "just as Other cultures are only observable from the perspective of a culture with which it is contrasted, so also people see their own culture from the supposed vantage point at which they imagine others to view it". Building on these views, I suggest that the Bengali negative self-image finds its ground in the well-established mass media view of Bengalis as lacking the basic necessities of life and of Outsiders as providers. In addition foreigners are unambiguously imagined to hold unfavourable stereotypes of Muslims. When my informants describe themselves as "thieves", "greedy", "destitute", they are reflecting what they believe to be our collective view of themselves.

This kind of negative self-definition is strategic in two senses. First, in view of the *dhorm*ic emphasis on charity (obligation of the rich to give) as well as the Bengali practice of relating to others in an ostentatiously hierarchical manner, the ubiquitous references to misery (by people of all economic categories) are affirmations of inequality in anticipation of patronage (Maloney 1985,see Rolt 1991:18) or just a way to incite compassion. Second, presenting a definition where cultivators appear as thieves and their means of production and fetishised commodity—land—as mud, the ideal of abundance on which the Bengali moral economy is based[15] as amounting in reality to hunger, may be a housewife's way of pointing to the lack of fit between the model and the praxis. It may also be an attempt to dissociate maleness (of cultivation) from positive attributes. Further, it is possible that my informant was attempting to deconstruct the myth of consensus (apparent in self-congratulatory presentations by men) by assuming the role of (an interpreting) commentator on the dominant model. Her position as an elder matron, the absence of men from the scene and the surprise of an unanticipated encounter may have prompted her particular version of the Bengali self-image as defined by men. Commenting on the articulateness of women, S. Ardener (1978) argues that women's ideas of the dominant model and their view of the world around may find a mode of

---

[14] See chapter 3 and 11, n.19.
[15] See "Livelihood—the idea of well-being" in this chapter.

expression in forms other than direct expository speech, as is the case above. Indeed, in the community where I lived, most women expressed discord less directly—becoming mad for a period of time (*pagol hoye jawa*), turning ano-rexic, running back to their father's home, refusing to cook, deliberately cook-ing unpalatable food, practising abortions, refusing to talk—to name only the salient manifestations of mute dissidence. It is not for lack of an appropriate linguistic code provided for women in Bengali culture. On the contrary, on the occasion of viewing the bride "the way of saying words" (*ki bhabe kotha bole*) is one of the accomplishments tested thoroughly by male suitors. Ideally, this should be in a mode counter to the male self-assertive firmness of speech. A bride is asked to read a few words from the Koran, not to prove her verbal in-terpretative skill but the vocal maleability and "sweetness" of her voice to in-dicate her capacity for a smooth encompassment. Thus the housewife in my example violated the women's *dhormo* (norm of hospitality, speech, modesty) and inscribed her self into this text.

In other encounters the Other (anthropologist invited for a sumptuous meal by an affluent *matubor*) may be placed in a different context and the treatment she receives is thus motivated by other purposes. As a political rival's exotic guest she may be seen as a potential mediator—one who disseminates strate-gic information; in this case an emblematic definition of the collective belong-ing is appropriate ("We are not as poor as you foreigners believe.")[16].

What I want to stress by these proliferate moderations to the original Du-montian model is the flexibility of *dhormo* and that the concern with distinc-tion and rank that so prominently preocuppies my informants also relates to the interlocutor. Like Tamil and Sanscritic lyrics, the manner of constructing definition and its meaning—"who the people of this land are", depends on who says it to whom, when, why and where. As Ramanujan (1989) reminds us "In such a world, systems of meaning are elicited by contexts, by the nature (and substance) of the listener". Had I searched for the meaning of the local definition of "Bengali", in the structural contrasts between encompassing and encompassed units and in addition also searched for its replicas in other do-mains of culture I could have arrived at a more coherent (i.e. unrefracted) still-life portrait where culture appears as a homogenous, self-contained system de-termined by the (one) structural model. But in that case, it would give an im-pression that the woman who defines her *jat* and *dhormo* to the exclusion of herself and others who claim that "women have no value", accept their "muted" position unreflectively. (And also, that the symbolic structures—rep-licated in words, domestic space, clothes, denote social life unproblematically, in a direct way.)

Recent anthropology abounds with perspectives which re-direct attention from the structure to process, from rule to strategy, from language to speech. Goffman, Cohen and others whom I shall cite in the course of writing (Fer-

---

[16] For another pragmatic category—that of a creditor—of placing a Westerner see chapter 11.

nandez 1985, Jackson 1983a, Karp 1987, Kondo 1986, Schwartzman 1978) propound epistemologies that place the meaning of culture in interaction and dialogue (or in practice in the case of Bourdieu 1986). This is in consonance with my informants' inclinations and therefore I borrow their insights and vocabulary to depict some of the ephemeral, processual phenomena that cannot be described in structural terms except as anomalies, but which are essential aspects of social life.

Belonging and becoming: transformations

In this section I shall consider the transformational character of *dhormic* principles in local discourse and praxis. First is the formal expression of encompassment in kinship terms. Second, I attempt to explicate the process of transformation the villagers employ when they are confronted with humans of non-Bengali pedigree. The third aspect of *dhormo*—the consubstantiation of people and the land of origin— produces an explanatory frame of reference alternative to Islamic ideology. Being born in a particular region inhers moral attributes which may contradict other *dhormic* tenets. Last is a reflection on the *dhormic* view of the good life.

Kinship dyads—extension of sameness

The organization of difference and the form of ranking discussed so far theoretically is elaborated in the Bengali etiquette of kinship behaviour. In Bangladesh, the larger kinship network operates according to a prescribed pattern of dyadic relationships. These range from avoidance (e.g. a man with yBrWi, a woman with HuFa) to deep affection (a woman to her Mo). In his study of kinship, Aziz (1979), apart from naming the prototypes of each form, specifies the types of behaviour expected from each dyad in terms of strictness/ mildness of avoidance; he also distinguishes between a range of emotions along the continuum erotic—filial affection (ibid.,110–120). Elsewhere he claims that "dyadic role expectations are more pronounced in Bengali society than in many because of the extreme gender role expectations … which have ramifications in the whole constellation of inter-personal contact within the family as well as outside" (Aziz 1985:70–72). Again, it is important to remember that the "hierarchy by structure and content is always in a potentially dynamic, complex interaction" (Roland 1988:219) and so, framed in Dumont's (and also Ardener's and Hastrup's) transformational perspective, one can say that a wife in Gameranga, experiences various forms of encompassment by various members in her affinal home and herself employs varying forms and levels of vigour in encompassing her male and female children, daughter in-law etc. at different stages of their life-cycle.

The kinship terminology as I will show in a subsequent chapter (11, n. 22), is widely applied to non-kin. Thereby a form of distance or closeness inbuilt in a particular dyad is translated to social interactions beyond one's kinship net. To invoke empathy a person may be addressed as "father" or "mother"; to solicit help one approaches the potential benefactor as "father's brother" or "mother's sister".

Similarly, the acts involving outsiders are assessed in terms of a dyadic relationship, e.g. guests–hosts, old guest–new guest, poor–rich. Before an evaluation is undertaken the interactors are located in the encompassing and encompassed scheme. For example, stealing from an outsider is less condemnable than from a neighbour, generosity to a low-ranked person counts on a different merit scale than kindness towards a relative equal.

Alien jat—management of otherness

In a practical moral context, *dhormo* is also contained in the way people deal with the strange, unfamiliar and alien. In the search for compatibility and homogeneity people in Gameranga always start with a neat dichotomous classification (Marriott 1976) so as to establish a common platform for mutual negotiations and from this they gradually seek to transform (encompass and ultimately absorb) diverse bodies with heterogenous inputs[17]. With regard to the presence of the anthropologist, there was a marked concern to gradually transform what was diverse in her way of being (and seeing) until she could eventually be incorporated[18]. This ran parallel with the rising awareness of dangers as well as advantages intrinsic to the mixing, or fusing in some way, of categories which in the local view should be kept apart (Douglas 1966, Tambiah 1973).

In homely discourse *dhormo* (appropriate behaviour) is reflected in terms like "the human" (*manush jat*), "the Islamic" (*Mia, Mussulman*), "people of this land" (*ei desher manush*), the "male" (*purushlok*) and the "female" (*meyelok*). In moral discourse these terms are often introduced and presented in opposition to the features and forms of life of the non-human, the non-Islamic, the foreign, the un-womanly, which altogether tend to be featured as of inferior quality, unbecoming or inauspicious in some way. In the villagers' judgement, any slight visible or suspected distinction from the collective self always retains a negative connotation. However, this negativity always depends on where and in whose *jat*'s collectivity the encompassing subject places herself or himself in a particular context and situation, and it is also relative to the degree of inclusion. In this way most of the evaluative, i.e. moral, statements can be transformed to their opposites without being necessarily ex-

---

[17] Similarly, with respect to Indian outlook, Ramanuyan (1989) claims "Not unity (in the Aristotelian sense) but coherence, seems to be the end".
[18] The process is described in more detail in Kotalová 1986.

perienced by the Bengali speakers as contradictory or anomalous. For a speaker who asserts male values, all female attributes are rendered as inferior, lacking or failing at least, but when a question of the Islamic features of the Bengali is considered, both males and females of Muslim *jat* are equally and indisputably superior to Hindus or Christians. An outsider to the *desh, dhormo* and *purush*ness, like a female anthropologist, is an epitome of negatively loaded difference. Indeed, derogatory comments were habitually passed as to my way of bathing, eating, clothing, combing, walking, belonging, laughing and of relating to animals, Hindus, lepers, "black" children …. But often, the debate on my strange habits and tastes would be concluded by a statement, "after all she is a human being", as if the commentator wished to dissolve the negativity of my otherness (imposed by the boundaries of both *jat, shomaj, dhormo* and geography) by extending her or his vision to all imaginable different forms of life, beauty, speech, love—all humanity has to offer. And, as soon as my physical appearance resembled that of a woman (after some adjustments of hairstyle and body embellishment) and my speech that of an adult, I was re-shuffled from the more generalised category outsider—*bideshi* (or *notun bou, shadha manush, ranga, redmanky, Singapur* —"new wife", "the white one", "the pink one", "red monkey", "one from Singapore") into a more specific, familiar category of a "woman" rendered occasionally as "*bun*", "*sister*" (sister) and in the presence of other outsiders even appropriated as "*amra memsaheb*" (our memshaheb). Hereafter people started to evaluate me more consistently by local standards of femininity and simultaneously I have been rescued from the third person pronoun (*uni, she*) and shifted to the second person—*apni*—whenever reference was made to me in my presence. Fernandez (1985), drawing on Benveniste and Ricoeur, writes of "turn-taking" when in conversation the "empty" category of the third person is filled with the subject "I" or "you", a turn that grants both interlocutors the possibility of mutually exchanging their roles whereby "I" becomes "You" as "You" turns to "I". Locating this process of intersubjectivity in Bangladesh, I would rather propose, "absorbed otherness", borrowing from Khare (1976b), because it is as far as the "turn-taking" was managed along my stay in Gameranga and it is as far as the domestication of an alien can go in the place (*desh*) where shared forefathers, soil and blood are the premise of true belonging.

A further example of how a shifting perspective, guided by a consideration of belongingness affects judgement of beings and their acts is the fate of a rabid dog, who appeared in the precincts of our household and attacked a calf—the most venerated of animals. In the discussion I overheard thereafter, it seemed of great importance to establish the dog's provenance, not in terms of individual ownership, but as to whether it belonged to our *para* or another. After a small boy attested to having seen it around the distant *para* where his *mashi* (MoSi) lives, the dog was beaten to death. It was clear, that "being of here" would have been a mitigating circumstance and could have saved the mongrel's life. It seemed that in that particular instance, the human:non-human distinction between *jat*s was subordinated to a regional criterion of sharing[19].

Desh *and* bidesh—*insides and outsides*

As previously mentioned, whenever an action or belief cannot be framed within Islamic tenets, those informants who would admit a discrepancy are quick to refer to the *desher achar*—"habit of this land"[20]. The regional code under consideration thus provides a further refraction of the dominant Islamic ideology that permeates *dhormo* and permits social actors to asert alternative claims.

For the Muslims, *dhormo*, in addition to its genetic–anatomical origin, inheres also in *desh*—regional substance: people occupying a common space also share the *dhormo*. While the salient generalized features and activities held as appropriate for Bengli Muslim *jat* include characteristic physical appearance (notably of men)[21], belief in Islam, Bengali language, cultivating and eating rice, wearing lungi, insulating womenfolk, the *desh* denotes a more specific physical setting and its population. This spatial referent of a person includes dialect spoken in the area, quality of water and of rice (this being related to the soil *jomi*). Separation from one's land, water sources and rice yielded from the fields that surround it, is always experienced as an immense discomfort, difficulty (*koshto*) and is generally associated with inauspiciousness (*oshubida*) and suffering (*khuda*). To make use of food, water (for drinking as well as for ablutions), women and medical services abroad (*bideshe*), is believed to have detrimental consequences for a man's wellbeing. Young men may be instructed before embarking on a journey to avoid touching un-known people. Whenever a team of young labourers from Gameranga embarked on employment as paddy-cutters in another district, a *kobiraj* always followed "to protect us from infatuations of erotic love". Golomb (1985:134), who noticed a similar dislike for tasting new foods and anxieties about travelling among Thai of various religious affiliations, explains this cautiousness by ref-

[19] This extends to the classification of domestic animals in general; a cat (*biral*) and a dog (*kukur*) occupy the lowest rank among domestic animals, because they are considered to be polluted ("dogs eat faeces", "cat hair causes diphteria"). They are only tolerated if their household belonging, (i.e. where they get leftovers habitually) can be established.

[20] This seems to be a case of "boundary overflow"-management pointed out by Tambiah (1974) and picked up again by Marriott (1976). Both advocate re-consideration of dualistic and boundary-oriented theories in favour of an interactionalist perspective. In their view the South Asian understanding and praxis of categorizing humans and other genera, arises out of transactions and transformations. The process "starts, but rarely stops, with neatly branching taxonomies ... instead, they run, ... to complex ... arrangements, ... often to lattice-like cognitive structures that provide for all manner of intersections among ... categories through remixtures of previously differentiated substance-codes" (Marriott ibid., Tambiah ibid., see also Ramanujan 1989).

[21] The application of a red mark (*tika*) on the forehead by Hindu women is the only bodily clue to *dhorm*ic difference between Bengali women. Men, on the contrary, employ quite a range of external signs marking them as Muslims or Hindu (see Aziz 1979:19).

erence to the medical humoural theory shared widely across religious boundaries. Bengali share with Thai the humoural medical outlook but their view of the consubstantiated nature of humans and land, as is clearly seen in the denotation "Bangla*desh*", reinforces these anxieties. This peculiar conjunction of *desh–bhat–pani* (land–rice–water), occasionally extended to *tel* and *mach* (massage-oil and fish) is expressed in an adage "*Jhole, tele, bhate—bengali*"—"Water, oil, rice—that is Bengali".

The anxiety about dissociation between humans and their land persists even nowadays when a large number of Bangladeshis emigrate or travel abroad. The often experienced delays with passports and other bureaucratic hassles may provoke a fatalistic "If rice and water do not want to release you, there will be no departure" (*Bhat, pani na charle jawa nei*) (Guhathakurta 1988). The reluctance of Bangladeshi anthropologists to do fieldwork in non-Bengali territories is probably related to the same "metonymic view of humans in nature" (Ramanuyan 1989).

The territorial dimension of consubstantiation is also a vital consideration in marriage arrangements and explains the reluctance to exchange women from areas beyond a certain boundary as discussed in chapter fifteen[22].

Livelihood—idea of well-being

As the original meaning of the word suggests, *dhormo* derives from the semantic field of nourishment[23].

The moral rhethoric and economic practices of villagers are rooted in an expectation of prosperity (consisting of fertility, abundance, indulgence,) as a conceptual starting point in contemplating their life and land. Most villagers experiencing nowadays a wide gap between what they are and what they could be, view the proper moral–economic order in terms of the "approximation of actual conditions to timeless, dimensionless, and metaphorically expressed ideal" (Greenough 1983). In urban transport this ideal is communicated via the painted panels of rickshaws. These paintings depict the idealized village where cows are healthy and fat, the rivers swarm with fish and every house has a corrugated tin roof. People in Gameranga today locate the state of prosperity in the past, as is apparent from the stories landless villagers have to tell about the lost riches of their fore-fathers. In villagers' autobiographical accounts, becoming poor is always related to once having been rich. This placing of the state of well-being in the past is not just a matter of nostalgia for Time Past (*mela, onek shomoy age*). In 1888 Lord Dufferin's (1880:12) report based on inquiries carried out in Bengali provinces notes that "houses [are] larger in East Bengal than in the Western district of Bengal" and that people of East Bengal wear "better clothes, eat better food—not infrequently flesh—and can afford to remain idle and to amuse themselves for days together".

---

[22] See chapter 15—"Spatial distance between affinal *gushti*s and provenance of wife".
[23] See chapter 16 and 17.

Even if we narrow the geographical perspective to the Faridpur district and move to the first decades of this century, the South and particularly the area that encompasses Gameranga was reported as its most prosperous and progressive region. (Gazetteer of the Faridpur District 1925:38). The following portrait of a cultivator dates from 1916:

"... nature is bountiful to him, the soil of his little farm yields in such abundance, that he is able to meet all his desires without excessive work. He can produce the food of his own family and sufficient to purchase everything else which he requires from a few acres of land that he can cultivate unaided without overwork."[24].

It should be stressed that in the moral discourse of peasants the idea of well-being which imparts *dhormo* extends beyond subsistence to include emotions and bodily states which indeed, are not perceived as having a separate existence.

Summary

As I have shown, *dhormo*, as a particular way of seeing and of being, is inseparable from *jat* and in this sense, it is viewed as an innate, ascribed, static category—it is "that which is firm" (Khare 1982). Yet, in villagers' moral discourse, it is also used to denote a normative, moral and intellectual goal to be achieved—"a bundle of interconnected attributes, powers and potential actions"—(Inden 1976:19) a praxis, that dynamizes its "firmness". It is something that is intended to be lived up to, struggled for, incessantly activated, compared with its opposite—*odhormo*, in order to attain that desirable wholeness and perfection of lifestyle.

Inden's rendering of the Hindu meaning of *dhormo* in mediaeval Bengal is not too different from the meaning Muslims in Gameranga impute to it nowadays. Hence, "only when realized through actual behaviour ... dhormo is believed to bring about well-being, good fortune and prosperity" (ibid.). The people, among whom I did fieldwork, while placing the actual experience of well-being in the past, relegate its possible revival to the metaphysical realm of afterlife. It will be then, in the future that a person's mundane striving will be judged and rewarded by a passage to either a prosperous garden or to hell (*behest*). Their daily strivings are reflections of these possibilities. The routine choices and decisions are necessarily compromises between *dhormo* and *odhormo*, i.e. impeccable and errant ways of seeing and of being. Therefore as Inden (ibid.) argues, *dhormo* is not only a "synchronic state of being" derived from the essence they share" but also "a diachronic process of becoming" (ibid.).

---

[24] From "Economic Life of a Bengal District", Oxford University Press 1916, quoted in the Gazetteer 1925:38.

CHAPTER 8

Embodiment of *dhormo*

Embodiment is closely linked to the concept of habitus. Both analytical concepts were introduced by Mauss 1934 (1950:372) and received significant elaboration by Bourdieu (1986).

In both body is viewed as "original object upon which the work of culture is carried out, and the original tool with which that work is achieved ... It is at once an object of technique, a technical means, and the subjective origin of technique" (Csordas 1989). This chapter focuses on the body as object. I wish to present the way *dhormo* is maintained through embodiment, i.e. how objective structure, regularities, are "inscribed on the body". In doing so I shall focus on gendrification, i.e. the process through which the physical bodies of girls and boys are processed in order to match their respective *dhormo*. Following the sequential order of my informants' way of presenting themselves, I shall commence with the way mothers in Gameranga[1] inculcate in their children moral, objectivist categories, e.g. the conventional ideas about and habitual pattern of body use, from the moment of gestation up to the biological mark of maturity.

As I am going to show, the relatively unspecified body of an infant is systematically feminized or virilized. The fundamental principles of femininity are reinforced by didactic narrative in the form of sayings, maxims, denouncements of heresies and, of course are indirectly incorporated through the experience a child has of its mother and father and of the asymmetry in their relationship. In the case of girls, the genderized world which has been successively absorbed is enacted again when her body is re-defined through the wedding ritual[2]. It re-appears constantly in her "manner of standing, speaking, and thereby feeling and thinking" (Bourdieu 1986:93).

Discussing cultural learning, Bourdieu (ibid.) uses embodiment to argue that the vision of the world and its divisions is learned systematically with and through the body, whereby a whole cosmology, an ethic, a political philosophy are transmitted, without necessarily attaining the level of discourse. What Bourdieu claims for "totalitarian institutions" (as treated by Goffman) applies equally for the non-writing, non-reading communities who, lacking any other

---

[1] As noted in chapter 2, Bengalis start any interaction by categorical statements enhancing distinction and hierarchy, (i.e.by the objectivist aspect of culture), which they later dissolve or deconstruct in some way. Categorical divisiveness is thus typically turned to contextual relativity. Cf. chapter 7 (n. 17).

[2] See chapter 18.

means of recording and objectifying the structure (of divisions), treat the body as the memory and "entrust to it in an abbreviated and practical (i.e. mnemonic) form the fundamental principles of the arbitrary content of culture" (ibid., 94). An important consequence following from this is, "that knowledge is never detached from the body which bears it" and therefore, "knowledge can only survive in its embodied state" (ibid., 218).

In South Asian ethnography, considerable attention is given to the use of the body[3]. Many of these studies have focused on the question of how groups in a religiously pluralist context conceptualize and express their differences through different modes of presenting the body (Das 1985, 1987, Hershman 1974). My previous essay on this subject shows how the body is used as the main instrument in self-construction and self-presentation in the process of mutual assessment and of learning to know the Other during anthropological fieldwork (Kotalová 1986)[4]. The theoretical positions underlying anthropological studies of the body in South Asia range from dualistic assumptions stressing the distinction between the body as biological substance and the body as a cultural construct ("a system of moral relations"—Das ibid.), to the monist notions which, following Marriott (1976), seek to eliminate the distinction between physical nature and cultural behaviour. As may be recalled, according to the proponents of monism, body substance and cultural behaviour are cognitively non-dualistic, each is immanent in the other, each is inseparable from the other, each is a realisation of the other (Davis 1983:2). One expression of this claim in Gameranga is the assertion that "people are what they eat". A corollary of the dualist proposition is the assumption that bodily experiences are themselves culturally defined, and therefore derive their meaning as human experiences from the cultural definition given to them. Further implications are that the meaning of a human action "comes from outside the act itself" (Das ibid.), that the body symbolizes something beyond itself (Jackson's critique 1983a), that has been induced in the past and from above. On the contrary, the monist (or transactionist) stance, in emphasising body use, locates meaning in the experience of human interaction. In effect the cultural meaning emerges from and has to be negotiated in dialogue, be it an event of monetary or commensal exchange, a combat, sexual intercourse, a prayer, delousing. Given the pervasive mode of anthropological learning through dialogue, the shift of emphasis from the text (be it a structural metaphor or any other organisational scheme or conceptual category) to its use— the event of reading, translating, paraphrasing or fixing in writing—becomes compelling.

I wish to take the middle way between these theoretical positions, viewing the physical body (as speaking, hearing, moving in space, posturing in a ritual action, experiencing pleasure and enduring suffering) and cultural knowledge

---

[3] Das 1976b, 1985, 1987; Hershman 1974; Inden/Nicholas 1977; Kakar 1984; Lindenbaum 1968; Obeyesekere 1981.

[4] See also chapter 3.

(concepts, rules, symbolic schemes, divisive structures) as mutually affecting, merging and conveying spheres of reality. Following S. Ardener (1978), Hastrup (1978), Parkin (1988) I prefer to think of simultaneities and "interlocking of metaphors" when considering the physical/conceptual dichotomy as well as a large number of the structural oppositions following from this.

Constructing gender: pre- and post-partum

In Bangladesh preoccupation with the sex of the child starts during early pregnancy. Predictions are based on various experiments[5], on beliefs regarding bodily changes in the pregnant mother and on the interpretation of dreams.

In Gameranga, dark nipples in an expectant woman indicate a son, brown nipples a daughter. If the son has a short penis this denotes that the next child will be a son, if he has a long penis a daughter will be born next (*choto nunu, tarpor chele hoy, borota nunu tar pete meye hoy*). The preference for boys is evidenced in demographic studies which indicate a 35–50 per cent higher mortality rate for females under five years of age (Lindenbaum 1975). How is this difference accounted for in popular language?

Gender preference for male infants is evident at the very moment of delivery. The announcement that a child has been born, is immediately followed by the question "A girl or a boy?". The overt disappointment over a newborn daughter may be mitigated if she is light-skinned (*shadha*). Skin colour is given almost equal attention as sex in inquiries about a newborn child. Generally, however, it is accompanied by sayings like "to get a daughter, one's face blackens" (*meye holi, mukh khalo hoye jai*), which suggests that the mother's face becomes ugly, contrary to the effect of "having a son (when) one is happy" (*chele holi kushi hoy*). When Rome, a young mother of a girl and a boy, was about to deliver again, her husband was absent on business. When her affinal female relative arrived from the neighbouring *para* to see how far the delivery had proceeded and found another daughter had been born, she bemoaned, "A girl? Her father will be angry", and in response to my question she explained, "A girl, what for? She will leave one day; here she will stay like a guest fed for others". Not all the depreciatory comments however, were directed toward the sex. The midwife (*dhoruni*), who attended the delivery,

---

[5] The size and shape of the mother's belly and creases along the left side of her hand are likewise predictive: if her navel resembles a betelnut a daughter will be born; long lines on her hand indicate the number of sons, short lines the number of daughters. Dreams filled with long vegetables or snakes indicate the birth of a boy, round objects a girl (Lindenbaum 1968). Various tests aimed at the same end have a long tradition in the subcontinent. In his account of the manners and customs of the Muslims of South India in 1832, Shurreef (1973:1) writes "… they perform a certain experiment, from the result of which they predict the sex of the expected offspring; that is, they press out a few drops of the woman's milk on a piece of yellow cloth; and if, when dry, it leaves a white stain, they conjecture the child will be a girl; but if a yellow mark, they suppose that it will be a boy". See also Maloney 1981:165–166.

remarked, "It is a gift from Allah, of course it is appreciated, it is only a pity she is so dark". There is a generally held opinion in Gameranga that "having daughters one needs a lot of money" (*meye holi taka dorkar*).

Gender differentiation is imposed by early interventions on the infant's body. Studying birth practices among the Muslims in Jamalpur, Blanchet (1984:119–120) observed that "the umbilical cord of a boy is cut nine fingers from the umbilicus but that of a girl only seven inches", and that the "boy's hair is shaved after nine days and the girl's seven days after delivery" … "It is because boys should live longer and in everything be ahead of girls", Blanchet's informant explained. The fee to the midwife (*dai*), if any, is double for delivering a boy. Elsewhere in Bangladesh two goats should be sacrificed for a newborn son while one goat suffices for a daughter. In some parts of Bangladesh an iron earring is inserted into the newborn child's ear to frighten the spirits; the midwife pierces the right earlobe of a boy and the left of a girl (Lindenbaum 1965)[6]. In Gameranga, this custom was practised only by one mother of a boy; she was of a very distant provenance and thought to protect her son from envious looks (*kharap drishti*) by marking him as a girl, i.e. less valuable.

After the first bath of the infant on the day of delivery and after the placenta has been buried and the floor of the place of delivery (*attur ghor*) mudwashed, the baby's body is massaged with heated mustard oil, the head receiving the main attention. Particular care is taken with certain features of a girl's face. Mere, my neighbour, pressed her newly-born daughter's forehead with her palm to make it flatter, and with the help of oiled fingers moulded her nose repeatedly to make it narrower ("*nak bhalo kuti hobe, shundor*"). The practice of daily pressure with a heated cloth to round a newborn girl's face and raise the bridge of a flat nose has been noted elsewhere in Bangladesh (Lindenbaum ibid.). It is to form her, at least in part, in the ideal of universal female beauty in the subcontinent, which is a full round face, straight narrow nose, fair skin and long black hair. Apart from massaging, a magic make-up is an indispensable part of the child's body care. Black coal (*khajol*) or soot from burnt vegetable stems is used to encircle the eyes, and a large round spot is applied asymmetrically on the infant's forehead. Women believe that only in disguise can their newborn babies face the world populated by evil spirits and the evil intentions by humans. Uglification is aimed at deflecting flattering comments on the child, which are invariably believed to be charged with the intention to harm. Protection of infants is compounded by amulets (*tabij*) tied around the forearm, neck or waist of the baby. Soon, a girl's wrist is adorned with a pair of glass or plastic bangles (*churi*) and both her ears are pierced to be hung with earrings (*kanbela*). Both bangles and earrings make up the essential paraphernalia of young virgins and are perceived as a woman's basic needs even by the poorest of village women.

---

[6] Association of women with the left,—the inauspicious side, and men with the favorable right in Bangladesh has been discussed in an illuminating essay by Lindenbaum (1968).

Private parts

At this stage, attention is also given to the hardly visible breasts (*may, don, dudh*) of a baby girl. Mothers pull and squeeze the nipples (*botha*) of their daughters to make them "soft" (*norom hobe*). The attention given to a baby girl's sex organ is the reverse. Its exposure is considered more shameful than exposure of the male organ and women who attend a female baby make an anxious effort to keep her pubic area covered by a rug. My own omission to cover a girl's baby's belly when taking photographs or while baby-sitting in-furiated most adult women—"how disgusting" (*ghirna*). The vagina also re-ceives least attention (contrary to the head) at bathing. The effort to conceal a girl's pubic area is motivated in part by the belief that it is through the vagina that *shoytan* (devil) finds its way into a woman and that the newborn child is particularly liable to draw evil. In contrast, a boy's penis (*nunu, bhashi*) is the object of favourable attention by all women. Mothers, sisters and old women attract the boy's attention to his *nunu* by kissing it, masturbating and by exag-gerately clear pronunciation of the word or sayings like, "Is it not your pe-nis?—you are my husband" (a 40 year old matron to her nephew of 4). In an-ger they may threaten their mischievous sons and grandsons with a gesture of castration or with words like, "I shall cut off your thing", or just, "Shall I cut it off ?!" While the linguistic term for the vagina is hardly ever pronounced by adult women (when the problem of covering her pubic area arises, reference is made to her "belly"—*pet*), there exists a distinctive term for the penis of a small boy (*nunu*) and of an adult man (*dhon*). Another word used to designate the male sex organ is *raja*—the king, power, authority—which is also the brand-name of locally sold condoms. (Birth control pills are sold under the name "Maya"—affection, longing). The first verbal skills and body con-sciousness of children are trained by interrogations about features of the child's head such as, "Where is your nose, your eyes, mouth …?" to which the child is to respond by pointing to the corresponding features. For male re-spondents such an exercise always culminates in, "Where is your penis?" (*tomar nunu kothae?*) to which the surrounding female audience responds with cheerful approval.

Bodha is the local lexeme for vagina and in Gameranga its use is restricted to the domain of insult. In the initial stage of fieldwork, before I was able to grasp the local dialect, *bodha* was one of the first words I could distinguish along with *bhat* (rice, food) or *khawa* (eating) and *taka* (money). *Bodha*, so frequently shouted by infuriated children, is just whispered by girls (on the rare occasion of teaching the anthropologist the forbidden vocabulary), and unmentionable by decent adult women[7].

---

[7] Thus a girl of 4 may call her father "oh *bodha*!" after being scolded, or a girl of 12 may refuse to do a job by shouting at her mother "*bodhar meye!*"—daughter of a cunt.
In medical contexts women refer to their gyneacological problems by pointing to the lower abdo-men.

According to Maloney (1981), the term is derived from *bhodai* (cf. Sen 1971), the word denoting a "fool" or "somebody unfit to have penis". This part of the female anatomy is thus equated with a lack or voidness. A similar negative association is reported from the Punjab where the term for female genitals (*chuta*) is linked with the general term of impurity (*chhuta*) (Das 1979). It is apparent that in both neighbouring cultures the source of impurity is seen in the biological formation of women.

The construction of a self-image (and world-image) by the opposition between what is masculine and feminine obtains from these seemingly insignificant, accidental forms of domestic communication. Beyond the domestic sphere this is replicated in political slogans and in advertisements. Local trademarks of birth control devices illustrate the point: condoms are sold as "Raja", birth control pills as "Maya". The latter, according to a maxim in Gameranga is exactly what men are lacking—*"purusher kono maya nei"* (men have no compassion).

Childhood and view of human maturation

As I have shown, the cultural marking of children as male and female by linguistic differentiation and different treatment of the body starts early. Deliberate sexual segregation or any other intervention in a child's development is minimal at this stage, because childhood (*shishukal*) is equated with the state of non-reason (*obuj*). Mischief, temper, tantrums, abusive language, manifestations of infantile sexuality like sexual games of toddlers or playing with the sex organs are tolerated and when such events are witnessed and reported, mothers react with amusement or explain, "She does not understand", "She lacks understanding" (*kitchu bujje na, kono buj ney*). Because of that, and because child development is perceived as an organic process, regulated by nature and God (and therefore apparently beyond parental control), the shaping of a girl's body is never brought to the level of independent discourse (for example, as gender didactics or apprenticeship of culture) apart from statements like "it is for her good", "it looks well". Yet, as Bourdieu (1986:95) points out in dealing with "the hidden persuasion of an implicit pedagogy", "the whole trick of pedagogic reason lies precisely in the way it extorts the essential while seeming to demand the insignificant" and the very state of non-reason seems to be the optimal set up for "durable impositions of the schemes of perception ..." to be effected. Within the scheme of "diffuse education" (Bourdieu ibid.,200) the opposition between the concealment of girls' genitals and fondling of the boys'—physically and verbally—re-appears later as a complementary opposition between muted female sexuality (extended into social and economic impotence entailed in the twofold meaning of *lojja*—emotional shyness, social modesty) and assertive male sexuality extended into political, economic and religious extroversion and conceptualized as *ijjat* (social prestige and the physical ability to defend it).

There is, however, an additional dimension to the popular idea of human development, related to the local meaning of "understanding". The child's maturation is generally perceived as a gradual understanding of the rules relevant for association with others and therefore children in Gameranga are not encouraged to develop a particular skill or proficiency apart from this. After the age of 6 or 7, the "unknowing" and therefore irresponsible child enters the cycle of life stages which frame a person's moral responsibility to others. This is not entirely due to the supreme agency of God ("*Allah jane*") or biogenetic determination ("*babar moto chele*") embedded in the notion of shared substances. Rather, it is because the conception of "an individual as a unique being of intrinsic worth ... autonomous, self-fulfilling ... with private interests, wants and goals ... a being valued as the elemental social unit" (Davis 1983: 81) does not enter into thinking in Bengal. As others have noted before, the "personal esteem of an adult bears little relationship to developing abilities and to being successful in work; rather, it is dependent on success in fitting into the group and carrying out one's role" (Bangladesh 1980:38). The local understanding of "the understanding" and of knowledge in general has no other context in Gameranga than a capacity to relate properly to people. Therefore, the attention, albeit very casual, given to a child's performance is directed to such motor and verbal skills as enable it to reach others. Stretching out the proper hand to take a piece of food, games of 'give and take' and first attempts at walking (towards other), bring warm responses from caretakers. Toilet training, eating habits and the proper presentation of one's body, important not least in terms of pollution, are further areas of focused pedagogy. Injunctions here are related to the proper distinction between right/left hand, general touchability of persons and objects, and behaviour with feet which, together with the left hand, constitute those parts of anatomy to be eliminated from social contact. It should be noted, however, that even in these areas, mothers never direct the pace of a child's development, neither do they compare their children's achievements because age is not an issue in the capacity to act maturely[8].

With its first steps a child's world expands beyond the compound boundary and hence space is introduced as a new factor to exert an anonymous, persuasive pedagogic action (Bourdieu 1986:90–91,94). At the age of four or so, carried by their older sister or walking in the company of elder siblings, children start to explore the precincts beyond the compound boundary. This is marked for both sexes by a change of dress habits. While infants and young children, even girls, go without clothes of any sort, at this stage of increased mobility they will start to wear a lower garment. Girls begin earlier than boys to wear

[8] There is however a culturally standardised way whereby a boy is turned Muslim. It is done as part of the circumcision ceremony which also marks a boy's entry into manhood (see further chapters 11 and 18, n.5.).

the universal toddler apparel—short pants. A slight difference in the pants' design is another marker of sexual identity. Given the habit of shaving children's heads it is sometimes difficult to tell the child's sex from facial features. Pierced earlobes and a pair of bangles, the distinguishing mark of girlhood at infancy, are now extended by a garment tailored in a particular manner. Her mobility requires an increased degree of concealment, and thus, while boy's breeches are loose, the wide legs of girl's shorts are gathered and tied by a string or rubber band around her thighs. The potential danger emanating from her genitals[9] is thus controlled by total encasement of her lower abdomen around the waist and thighs.

Boys and girls alike roam through the village freely at this stage. Girls participate in mixed competitive games—as losers usually, as their hips are burdened by younger siblings—but there is no significant segregation yet regarding male/female activities. Play and participation in subsistance activities may take girls as far as the market to sell milk or vegetables or to do shopping for the family; they may go fishing in the canal or collecting spinach (*shag*) in the jungle—areas which will be strictly prohibited to them in the near future.

It is at this stage that a girl enjoys maximum freedom. By exchanging goods for money at the market[10], fishing, boating even climbing trees, she is now exploring the alternative to the domestic sphere of her future. This period, when the male stage is open to girls, is brief, yet extremely important, because this world generates the dominant discourse and her undertakings in it persist as an experience in her memory and possibly also as an inner conflict, when her freedom of movement is curtailed and her verbal competence muted.

Bodily appearance: cosmetics, adornment, hair-care

Along with increased concealment of impure body parts goes greater concern with face and hair. Even very young girls are highly conscious of their looks and employ various beautifying preparations to correct imperfections or enhance their good points. Lipstick, powder, red laque (*alta*) and eyeliner (*khajol*) are the main beautifiers which every girl covets and contrives to get and apply. While children of both sexes still mix freely (*mela mesha*), the girls mark their state of becoming—the sexual desirability associated with a marital future—long before it is marked biologically. At this time, jewellery is worn to mark body extremities. The strings often kept in earlobes since they were pierced may be removed and real earrings (*kanbela*), usually of brass (*pitel*), are drawn through. Earrings are essential female paraphernalia, and the quality of the metal—gold, silver, brass—is seen as a direct statement of a

[9] Danger relates to a female body in two ways. A woman's sexuality attracts malevolent supernatural forces if uncontrolled (untied) at the same time as it emanates dangers, particularly at the time of menses and parturition—the period of greatest vulnerability.

[10] It should be noted that the daughters of well-off households do not get involved in male activities at any stage, but these were underrepresented in Uttor Para.

woman's value and, after marriage, also of the position of her husband. Glass bangles are another essential part of a woman's accessories. The arrival of a Bede woman, who goes from compound to compound selling trinkets, is a welcome opportunity for girls to purchase new bangles and freshen up their appearance. Ideally, each wrist should be adorned with a number of bangles[11]. The expectation of verbal reticence in mature women is coupled with sonal adornment: the tinkling sound of the bangles is often the only sign of a woman's presence.

The importance of hair is manifested on the sixth day after birth when the pollution of birth is removed by shaving the infant's head and pairing its nails. Throughout childhood the hair of children is regularly shaved off. It is be-lieved that frequent shaving makes hair strong and black. It is also considered easier to keep a child's head cool and, lastly, it is the solution to heavy infesta-tion if manual delousing fails. For a girl, the habit of head-shaving ends when she reaches about nine years of age. It coincides with her gradual preparation for womanhood. Hair together with skin colour of a girl are the only aesthetic criteria considered in marriage negotiation. Skin colour can hardly be light-ened except occasionally with powder, but hair can be grown long and black-ened and oiled to correspond with the ideal. Regular oiling with coconut oil and occasional smearing with the crushed leaves of sim tree (*shimir pata*) is practised to enhance these qualities. The importance of oiling extends far be-yond mere cosmetic considerations as it denotes a general state of auspicious-ness and purity. Oil-less hair in a married woman denotes menses, post-par-tum period, insanity, poverty or absence of a male guardian, i.e. conditions of vulnerability and lack of self-control. Any of these states, marked by a wider range of signs, is frequently expressed by women pointing at the head and saying that if they do not oil their hair they will go mad, their head will spin (*ghura*i) or they will go blind (*chakhor da*i)[12].

Adult women, by now emulated by their daughters, care for their hair by combing, delousing, moistening and mud- or soap-washing. They moisten their hair daily as a part of the ritual midday immersion in the water tank or canal. A thorough hair wash with application of mud or soap is linked to the post-menstrual purification bath and by extension "the latest hair-wash" is taken as a mark of the onset of pregnancy[13].

[11] The universal popularity and indispensability of bangles in the subcontinent is evident from the following note in Bombay Handbook (Steinmeaz 1977): "No self-respecting Indian lady, even of the poorest circumstances, considers herself fully dressed unless she has a few bangles on both arms. For those who can afford it, gold and silver are "de rigeur". For the rest, colourful glass bangles are a must. The bangle-wallah carries his multi-coloured glass and plastic bracelets, usually strung on twine or rods suspended from wooden frames, right to the lady's doorstep".
[12] Women always wondered how I could stay alert without oiling my hair and they approved when the grease of my unwashed hair gave an impression of shine.
[13] Most women considered my questioning the length of their pregnancy as indecent and would just cover their face; those I knew more closely would answer by reference to the last "time of washing head" or "sari" which is a way to indicate the time of last menstruation.

Length is a further sign of beautiful hair. A girl's hair should be allowed to grow long before the onset of marriage negotiations. When a young man, accompanied by his relatives and friends, returns from the viewing of a girl as a prospective wife and is interviewed by the neighbours, the first impression he is likely to communicate is the length of the girl's hair (while the accompanying guardian always stresses signs of affluence of the prospective in-laws). At the beginning of fieldwork, women would comment incessantly on my shoulder-length hair and fringe. They untied their own or their daughters' knot and displayed the length to emphasize my shortcoming and to set an example for emulation. Small girls comb, oil and re-arrange their hair in different hairstyles many times a day. Each has a number of bright coloured ribbons and plastic clasps to facilitate hair arrangement in various styles. However, the standard and only coiffure of adult women is hair parted in the centre, tied back and twisted into a knot. Looseness, apart from of the indispositions given above, is condoned only as a follow-up of midday bath (*ghosol*), which, together with collective delousing in circle, constitutes an interlude in women's daily routine. But a woman who leaves the precincts of her compound after sunset, without properly knotting her hair, makes an ideal prey for malevolent spirits[14].

Early adolescence

As girls mature, they are gradually separated from the company of boys and restricted from entering male precincts. At this stage a young girl's garments consist of *salwar* and *kameez*. Shorts are not suitable any more and are replaced by a lengthened version—*salwar*—baggy trousers with the gathering of excess cloth moved from the thighs to the ankle. The upper body is now covered by *kameez*—a loose, slightly fitted tunic hanging over the *salwar* to the knees. It has short sleeves and two side slashes from the waist down. Modesty is ensured by double coverage of the abdomen to the knees and the addition of a scarf—*orna*—to cover the head and bosom. Girls who do not attend school, or are too poor, may wear any second-hand US-made stuff instead of *salwar-kameez*, provided that the legs and breast are entirely covered. The performance of the last major beautifying operation coincides with this increased multiple concealment and the cessation of hair-cutting. The girl's nostril is pierced for the insertion of a nasal trinket (*nat* or *phul*). In contrast to boys, whose spatial horizon continues expanding and the improvement of whose skills centres on boating, fishing, husbandry, and marketing calculations, the girls gradually withdraw from the areas beyond their *para*, and the hearth (*chula*) becomes the central point of interest. Their outings are restricted to fetching water, shopping in the village shop (*dokhan*) and visits in

---

[14] See chapter 3.

the immediate neighbourhood. Girls who attend school always walk together in a group (separate from the groups of schoolboys), a pattern they share with the boys, though lack of company would not impede a boy from moving around.

By now the girls know that submissiveness, self-effacement and self-sacrifice, conceptualized as *lojja*, are the tenets of womanhood and that subdued (or no) speech or laughter, slow graceful gait with short steps and veiling are its physical expressions. It is the moral equipment which has been by now instilled by the diffuse education (Bourdieu 1986:200) reviewed above. On the contrary, talking with boys on the path, accepting sweets from them, too much laughing in the presence of men, indicates "looseness". By now mothers expressly concentrate on training their daughters in these skills which will in future render them 'good' daughters-in-law. To be protective, conservative, and to save, store and preserve things are the basic requirements (the tenets of women's *dhormo*). The feeling of *lojja* is now developed. In addition to the embarrassment experienced by both sexes at the violation of cultural norms (i.e. shame), the girls internalize it as a dominant virtue—an emotion of modesty and shyness. The bodily focus of *lojja* is the face (*mukh dekha*). More specifically, a face which turns red (*mukh lal hoye geche*) indicates the first sense of the emotion—embarrassment or shame. The latter sense manifests itself through averted eyes, head inclined to one side and a subdued voice or silence—a posture which girls learn very early. Both "orient the individual to the reaction of others: he (or she) wants their approval and fears disapproval and ridicule" (Obeyesekere 1981:79). As I said, the restriction and control of girls are no longer a matter of implicit pedagogy, neither are they limited to making offensive body parts invisible. As an interiorized moral force they are now expressed from inside, and a spiritual quality is added to increased physical restraint in the form of elementary religious instructions regarding compulsory prayers (*kolema*) and fasting (*roja*). Writing on Indian childhood, Kakar (1978:62) refers to this stage of girls' development as "a time of instinctual and emotional volatility" and notes "It is precisely at this development moment, … her training in service and self-denial, in preparation for her imminent roles of daughter-in-law and wife is stepped up". As a result, her "self-esteem falters" and the girls in these years of early puberty tend to overconform to the prescriptions and expectations of those around[15].

Indeed, the most ardent and consistent censors of my appearance and behaviour in Gameranga were the girls of this category—novices to womanhood. Earnest reprimands were addressed to me about precisely those features and endowments in which they expected a complete woman to excel and in which I was conspicuously lacking. Length of hair, head covering, way of walking and talking, quality of jewellery and colour of sari define the category of their imminent aspiration—*notun bou* (new wife). In fact any slight devi-

[15] For similar observation of identity "confusion" among girls in Punjab, see Das 1979.

ance or lapse in demeanour of any woman occupying the category to which they aspired was immediately pointed out and publicized. Non-conformity could even be punished by physical assault as in the case of a young female beggar who came to our compound. She was dishevelled and uttered her supplications in a hardly intelligible high-pitched sound, typical of deaf-mutes. She was known as *boba*. A group of girls surrounded her, pounced on her, pulled her hair and finally painted her face with red lacque (*alta*). Although an important category of citizens, beggars (children or the aged of both sexes) are rendered invisible as persons. After giving alms and receiving blessing no exchange is pursued with a beggar. It seemed that the agitated reaction to this particular woman was provoked by a combination of youth, deviant speech (loud animal-like sounds) and lack of escort—the epitome of what these girls did not want to become—and therefore marked her off as an undesirable category.

Late adolescence

While villagers take an indulgent attitude towards the progress of their daughters and sons during early childhood and do not compare their speed of development, it is generally believed that daughters reach maturity earlier than sons (Aziz 1985:50). A woman's maturity is signalled by the onset of the menarche[16], an event which separates her definitely from non-related men as well as from the status of *nabarlok* (immature). Inclusion into the "understanding" category of *shabarlok* or *dangor* (or *shaena*) corresponds further to a girl's withdrawal from places occupied by non-related men and a more permanent attachment to the hearth (*chula*). This latter shift with respect to space seems to me the main indicator of gender difference in Gameranga—a re-orientation from which other marks of gender distinction and complementarity spring and which constitutes the key marker of complete Bengali Muslim adulthood.

When asked to explain the meaning of *dangor meye*, which is the local synonym for a mature unmarried woman, female informants provided shorthand definitions like "the blossom has ripened", "need for bathing", "time for wedding", thus summarizing the core events linked to the appearance of first menses. The dispositions of a boy at the corresponding life stage are specified in terms of physiological change and the subsistence skills linked to them: thus growth of facial hair should indicate a son's readiness and duty to cut paddy (*dhan khati hoy*) and look after animals. Emphasis is laid on the understanding of and assumption of general agricultural and marketing responsibilities (*kaj bujte hoy*) entailed in the position of householder. The corresponding skills and duties of a girl are not expressed verbally but her attachement to *chula* implies cooking as a core aptitude. The age appropriate to the *dangor*

[16] See chapter 17.

stage is 12—15 for a girl and 16—18 for her brother. Because the exact onset of menses is unpredictable, the ultimate phase of a girl's maturation is closely monitored. At this particular phase, her body is associated with a sprouting bud. The symbolic association of an edible plant with a woman's body, and sexual intercourse with food consumption, are clear from the categorization of pre-adolescent girls. The image of growing paddy (unharvested, unprocessed rice, future food to be consumed) is used to define a category of *auisya*-girls who, like *aus*-paddy[17], are expected to be ready for harvest in three months, and a younger category of *amuinya*-girls to be harvested, like *amon*-paddy in six months (Aziz 1985:50). The ripening process of young girls culminates with menses which is metaphorically referred to as *phol dekhe*—the flower came out in blossom.

While emphasis on the menarche as a marker of change in a girl's behaviour is expressed by reference to botanical species, the glosses denoting the actual process of bleeding are void of positive euphemisms: "being sick" (*oshuk*), "having one's body in bad condition" (*shorir kharap*), are primary referents, while more literal denotations—"blood breaks off" (*rokto bhange*), *haez* (arabic for menstrual blood), *mashik*, *mins* (corrupted English) or *ritu* are used only in explanatory situations. All these glosses suggest a state of indisposition and vulnerability which periodicizes the life of a woman between menarche and menopause. The implications of this association bring about a range of ritual observances (linked to the assumption of women's hidden powers) by adult women[18]. Relevant to the universal imperative of marriage for women is that union with a man is to be synchronized with the first occurrence of the menses[19]. The abruptness of the metamorphosis was noted by other outsiders in Bangladesh:

"We saw several girls go through these changes during the year that we were in Jhagrapur. Girls who in the beginning had been running about freely, often naked-breasted and wearing only a skirt, had become little ladies by the end of the year, wearing saris and restricting their exuberance. They were now waiting to be married off" (Arens, van Beurden 1977:54).

Summary

As I have shown, maturation (*dangor hoye geche*) is broadly understood as readiness, both physical and mental, to relate to others, a faculty that for both women and men is sealed by marriage. The knowledge of how to relate and how to belong is particularly important for daughters in view of their departure from the familiar world of the father's house. This knowledge, transferred

---

[17] *Aus*—early summer rice, or, literally "ripening-in-a-short-time rice"; on the contrary, *amon*— late summer rice.
[18] See chapter 9.
[19] See chapter 17.

explicitly by way of narrative, is also conveyed by countless non-verbal codes inscribed on the body ("the body is ... continuously mingled with all the knowledge it reproduces ..." Bourdieu 1986:218). Social maturation has also a spatio-temporal dimension given by gender (Moore 1986:61). Paradoxically, for a girl the transition to adulthood coincides with bodily confinement and restrictions on movement. While the space of the world opens out before the growing boy, it shrinks abruptly for the girls to the homestead and the kitchen, a shift in the use of physical space which is to dominate all female activities. It is the interlocking of the bodily and the spatial, condensed in the notion of purda, that shapes the experiential reality of becoming a woman, the process of learning to belong.

Gender distinction in maturation is further affirmed by metaphors refering to natural habitat such as the means of subsistance or of dwelling. Girls are affirmed by the reference to ripe paddy while boys by the ability to look responsibly after cattle and manage the harvest. A corresponding pattern of gender distinction is imposed by the organisation of domestic space[20]. As Bourdieu (ibid.,90) put it,

"The house, an opus operatum, lends itself as such to a deciphering, but only to a deciphering which does not forget that the "book" from which the children learn their vision of the world is read with the body, in and through the movements and displacements which make the space within which they are enacted as much as they are made by it".

---

[20] See chapter 18.

CHAPTER 9

Administration of *dhormo*

I shall elaborate here on the *shomaj*'s judicial role, since it is through jural practice that the discourse on reason, gender and morality is most saliently brought to light. I will also show how the *dhormic* tenets ("that which is firm") are produced, reproduced and manipulated through the course of the hearing session. A case of a female plaintiff will illustrate the tension involved in winning the case but loosing one's reputation.

Dominance: fear and *bichar*

The Bengali understanding of effective dominance—the duty of superiors (husbands, masters, parents) to judge and punish (wives, servants, children) is based on the premise that unless there is an authority to be feared or if deserved punishment is omitted, society will collapse (cf. Dumont 1980:302). This insistance on punishment was stressed by my informants as often as was the necessity of fear for the maintenance of order. The lack of fear is seen as a defect of character—"a person who has no shame" (*kono lojja nei*). On the other hand there is equal emphasis on superiors to be, like parents, protecting, sustaining, nourishing and understanding.

Within a community (*para*) the encompassing disciplinary authority is diffuse in its representation—*shomaj*. The jural function of *shomaj* is explained by reference to the belief that *dhormo* can only be sustained if each unit (category), for example "women", "*bhodrolok*", domestic animals, "a family"—upholds behaviour inherent in its substance (Davis 1983:147) and that the fear of punishment is indispensable to this balance. Notably, in Gameranga, *dhormic* behaviour is related to the maintenance of boundaries.

Like every discourse, *dhormo* inclines toward an implicit negativity (Boon 1987:232). Thus, it is most vividly and frequently realized and experienced in its absence— *odhormo*, the failure of humans to act in accordance with their natural substance and rank (Davis 1983:147). In this case, as the leading *matubors* claim, *dhormo* is to be re-created. The conflict-solving sessions and public hearings (*bichar*) serve that purpose in Bangladesh communities.

Bichar—multilevelled performance

Bichar means "judgement" or "discrimination" (Inden 1976:45). These are also the qualities that point to the competence of a *matubor* to relate the events of life to *dhormic* tenets as well as to his verbal articulateness[1]. The former is concerned with the particular case that had sparked a conflict leading to the session; the latter skill points to the performative, expressive aspect of the jural-political action.

As any event of communication, *bichar* is multilevelled. Drawing on Bruner (1986), we can recognize at least two levels of narration in *bichar*. First, there is the past story that narrates a case of misconduct. Its plot (the subject matter that has occasioned the session) consists of sequences which are told and re-told, questioned, doubted and contradicted by the victim, culprit and judges in the course of hearing.

Second, there is the act of narrating ("the communicative process that produces the story in discourse (of *bichar*)"—ibid.). This process comments on the constitutive story at the same time as it provides messages about how it should be interpreted[2]. In this perspective the public hearing (and any judgement for that matter) can be seen as a narrative within a narrative built on at least a couple of frames: the literally frame and the situational, circumstantial frame.[3]

In view of this, it can be claimed that to define what is right and wrong with respect to a particular case that appears at *bichar*, is not the only concern of the session.

Equally important is its expressive form—the verbal competition, to which the concerns of the victims and the culprit may be marginal. Thus although the decisions taken by the council of *matubors* about petty crimes are quoted as official statements about the proper order of society (in general), the *bichar* provides simultaneously the opportunity to display political ambition in verbal competition—a prominent case of semantic creativity.

We can say that the event both regulates as well as generates the behaviour that occasions *bichars*. *Bichars* in Gameranga are as frequent and anticipated

---

[1] Sometimes a villager known for his rhetorical skill may be asked to participate in the session although he does not belong to the core *shomaj matubors*.

[2] Concerned with an African culture Parkin (1984) characterizes the process as one where the speakers "have to adapt quickly to the changing demands and responses of audiences alternating between set and innovative speech". They do so by changing the voice, intonation, intensity and, tempo of speech and gesticulation, by repetitions, pauses, dismissing others' comments as irrelevant and so on. By these slight shifts, those in control of the procedure produce messages (quite apart from the subject matter of the hearing), suggestive of how the story should be interpreted.

[3] Writing of transformations in children's plays Schwartzman (1978, drawing on Geertz), identifies a corresponding distinction between text, i.e. the particular behaviour marking an event and context for interpreting this. Referring to Ramayana and Mahabharata Ramanujan (1989) discerns similar structure in the classical Indian texts: "Every such story is encased in a metastory. And within the text, one tale is the context for another within it. Not only does the outer fram-story motivate the inner sub-story; the inner story illuminates the outer as well".

as are the disputes and violence that causes them. Their ubiquity depends on the shifting emphasis on one or other aspect of *dhormo* and the power placement among the *matubors*. Because *bichar*s are enactments of the status quo of morality and because morality, as well as power, is subject to constant, albeit subtle shifts, each new emphasis has to be objectified, i.e. performed and re-told, in new *bichar*.

It is via *bichar* that the authority to speak and "be listened to" ("*tar shobai mane*") is communicated and identified with a particular speaker. As a prestigious verbal discourse it determines who among the *matubors* has the skill and authority to speak. Whose interpretation and definition of *dhormo* will be accepted as legitimate largely depends on the manner of presentation. Hence the *bichar*'s relevance in re-structuring objective power and authority[4].

The social status, personalities and life experience of the *matubors* who preside over the hearing vary and so do their interpretations of *dhormic* tenets, received from the texts. *Matubors* are further divided by their varied involvement in political factions, patron–client loyalties and by their unequal emphasis on and respect for fundmentalist interpretations emitted by local *madrasa*. *Bichar*s thus serve to a high degree as a public display of the current division of power among the powerful *matubors*. In the struggle between the *madrasa* and *shomaj* for authoritative knowledge and influence in the more secular sphere of life, the former has been losing its previously unchallenged position. My urban informants, natives of Gameranga, have observed that "never before was there so much criticism against *madrasa* openly voiced as there is now". They all agreed that it was the moulana's son's illicit love affairs that discredited not only his father but the whole institution. This shows that personal lapses can affect the political position of something as unchallengeable as the bastion of Islamic knowledge (and hence the content of *dhormo*).

Procedure

As earlier mentioned each *bichar* is as much an occasion to search for truth and administer punishment as it is an expressive act, a paramount verbal contest. The whole procedure is aimed at reaching a compromise acceptable to both parties but also at serving the private political interests of the matubors. It is opened by the presentation of the case by a *matubor* representing the patriline (*gushti*) of the accusing party. After guilt is determined and acknowledged, a decision is to be taken as to the form of compensation for, (i.e. the amount of money or land) the injured party to be exacted from the criminal.

---

[4] Commenting on the work of village leaders (*shordars* or *matubors*) van Schendel (1981:217–218) speaks of the traditional competences and aims of decision making (work of reason and evidence) as "scheming, face-saving and compromise" and contrasts it with the "straightforward, crude" strategies "keen on quick returns" that characterize the methods of political leadership increasingly employed by "new village bullies" who established themselves after the liberation war in 1971.

Physical punishment is not infrequent[5] and severe breaches of Islamic tenets may lead to the temporary exclusion of the culprit's family from *shomaj*. Complicated cases may expand into several sessions and although there is a strong preference to keep all conflicts within the *para*, complex land disputes and murders are forwarded to the police. There are also cases which remain unconcluded on the grounds of shaky evidence.

The conclusion of a case is marked by the guilty party asking publically for forgiveness, which is, apart from a verbal statement (*map kora*), expressed by touching the feet of the wronged person (provided the offender is junior to the injured).

Involvement of women in *bichar*

Judgement, discrimination and verbal eloquence in extrahousehold contexts are the very attributes women are believed to be without. Women are involved in the public discourses of the village as mere receptors of *madrasa*'s exegesis of the liturgical portion of *dhormo* a few times a year; in addition they may participate indirectly by, among other things, generating gossip. A woman who displays some of the above qualities, for example by giving her opinion on public affairs, or one who is known as opinionated, is ironically referred to as "*matubor*". However, the *bichar*s do involve women, mostly as a victimized party. Cases of sexual abuse, illicit sex, and also physical violence by non-husbands[6] are the most obvious examples. A woman's case is usually brought to the council by her guardian, be it her father, uncle or an adult son. The former two kinsmen may represent a daughter in her natal village, sons and husbands are in charge of the wives in their affinal homes. Widows, who lack an authoritative guardian, are the most susceptible to sexual and physical abuse by men. They are those who plead directly without any intermediary.

To provide an insight into how "encompassment by muting" is achieved during the most public of political–moral actions of the *shomaj*, I shall specify some of the details that may shape the event. During the interrogation, the person interviewed stands a few meters apart from the *matubor*s, who are seated in chairs or on a mat, often under the shade of a tree or on the veranda of a *matubor*'s house. In answering questions, the interviewee employs a subdued tone of voice and keeps his or her eyes averted from those addressed. Women usually appear in *burka* which totally conceals their body; their face is hidden behind the veil. Those who cannot afford one, swathe their body in a sari and

[5] This ranges from physical exercise performed in front of the *matubor*s, beating with a bamboo cane and once a *bichar* where I was an onlooker decided to pluck out the eyes of the thief who managed to escape in the meantime.
[6] Wife-beating is considered a legitimate right of husbands, according to the *dhormic* order, therefore conjugal maltreatment never appears before the village court, unless it causes death or has side-effects which may implicate claims on property in case of divorce and the like.

draw its end over their head and face. A woman never stands facing the judges; her body is turned to them laterally with her right side. She is supposed to answer questions but not to voice her opinion. She may not even be called to the subsequent sessions where her case is handled. Not all women who wish to "talk" are given the chance. In two cases of physical injury[7], one widow was hospitalized (because her forearm was broken) when her case came up and her son had to come from his home in the district town to represent her. The other widow was heard by *matubor*s from the inside of her house because her only sari had been torn into pieces (by the accused party—her Hu-BrSo) and therefore she had nothing to screen her face with but the latticed walls.

Both men and women clearly occupy a deferential position during the hearings but what makes it different for women is that for them the situation is framed with additional expectations which either impede the clarity of their voice or totally silence it. Indeed, men say, the hearing of women is difficult, because they are too shy (*onek lojja hoy*). *Lojja* is the supreme female quality shared to some degree by all women (and men); *bichar* is the situation that requires shyness to be displayed in a conventional stylized manner as described in chapter 8. As elsewhere in South Asia, a woman is not supposed to interfere with political affairs between men, particularly with the men in her affinal home (Sharma 1978:4). *Lojja*, interiorized in childhood, and the institutionalized veiling of wives are the prime cultural devices to ensure that women's political and sexual attention is turned from the public to the domestic sphere (Sharma ibid.).

Women, however, are not prevented from attempts to bring a legal case for extreme violations of the moral code. Sometimes, a woman may even be encouraged by a male relative to enter into litigation in expectation of an eventual profit for himself. And, as ability to protect one's womenfolk is a part of a man's *ijjat* (honour), it is in a *matubor*'s interest to see to it that the injuries of unprotected women within his *gushti* are compensated. Each *para* in Gameranga has a few women who were pointed out to me as having once won a case; such an event is remembered even fifteen years back. So, it is not that the words of women in *bichar* are totally ignored, but saying of these words is embedded in technical obstacles which establish a premise for silence. It

---

[7] One was an older well-off widow who had her only son settled in Khulna. She lived by herself in a spacious house and yard surrounded by the much poorer dwellings of her husband's *gushti* members. A quarrel arose with a young affinally related man in her *bari* when she objected to his habit of urinating too close to her hearth (*chula*). In a rage the young man broke her forearm.

The other was a poor widow living with a married daughter and a *ghor jamai* ("son-in-law of the house") and another two unmarried daughters. A quarrel (*jhogra*) blew up when she attempted to prevent her *deor*'s (HuBr) son from felling a tree which grew on the border of their backyard. The young man scratched her face, twisted her hands and tore her sari into pieces. Later, the woman lamented "If it had been my daughter he had beaten, I would not let it go in front of the *matubors*, but doing it to an old woman like myself, it is sheer *odhormo*". However, the *bichar* found her guilty of unduly provoking the young man and he was released even from asking her forgiveness.

should be added that *bichar*s, dealing with matters of minor importance with respect to the political relationship between leading *matubor*s, are held in the courtyards (*uthan*) of the household of the accusing party. For a woman directly involved as an accuser, this means that the private, familiar place, which in normal circumstances constitutes the locus of female competence and creativity, is re-defined as a public space with corresponding consequences for her when she voices her interests; from this spatial re-definition of the private, follow others: of competence, knowledge, bodily posture, self-perception.

Zahera's case

Although disputes and fights which end up before the *shomaj* community council are recurrent feature of life in Gameranga[8], the session itself is an extraordinary event, an interference with the flow of daily life. It is a staged performance whereby fit is sought between *dhormo* and social action (Davis ibid.). Its difference from ordinary communication is marked by rules regarding speech, spacing and body posture. The *matubor*s presiding over the session establish their authority and credibility by physical as well as symbolic distancing from the subjects of the interrogation. Female respondents protect their integrity and express submission through sartorial adjustments, but apart from screening their face and directing their answers past their interlocutors, additional factors impeding their expression come into play. For instance, the lineal interrogative style of communication (where leading questions and concise, straightforward answers alternate in a flow designed to lead ultimately into a conclusion) through which the authoritative knowledge is to be established is a style to which women are not accustomed[9].

Therefore, the range of things women can express is limited. The shift of spatial meaning in cases of minor domestic *bichar*s not only affects women's own performance but excludes other women from being a part of the audience, which could have provided for them a certain degree of support[10]. So apart from the *matubor*s' self-interests and the processual techniques that disadvantage women's claims, the experience of the hearing itself re-affirms them as incompetent, shy and dependent, which is exactly the view men hold of women. This applies even to those who leave the *bichar* as winners as is clear from the way these women enter village memory. For another part of Bangladesh, Bertocci (1972) reports that the name Pagli ("the mad one") at-

[8] And elsewhere in South Asia as Davis (1983:114,170) and Bennett (1983:202) show.

[9] As it runs contrary to the domestic style of communication, which is short-hand, circuitous, discontinuous, and gestural. See chapter 7 for Ardener's (1977) comment on muteness as the function of a person's position vis à vis the dominant discourse.

[10] This is the case in inter-household *jhogra* or a spirit possession of a household member; both occasions bring together an audience of both sexes, which in the case of *jhogra* means that both rivals find supporters among on-lookers.

tached to a *bari* whose female ancestor made herself infamous after prolonged and insistent litigation with a male relative over land a case from which she ultimately emerged successful. In Gameranga one woman, who did receive approving comments for initiating a legal case, litigated against her brother in her natal community. She won a piece of ancestral land from her brother and thus contributed to the expansion of landed property to be inherited by her son (i.e. her husband's *gushti*). The consequences for a woman's reputation of a legal victory over a man in an affinal community are different, as the case of Zahera illustrates.

Zahera, a widow of 45, was a servant in the household of a rich landlord during my preliminary trip to Gameranga. A year later, after I had settled "permanently" and inquired about her, nobody was willing to tell me anything. Later I found out that she was taken as the third wife of a man in neighbouring *para*. I started to see her, as she seemed to know a lot about the influential men in the *para* where I lived. As soon as my renewed acquaintance became known in my neighbourhood, both my landlord and the women in the *gushti* where I lived told me emphatically not to see her, as she was a most disreputable and dangerous woman (*dur nam, aro bipod de*). When after a short break, I attempted a surreptitious visit to the place where she lived, she had gone. Her co-wife told me, that Zahera had gone to visit her sister in the district town and I never met her again.

Her pubescent daughter who worked as a servant in a neighbouring house was a beauty with a reputation for being unusually free and responsive to young men's advances. Zahera's name sometimes appeared in women's disapproving comments on her daughter's laxness—"like mother, like daughter …"—and once, a woman confided to me in friendship that prior to her second marriage, Zahera was surprised in a sexual involvement (*kharap, shoytaner kaj korche*) with the 15-year old son of the house where she used to be a servant. Two years after I left the village, I enquired about Zahera from one of my informants, whom I met on his trip abroad. He started by re-stating again and again how dangerous Zahera was and his story continued as follows:

Two years prior to my fieldwork, Zahera—one of the widows in Uttor Para who provided some of the politically most powerful and respectable men with sexual services, found she was pregnant and took an unconventional course of action. She went to see all the *matubors* in the area even beyond *para* bounds and told them the thing and pointed out the man[11] responsible for her condition. Some of them were the alleged culprit's arch-enemies and some were also her ex-lovers. She managed to have a *bichar* set up with wide participation of influential men from all the *para*s and after several sessions the accused man—one of the politically most powerful and respected man in the *para*—was sentenced to pay compensation.

Apart from the costs of an abortion, Zahera was indemnified with cash of Tk 800 and a piece of land. Following the scandal, the accused man lost in subsequent elections the position he had been holding for years as the "*Member Saheb*" (i.e. the representative of the *para* in the government body of Union Parishad). In contrast to Zahera, his position was only temporarily jeopardized: at the time of fieldwork, when her name was still unmentionable, he had regained public respect and was re-elected to the post.

---

[11] "How did she tell them?" I interrupted my informant. "She said she had not washed her sari for four months and pointed to her abdomen".

Zahera's case was given by my informant to support the complementary male view of women[12]: dependent and shy as they may appear they are potentially dangerous, their lack of self-control leads ultimately to treachery and widows and divorcees are particularly susceptible. "Lacking any *lojja* she went around appealing to *matubors* by sticking out her belly"[13]. In these words my informant described his vision of the ultimate moral fall. During the hearings, I have been told, Zahera was dressed in *burqua* and acted as submissively as convention requires.

Zahera's case also fits well with the generally held Bengali belief in the divisibility of the person (Marriott 1976)[14], on which the assumption of the the hidden powers[15] of women is based. In Gameranga, these powers were wielded in particular by elderly widows (to which category a woman of Zahera's age belonged, albeit attached to a household as a co-wife) who have more life experience, self-confidence and time resources to devote to the intricacies of nonformalized power relations within and among households (cf. Morsey 1978). According to my informant, Zahera had gone through several abortions in connection with previous illicit involvements, but never raised her voice then, as the men involved were economically and politically insignificant. Clearly, it is Zahera's shrewdness (i.e. strategic calculative skill) that outraged my narrator most profoundly ("she knew exactly on what occasion to cast off her *lojja*").

Elaborating on various aspects of honour, Bourdieu points (1986:12–13) to the ideal of equality that operates in honourable contests. Accordingly, the offender challenging another man's honour should consider whether the man is worth of challenging, for there is no point in attacking the man who has no reputation to lose. Such a man "is incapable of pursuing an exchange" (Bourdieu ibid.).

Referring to previous occasions when Zahera dealt with her pregnancies surreptitiously, my informant affirmed Bourdieu's (1986:61) assumption[16]:

"What would have been the point of opening a case, making trouble for a man whom nobody respects; she could not have gained anything out of accus-

---

[12] It seems to me no mere chance that this piece of information was communicated beyond the time and locus of my fieldwork. Similarly, Nancy Tapper reveals (1988) that it was during the last week of her fieldwork in an Afghan community that the existence of a brothel in a neighbouring house was brought to her attention by her informants.
My experience of commuting at a later stage of fieldwork between my home and the hospital in the adjacent community corroborates this: people who would be reticent informants as my neighbours were willing to slip pieces of valuable information as patients, away from their home. These instances illustrate the limits on the access to local information by outsiders.

[13] Even a body altered by conjugal pregnancy is considered a shameful condition in Bangladesh.

[14] Cf. chapter 7.

[15] I am not referring here to the immanent powers associated with women's self-control (Wadley 1980), but a form of power exercised situationally (to influence superiors or persuade inferiors) (Underwood 1982) and the informal forms of power available to people whose access to the dominant means of expression is restricted (Karp 1987).

[16] Cf. chapter 11.

ing a poor man who has no name, elections or property to lose". As soon as a man of substance was responsible for her pregnancy, Zahera did not hesitate to discard *lojja* and publicize her sin, instead of resorting to abortion as before. It is her adoption of male logic in strategic calculation and her lack of decency in the manner she publicized her pregnancy rather than the pregnancy itself, that outraged so many people and that renders her dangerous.

Zahera's case, although exceptional in the degree of ostentatious assertiveness, provides us with a clue to how non-dominant groups in a community like Gameranga relate to *shomaj* and how effective (albeit temporarily), if properly timed, their intrigues can prove. It further corroborates the view held by some analysts of purdah (Sharma 1978), that veiling in its most familiar form in South Asia does not prevent women from using their sexuality strategically.

Summary

So far, I have presented *shomaj* in its jural role in particular situations occasioned by the failure of individual villagers "to act in accord with their own ascribed behavioural code" (Davis' definition of misconduct, 1983:147). As other observers of village courts noted (Jensen 1984/85), the decisions taken by a *bichar* are respected, in spite of frequent comments which convey a sense of injustice and partiality. In order to minimize doubts as to the impartiality of decisions the *matubors* emphasize the processual norm. Hence, the authority of the judgement is attained by rules of procedure suggestive of an objective, impartial process. A physical and symbolic distance is created between the jury and the subject of the hearing to convey that message but also to subordinate the individual to the collectivity of the *shomaj*. The form of subordination differs according to the sex of the person interviewed. Women are encompassed in a multiple system of muting which in the case of *bichar* does not so much depersonalize (as in the case of a new wife)[17], as renders them ineffectual, dependent in the very place which in the non-*bichar* situation may be an area of their competence. This undoubtedly disadvantages their claims. Morever, spatial conversion extends to the nature of the dialogue between *shomaj* (society) and the woman, where she is asked to speak in a manner and under circumstances, which tend to silence her. A wife is thus not only "told" to turn her political attention from the public sphere to the domestic (Sharma 1978); she is reminded of the indeterminacy of her belonging—her outsideness even in the domestic sphere itself.

In writing of the various consequences of the encompassing principle I have described a social reality which is shared by both the encompassing and en-

---

[17] See chapter 18.

compassed groups[18]. *Bichar* is a case where dominance as well as muting are attained through actual linguistic as well as spatial and sartorial means.

In order to see how additional meanings are generated I have extended the structural metaphor of encompassment with the reference to the metacommunicative function of social interaction. Whatever the specific contention that has led to *bichar*, the performance itself provides an insight into how the conceptual division of reality into encompassing and encompassed units applies in action as well as showing how the encompassed, though dependent, are not entirely powerless. Specifically with respect to my concern with the construction of gender, *bichar* also provides an insight into a broader cultural assumption about Bengali Muslim women vis à vis "society"—the community into which they are married—and how these assumptions operate and are transmitted through village narrative (interpretation of an informant's interpretations—i.e. how social facts become ethnographic data). As is shown by the case of the housewife who supplied the definition of her land and people[19] and also by the case of Zahera, no norms nor conventions prevent women from attempting to exert a degree of power over their lives, however illusory it may prove to be.

[18] See chapter 7.
[19] See chapter 7.

CHAPTER 10

Shomaj represented in prayers, funerals and food exchanges

So far I have explored the idiom *shomaj* as embodied in an assembly of *matubors* who seek to restore moral order in the secular sphere of life. It is enacted in a multilevelled process in which the normative code and power interests interfere and where women's voices are silenced by the application of a host of muting contrivances. In this section I intend primarily to deal with those concerns and activities that promote the image of *shomaj* as an undivided (Islamic) community. I shall do this by examining three forms of co-operative activities through which villagers attain a sense of equality as well as a link with the metaphysical sphere of the afterlife. Congregational prayers, management of death and food exchanges are the topics of this chapter. As I will show each constitutes a meaning for the participants not only as a manifestation of their equal dependence on God, but as an experience through which the conceptual and the physical spheres of reality are unified. Through strictly regulated bodily involvement in communal prayer and sacrificial strictures that precede communal eating, the participants find out and express the equation between self and world, body and mind. Synchronisation of the movements of one's body with bodily movements of other devotees brings out the abstract notion of belonging to a *shomaj* (and beyond) and the notion of what it means to belong, to practical realisation. On the other hand, the conspicuous speed and effectiveness in the treatment of a decaying body before burial expounds the notion of double separateness: of body and soul and of a person from its *shomaj*. Like *bichar*, prayers, funerals and commensal feasts are interactions whereby the participants attempt to assimilate the idea and the practice of *dhormo* and *shomaj*. In addition, each can be considered as a processes (of clarification) that "effects understanding through bodily technique" (Jackson 1983a).

Model of the community

More important than the territorial or structural status of *shomaj* is its symbolic representation as a model of community, of the shape of social life into which a member of a human *jat* is gradually moulded. In spite of endless rivalries, litigations and lack of corporateness, and in spite of the prevailing elusiveness attested to in the studies of Bangladesh village structure (Bertocci 1970, van Schendel 1981), there exists a pervasive feeling of belonging to a particular community[1].

The importance of community belongingness is clearly evident in the difficulty, if not impossibility, for an outsider to make itself at home in a *para* where he has no kinship ties. Even a person, who may secure entry to a community by buying a piece of land, "has a hard time to be accepted even after decades of residence" (van Schendel 1981:67–68, cf. Walraven 1985). His own and his family's misconduct is judged by stricter standards than the misdeeds of his native or in-married neighbours. In Uttor Para, theft of a neighbour's boat by a newly settled, but un-related man, elicited a violent response from the villagers and in the *bichar* that followed, the thief was sentenced to having his eyes poked out (*chok tola*). As he managed to escape, the sentence was recorded and attested on a piece of paper to be archived for "twenty years".

In spite of Uttor Para's reputation as the poorest, most quarrelsome and combative *para* in Gameranga, the villagers clung most tenaciously to the idea of "coming from Uttor Para". My own loyalty was recurrently tested in inquiries about which of the *para*s I liked best.

"Indivisiveness", "equality"

Etymologically, *shomaj* reflects the notion of "going together" (Inden 1976: 22), which for the Muslims in Bangladesh gains a specific meaning. It points to the 'umma Muslima'—a model of society with the principles of solidarity and equality based on the universal brotherhood of all Muslims. In this sense, *shomaj* alludes to an abstract membership in, and belonging to, a Muslim community beyond one's land of origin (*desh*). In a narrower sense, *shomaj* is the symbol of male collectivity through which the community is defined and its boundary maintained. Unlike caste hierarchy and endogamy, which is pronounced in Hindu social ideology, official Islam propounds an ethos of equality. At the level of *shomaj*, kinship, status and economic position count ideally as secondary factors (Jensen 1984–85:149) and the actual rank preoccupations and competition within and between *gushti*s are symbolically dissolved. This effort to activate a sense of equality and to shift away from "division by hierarchic encompassment" shows that there exist multiple ideologies and texts within *dhormo* that structure subjective experiences and which people may use to assert a variety of claims (Abu-Lughod 1989). The performance of col-

---

[1] In conversations beyond one's home, this attachment is expressed by reference to the geographical area of one's birth, not to a particular *shomaj*. *Shomaj* is a diffuse, neutral category for one's collective sense of belonging which can be filled with various meanings; one's *desh* (land) on the contrary is irreplaceable. This is, of course, a male perspective on belonging; for women, who are transferred after marriage, the concept of belonging is split: while politically, their interest lies clearly in the affinal home, their emotional affiliation is more doubtful.

lective prayers (*jumat*) by householders is one means through which the dissolution is realized. Another major occasion on which the Islamic emphasis in
dhormo and collectivity of *shomaj* comes into play are funerals and memorial
prayers for the dead (*namaj-zanaza*). Whereas regular private prayers (*namaj*)
mark off particular times of the day, funerals are a rite of passage—a person's
passage from a social form of life to a metaphysical after-life—marking particular time in a person's life.

Congregational prayers

Five times a day all villagers hear the *ajan*—a sound emitted by a religious
functionary (*muezzin*) from the mosque which calls the faithful to public
prayer. The imperative verb—"Look alive" or "Come" (Cragg 1956:105)—
has a form of common singular which does not distinguish between the mas-
culine/feminine addressee in Arabic (the idiom used for that purpose in Bangladesh). In practice, women in Gameranga are forbidden participation in collective prayers (*jumat*)[2]. However, as prayers may be performed privately
(*dua*), the prohibition does not prevent them from fulfilling Koranic obligations.

The word for praying—*namaj pora*, "reading of a prayer"—suggests that
somewhere there is a text to be invoked and interpreted. Its recitations are silent, internal evocations of memorized Koran, which each reciter exteriorizes
through his or her body and face. The face of a worshiper expresses concen-
trated attention and sadness, the latter is the emotion invoked sonally by *ajan*
and perpetuated throughout the performance. Prayers are not mere recitations.
Private or collective, they are distinguished by high elaboration and stringency of performance. Each prayer is preceded by an ablution (*ghosol, wudu*),
whereby the worshiper purifies his or her body with water. Doing so, he
washes particular body parts (orifices and feet) in a prescribed sequential order, thus modeling the soul-cleansing to come. The experience of prayer is enacted as a series of bodily postures (*rakat*)—standing, bending, prostration—
accompanied by silent (inward) recitations. The prayer thus indicates the circumstances—of text, sound, natural substance and movement by which
dhormo is affirmed and produced by each believer. Thereby, prayer constitutes an instrumental metaphor that makes fluency of body movement analogous to the fluency (and extension) of thought (Jackson 1983b) and thus
"equates the physical and the mental domain of reality". The acquisition of
dhormo through embodiment discussed so far in the context of the child's socialisation[3], cannot be illustrated better than by the performance of prayer. In-

---

[2] As to the authorization to sound *ajan*, there are four categories of persons for whom it is unlawful according to Hadith: "an unclean person, a drunkard, a woman and a madman" (Shurreef:
1973:51).
[3] See chapter 8.

deed, learning to pray is an important step in a child's acquisition of "understanding".

During the collective performance the worshippers stand in several rows behind a leader, facing the direction of Mecca. This direction and movement in unison provide a sense of belonging derived from common faith and of corporateness unattained in mundane daily pursuits. At the same time as the devotee gains a sense of self with immediate co-practitioners (i.e. own *shomaj*) the prayer also provides participants with the possibility of traversing the boundedness of their community (its particular form of hierarchy) and of manifesting an adherence to the pan-Islamic assesment of universe (counterposed in daily practices to specific local interpretations of *dhormo* and ethnocentric outlook). Essential to Islamic prayer is the formulation of its purpose (*niyyat*) (Cragg 1956:109) which follows ablution and precedes posturing. It is for each performer to reflect over her or his imminent problems and needs, present them to God, solicit benevolence and secure favour. *Niyyat* thus welds a self-reflective, self-recreating element into the habitually exercised *rakat*s; it constitutes the sole improvised portion of this otherwise mnemonic technical action. In this way a prayer permits each person to discover in his or her own personality a way of uniting the personal and the social aspect of Being (Jackson 1983a,b).

The most widely attended of daily prayers in Gameranga is the late afternoon prayer. Whenever it coincides with a public event like *bichar*, or the Wednesday market, all activities are interrupted and men gather along the embankment of the pond for ablution and then assume the prayer position on the school playground. On other days, but particularly on Fridays, the *madrasa*s mosque is the obvious site.

Congregational prayers are open to all male Muslims in the community, even passing beggars can join them. However, neither men from the Bede settlement[4] nearby, nor the members of a *muchi* household[5], were ever seen to participate or to enter the mosque. There was no fixed order of placing indicating the hierarchy of the devotees; however, after a platform was constructed (of bricks left from the construction of the school latrine), the *matubor*s constituting *shomaj* started to gather there, squatting and talking; when the *ajan* reached them, they assumed a praying posture at the same spot, thus marking who the core men in the congregation were.

On Wednesdays during the afternoon market, a group of women[6] gather behind the bushes in the courtyard of an adjacent *bari*, watching this massive transformation from busy marketing into a pious stillness that follows the call of the *muezzin* and dissolving again into mundane material concerns after the

---

[4] Four semi-nomadic households of a Muslim sub-caste located at the outskirts of Dokhin Para.

[5] Scavenger, hide-curing caste.

[6] These are the female heads of households or young unmarried daughters whose fathers are occasionally absent, awaiting impatiently their male-relative—a cousine, an uncle—whom they entrusted with the task of shopping. Like a mosque, market is not accessible to decent women.

prayer is accomplished. In all its forms a prayer introduces a supernatural, out-of-the ordinary dimension into the course of daily business and preoccupations. As I said at the beginning, for the Muslims in South Asia in particular, it creates an opportunity to demonstrate a kind of self-aspiration to a universal extension (Pitt-Rivers 1979). As the most inclusive of formal male gatherings, and as a public display of an undifferentiated dependence on God, a prayer also provides its performers with an experience of equality. From verbal self-presentations it is clear that for Muslims in Gameranga, the traditional Others have always been caste-oriented Hindus; in effect for a Bengali Muslim a sense of belonging even today is construed by way of contrast with Hinduism (this in spite of the dwindling number of actual Hindu neighbourhoods). It seems, therefore, that this focus on equality, as demonstrated in male perform-ance of prayers, is associated with an assertion of the Islamic dimension in *dhormo* (this in spite of residual caste-mindedness prevalent in Bangladeshi Muslims' view of occupations) and in *shomaj*. The collectivist element of this performance rests in the fact that the participants follow mechanically the same formal structure. However, equally important is the emphasis on the unique in each worshipper's particular worries, desires and strivings—that which is given expression in formulating silently one's intention with each particular prayer. So in spite of its commonly structured scheme, it allows each person to discover a way of being self while interacting with others (Jackson 1983a).

In prayer the worshipper attempts to balance two sorts of aesthetic forms—the memorized structure of verbal text is to be harmonized with the physical structure of bodily movement (within habitus). This uniquely silent and har-monised performance provides thus a meaning for its reciters not only as a manifestation of ideal social states—togetherness, equality, belongingness to *umma* Muslima, but in a more concrete sense it serves to abolish the separa-tion and hierarchization between mind and body, emotion and intellect, self and the world. In this lies the therapeutic and pragmatic power of ritual activi-ties.

Funerals

I have previously mentioned that apart from *bichar* there are other, less noticeable ways *shomaj* enters the consciousness of villagers. As an internal-ized authority, *shomaj* is implied in threats women recall of denying them proper burial when their time comes. This is frequently given as a reason for refraining from actions which the *shomaj* or *madrasa* condemns[7]. Transgres-sions of *para*'s boundary but also transgressions of various moral precepts through acts of adultery, theft, singing, dancing, listening to Radio Bangla-

[7] Cf. chapter 5.

desh, taking of life, submitting onself to sterilization, etc. are all examples of activities propounded by the *shomaj* establishement as meritricious or non-Islamic. A pious old man in Uttor Para, whose *bari* had been for generations linked to *madrasa*, was particularly feared and often quoted, as he used to make rounds throughout the *bari*s, threatening mature girls and wives with the worst imaginable punishment—denial of a proper funeral.

The persuasiveness of this particular threat capitalizes on two mutually related beliefs. First is the promise of salvation that negates individual extinction, the second is the split between body and soul on death. Both preoccupations are directed towards the central existential problem which the thought of death invokes, namely, what form of continuity exists beyond a physical death? The problem of salvation, as well as the process and method of attaining it constitutes one of the distinctive features of a Bengali Muslim *jat*. The preoccupation with disposal of the bodies of dead is of central importance, as evidenced in the inquiries villagers addressed to me with respect to my own and other *jat*s. I was relieved that for once I was able to accord with my hosts' notion of humanity when I related the Roman-Catholic praxis. It was with surprise my informants heard that "we" too bury our dead. As they continue to associate all non-Islamic practices with Hindus, they thought "my people" also burned their deceased—a practice regarded with horror.

A great deal of my informants' thought is directed to the contemplation of death. Unlike infertility, an individual death is not conceived of as an absolute finality, rather as a passage to another place to await the Last Judgement and finally to assume a new form of life. As Thorp (1982) also noted, it is much easier to discuss death than life with Muslim peasants. In my informants' parlance, the term "life"—*jibon*—is recalled in reflections on the various forms of "life"—a *jat* attainable at birth rather than in existential discourse. Life's meaning and the enforcement of *dhorm*ic behaviour are typically reflected upon and effected through imagining one's death, as if the ultimate purpose of all human efforts and solace in suffering were to attain admittance to Paradise. This world and the next thus merge in the idea that there attaches to each individual action in life a deterministic consequence (Keyes 1987). In effect, the meaning and moral load of daily actions is always measured with respect to their consequences for the afterlife. My informants remained unmoved when I became outraged and pointed out to them a case of blatant exploitation or injustice; instead they reminded me of God's ultimate jural authority, that it was not up to us humans to judge, and recalled in considerable detail the torments of hell awaiting the culprit.

Apart from this salvationist perspective that provides a basis for moral evaluation and life orientation, Muslims are enjoined to undertake merit making. The Islamic calendar and tenets[8] supply villagers with plenty of opportunities to punctuate their life with particular acts that produce positive merits (*pak*).

---

[8] The five pillars of Islam listed in chapter 6.

In spite of the invocations of God's omnipresent and ultimate power, the villagers in Gameranga, like Muslims elsewhere, seek to attain eternal life in paradise deliberately and often ostentatiously "through … prayers or specific good works, to acquire quantities of merit … to offset the quantities of sin … they may have committed" (Tapper 1987). Directed to pleasing God, this manipulative, calculating attitude towards salvation is at variance with the all encompassing fatalism asserted in the very denotations of their particular *dhormic* belonging: Muslim or follower of Islam is —"one who is in submission to God's will" (Ewing 1988, Weekes 1984:xxvii). Eager merit-collectors are suspect, as is revealed in a commment I once overheared, "Too much *dhormo*, (invites) too much Devil" (*Beshi dhormo beshi shoytan*).

Given the local recognition of the interior and exterior aspect of things, a person's behaviour (quantity of accumulated merits and demerits) is submitted at death to a double evaluation: of the community (*shomaj*) whose task it is to secure easy release of the soul, and of God who executes the final judgement[9].

The possible goals are imagined either as a joyous life in paradise or as suffering in hell. Paradise is invariably associated with the humid lushness of a prosperous garden, hell with dry heat of fire. Women would often remind me of the consequences of my unconcern with covering my head by graphically specifying the form of suffering that awaited me: "Each strand of your hair will turn into a snake voraciously biting your face while flames of fire will lick your body". Though both are considered matters of *dhormo*-management, the verdicts issued by the *shomaj* at *bichar* are ephemeral compared with those of the Day of Judgement administered by Allah. It is also of interest to note that the negative prospect—the form of life to be endured in hell is illustrated in more poignant detail than are the joys of paradise.

Recreation and assertion of shomaj

All adult Muslims in Gameranga are seriously concerned with providing and obtaining a proper burial. It is believed that the soul of a person whose body has not been properly purified and buried is transformed into a wandering spirit (*bhut*). This fate also befalls those who die an untimely death. A person who dies suddenly or violently, a woman dying in childbirth (the most frightening form of death) are equally succeptible to such a distressing metamorphosis. Muslim villagers remembered that the worst aspect of the disasters precipitated by floods was the fact of not being able to bury their dead. Instead, corpses were tied to banana tree trunks and floated down the waterways

---

[9] Since humans can conceal their motives, intentions and even acts from the *shomaj* but not from God, it is beyond the *shomaj*'s competence to identify all aspects of human experience (i.e. a person's internal experiences as well as outward behaviour); this task is up to an omniscient Allah. Nevertheless, it is up to the *shomaj* to judge whether a person deserves Islamic burial or not.

(Tham 1989). This corresponded partially to Hindu practice—the less offensive part of Hindu mortuary rites, whose central moment—freeing the soul by burning of the corpse—is otherwise recalled with great horror in Gameranga.

Death creates a gap and a separation from the human community—*shomaj*. Apart from the danger posed by supernatural beings (*bhut*), there is an interest in responding to the challenge to social continuity that the loss of a *shomaj* member represents. Of all life-cycle ceremonies, the funeral is the feast where the obligation to invite all *shomaj* (at least male representantatives of each household) is most pronounced. In relation to the ideology of death, Bloch and Parry (1982:5) remind us that the transformation (rebirth) "that occurs at death is not only a denial of individual extinction but also a re-assertion of society and a renewal of life and creative power". This emphasis on the problem of society's (*shomaj*) re-assertion necessitated by death is further evident in the manner of disposing of the bodies of persons who have not attained a complete social status or whose belongingness (in terms of marital status, *jat* identity) and moral profile is questionable. Their funerals are effected less elaborately than those of fully fledged social personae. In Gameranga, the death of infants or young children passes almost unnoticed; their bodies are just buried without any ritual attention. Mothers remained largely unmoved when talking about a child who died soon after birth. Surprised by such detachment I once asked a matron whose daughter-in-law's first-born baby died the day before: "Must she laugh when telling me about it? Is not she sad at all?". "What for? It had not yet touched her breast", my informant responded, alluding thus to the non-social status of the newborn, who had not yet been ritually incorporated into humanity[10]. An outsider like the anthropologist, not fully fledged into any of the existing social categories, occupies an interstitial status. Once when I was ill with a high fever, I overheard the question "Who will tell her mother if she dies?", among the women who surrounded my cot. Not much attention was given to this, but later when I recovered and asked a friend she admitted—hypothetically, the possibility of my death had been considered. They thought a messenger ought to be sent instantly to "my people" so they could collect my body and bury it elsewhere.

The bodies of social rejects are disposed of without ritual. For example, children born out of wedlock are left in the jungle to be eaten by jackals and dogs and as I said earlier, even women transgressing purdah are frequently threatened with denial of a funeral. From Jamalpur, Blanchet (1984:91) reports that "the corpse of a thief is sent floating on the river, treated as a desanctified body, the exposed decomposition of which disturbs no one"[11].

[10] Mothers in Gameranga delay the onset of breastfeeding for one to two days, believing colostrum—"spoiled milk"—is harmful to the child. A child who has not yet "touched mother's breast", i.e. eaten and established social contact, is considered less than human. A further passage into the social order of human *jat* is marked by ritual hair-and-nail-cutting on the 6th day after delivery. Then mother's milk is poured on its head to soften the hair before it is removed.
[11] Once during my stay in the village hospital I contacted the staff urgently when a floating object on the river appeared to me to be a baby. A nurse commented unconcernedly, "She must have been unmarried"—thus pointing to the mother's presumed sin.

Here Blanchet's comment of the *shomaj*'s role in funerary rites illustrates aptly their function in the restoration of social order: "The thief and the illegitimate child are social rejects. The shomaj, i.e. the community of men who act as gate-keepers to the religious society and to God, will not bury them. Here, the jungle and the river are regarded as untamed and can be contrasted to cultivated land which has been brought under the control of men. Only the latter environment alone is associated with civilization" (ibid.).

In Gameranga, when a person dies, people say "Allah took her", or "life has left it", and also "like a bird, it has flown back to Allah" (Thoorp 1982); or, they may make a gesture pointing to the sky. As Thoorp notes for another community in Bangladesh, it is only in the context of death that people view "… a person's spiritual reality and identity, as something dualistically separate from body". The meaning of the word "life" or "being alive" is thus approximated to "soul" (*ruhu, pran, jibon*). In order that the soul's separation and transition—the road to salvation—can procede on its proper course and that the dead and bereaved can hopefully survive the death (Keyes 1987), it is necessary for the body to be treated in a culturally standardized way. Funerals are the ceremonies concerned with this.

Procedure: division of labour and emotions

To ensure that the dead can face Allah, physical death is followed by two stages and modes of cleansing—ablution with water (*ghosol*) of the corpse, and spiritual purification attained by prayers for the dead person's soul (*namaj zanana*).

As soon as life has left a person, water is dropped in her mouth and her jaws are tied shut. Then the body is covered with a cloth, carried out of the house and placed on a mat or a bamboo stretcher where it is scrupulously washed with soap and hot water. It is particularly important to remove dirt from the orifices—mouth, ears, nose and anus. All work involved in funeral preparations is carried out by men, but a female relative is summoned to wash and dress a deceased woman's body. In the meantime a tailor (*dorji*) is sewing the new dress, a male team is cutting bamboo to line and reinforce the grave, another team does the digging and *madrasa* functionaries check that everything proceeds in an orthodox manner. Messengers are sent to relatives (for instance daughters married in surrounding villages) to break the news.

Women of the bereaved household are busy in the kitchen area boiling water for the last ablution as well as for washing bedding with which the body of the deceased might have been in contact. When the corpse is carried away, it is for women to restore the house and smear its floor with cow-dung.

Following the ablution, the corpse is wiped, scented, and wrapped in specially sewn white cotton cloth. When it is done no part of the body shows. For a deceased woman, more material is used, as her private parts require a double covering[12]. The scented and dressed body is placed in the middle of the court-yard with the head directed towards Mecca. An umbrella may be stretched be-sides to protect the deceased's head from the sun. A family member may squat alongside, facing the same direction, to recite from the Koran. At the funeral of a famous *kobiraj* (herbalist), it was his daughter who read the Koran by her father's body, while his son, leaning against a tree was weeping, overwhelmed by grief at the loss. Two senior agnates attempted to pull him away and con-sole him by referring to God's will.

Another funeral preparation that I observed closely, followed the death of an old mother from a pious, orthodox bari of *munshis*[13]. In both cases, women from Uttor Para, but also female relatives from surrounding areas, were present as distant, silent and shy observers[14] clinging together at the back. One was summoned as a "washing woman" (*douhani biti*). Women's (hesitant) participation, however, does not extend beyond the moment at which the body is carried away to the grave in a bamboo grove behind the house or a jungle-like place apart. Henceforth the funeral is exclusively a male concern—con-gregational prayer and the lowering of the body into the grave is a stage of the ceremony at which even my presence was banned[15].

Grief

Funerary work is notably well organized and co-ordinated—a unique and ex-ceptional case of lineal (*gushti*) and community (*shomaj*) corporateness. There is a marked concern with speed and exactness in measuring—the cloth, the dead body and the grave—unequalled in other ritual contexts.

This focus on effectiveness and *shomaj* co-operation contrasts with a marked lack of concern for ostentatious mourning. Although the atmosphere is solemn and occasionally a relative of the deceased bursts into weeping when she or he receives the news, emotional outbursts are not a prominent feature of funerals. Having known a large number of the funeral participants as my neighbours, I found them curiously impassive during the rite. In con-trast with the detachment at funerals, sorrow is expressed in loud crying or si-lent weeping at any time after the body has been placed in the grave. Abruptly and at any time a woman may burst into loud wailing, because she has remem-bered the death of a close relative. Many a female informant burst into tears whenever my inquiry led to her dead mother or to a daughter who died of cholera; another became upset recollecting a daughter who had been mur-

---

[12] Also extra digging is needed as the grave for a female corpse should be deeper than the grave for a man.

[13] One of the lower titles of a religious functionary.

[14] This is contrary to observations made by Blanchet (1984) in Jamalpur where women are totally excluded.

[15] Normally, I was encouraged to participate at *bichar*s and also went unrestricted to the market. Killing of a cow and burial were the most gender exclusive areas of the ritual realm.

dered. Some may express anger and blame another person alleged to have caused the death. Loud wailing always attracts other women who express their compassion in words and by intense eye contact. The post-funeral grief of bereavement takes the form of a loud stylized chanted lament interspersed with words confessing and evoking feelings of damage caused by separation and loss. Unlike men, women turn weeping into wept song. The musical quality of the lament recalls a Bedouin poetic form noted by Abu-Lughod (1986:198) among Awlad 'Ali: "Like the singing of poems, the chant takes the form of a short verse ... the words repeated in a set order following a single melodic pattern. The special pitch and quavering of the voice, more exaggerated than in singing, along with the weeping and sobbing that often accompany it, make this heart-rending"[16]. Men also may remember with obvious sadness a particularly loved relative in the course of a conversation but it is not expressed in the stylised manner of women.

At funerals male participants, while busy with digging, sewing and measuring (as if to counteract the rupture in the structure), may intersperse their work with conversation on casual, worldly matters (A man sewing the cloth for the corpse asked me whether the dead man returned money he had borrowed from me earlier, another urged me to ask my landlord for cooking oil for the meal to be cooked and served for the guests after the burial). The dead are remembered at a commemorative feast held on the 6th and and 40th days following the death, and at any time a memorial ceremony may be held to commemorate long departed parents or grandparents. These are, again male and *shomaj* centred commensal feasts from which women are excluded.

Disgust

The immediacy of death is not met with tears but spat out saliva. Unlike weeping, disgust (*ghirna*) is an emotion that is given overt expression at funerals. Disgust occupies a central place in the emotional repertoire of villagers in Gameranga. It is expressed in words or gesture as a comment on a variety of undesirable contacts (notably with respect to *jat* transgressions) and processes (decay of organic matter, parturition, menstruation, flatulence). In the realm of human physiology, a sick body and a dead body are viewed as repulsive objects, each representing various stages of transformation and decay. It is the contrast between the wholesome, "clean" body and its decomposing, broken and smelling variations that generates the idea of pollution and incites disgust.

A dead body should be buried within a day of death, and cases of delay (e.g. a crime that involves police intervention) are long remembered with regret. Villagers name explicitly the decaying process (that invites a reflection

---

[16] In Gameranga, similar ritual with the same poetical structure of text and melody is adopted whenever women wish to express and to draw attention to her disappointments, anger and sadness in contexts other than death.

on a rupture in the normal flow of things) in the climatic conditions specific to their *desh* as a reason for immediate and uninterrupted funeral work. Everything that may have come in contacat with the corpse is considered polluted and, as mentioned before, the person who undertakes the last ablution for the dead must bathe thoroughly. The purification of clothes and the house where the dead slept are other insitutionalized requirements. Except for washing male corpses, the removal of pollution is women's work.

Disgust (*ghirna*) on smelling or seeing whatever falls within the category of pollution (excrement, menstrual blood, pork, a carcass) may find individual expression in spitting. It is believed that even dirt perceived audiovisually may penetrate and harm one's body, in which case it should be rejected by spitting out saliva (Kotalová 1984). Disgust caused by a decomposing body is marked by copious spitting at funerals ("because of the smell"—*gondo hoy*), which is a way the participants get rid of the harmful effects emanating from the corpse.

Surviving death

Among Bengali Muslims the existential problem of finite mortality (broken belongingness to this world) and the practical problem of the disposal of the physical remains are combined in the ideology and method of salvation. Although the dead in Gameranga do not become venerated ancestors and the personal status of the deceased after re-birth remains largely unspecified, the journey, Day of Judgement and hoped for admission to paradise are of central concern. It is up to the *shomaj* to open up the possibility of transformation through a process that entails the double work of purification and a particular working style. Beyond the processual concerns, the loss of a family member brought to mind by the presence of the corpse in the home invokes profound emotions.

In trying to grasp the particular relation between funeral emotions and work I have initially assumed, in accordance with local exegesis, that the characteristic speed and remarkable effectiveness of the work together with the customary spitting are intended to remove impurity for the comfort of the bereaved. Apart from the disgust (which is given verbal as well as physical expression), there is the fear that unless the dead is properly (i.e. rapidly) buried, it will turn into a ghost (bhut). However, what my informants did not put into words, but what is implicitly suggested by the emphasis on God's will to discourage grief during a funeral, is an acute concern for "the fate and comfort of the soul from the point of death until the Day of Judgement" (Tapper 1987). By shifting the focus onto the dead, one can understand the absence, or postponement, of mourning as an effort to eliminate all that could retard the soul's departure. Both concerns stress a person's double belonging, the social and the metaphysical.

Because the point of Judgement is not more precisely specified than "as soon as the soul departs" it is felt that too lengthy and too ostentatious mourning obstructs its release. Tears, laments and other self-centred forms of grief lead to distraction from the fate of the deceased that may in the end prevent the soul's acceptance by God (Tapper ibid.). Instead, attention is focused on work and uncompetitive co-operation of *gushti* and *shomaj*. By shifting from various self-absorbing forms of sorrow to positive activities and a new form of interaction (an out-of-the-ordinary inter-household corporateness), the funeral helps the deceased to survive his death and the bereaved to overcome the immediate pain of loss. Since, as Keyes (1987) argues, "death poses not only a problem for society, but also for every individual who in viewing the death of another glimpses his or her own ultimate fate. To be assured that the dead person one has known in life has achieved some sort of immortality in death is also to be assured that one will oneself achieve such a state when one dies".

Commonness

Ultimately, to understand the matter-of-factness with which death is met in Gameranga, it is of importance to consider the local understanding of death in relation to its frequency[17].

On my arrival in November 1982, the boatman who took me to Gameranga told me that a cholera epidemic had taken the life of fifty people there in the previous two weeks (out of the population of ca 2000). The number shocked me at first, but during my stay I came to realize that death is a "domesticated" event, a part of the expected and the ordinary, and that the villagers even speculated from time to time on my own death. Once, when I returned from prolonged medical consultation in Dhaka, a female informant confided to me that she thought I was dead because my death was revealed to her in a dream. Another woman confirmed that people speculated on the reasons for my long absence: she heard that I would not return to the village because I was seriously ill and had probably died.

It may be that because death is so close and familiar it does not evoke the same fear and awe in my informants as it does in myself. Writing of deaths in peasant societies, various ethnographers draw attention to the shift in thinking of death in Western Europe[18]. Recalling Mediaeval Europe some scholars link the calmness in the face of "death in due time" to the absence in these cultures

---

[17] In my sample of 193 households, 184 married women reported the deaths of 446 children. A woman I used to visit in another village experienced 23 deliveries and by the time of our acquaintance had only three surviving children.

Maternal mortality in Bangladesh was estimated to be between 4.8 to 7.7 per 1000 live births (Schaffer 1986:6); in the recent World Bank Report (Staff 1991) the ratio is 6 to 8 deaths per 1000 births. The same report indicates infant mortality to be 110 (compared to 61,5 for the rest of Asia) while the mortality of children under five is estimated to be 188 per 1000 children.

[18] Myerhoff (1984) relies on Aries (1974) who quotes Solshenitsyn (1968); Bourdieu (1986) cites Proust; Cantlie (1989) recalls her experience from Assam and England. See also Bakhtin 1986: 398.

of the ideal of the atomized individual (with rights to good health, love, happiness, self-realization); rather than taking death as injustice, they accept it calmly "as if they were just moving into a new house" (Solshenitsyn quoted in Myerhoff 1984). Writing on "tamed deaths", Myerhoff (ibid.) joins a similar line of argument: "Later, as the concept of the individual emerges, distinct from the social and communal context, the moment of death came to be regarded as an opportunity in which one was most able to reach—and publically present—a full awareness of self".

To associate death with the attainment of self-awareness is in line with the praxis among villagers in Gameranga of recalling death and the after-world in the context of conversations about life.

Extra-household commensality

Apart from worship and management of death, the identity of *shomaj* is mediated in extrahousehold commensal events, whereby a sense of equality is made consubstantial through the act of sharing a meal. Because inclusion of cooked meat—qualifier of social distinction—is a requirement (of extrahousehold commensality) these feasts are not as unequivocally linked to the cosmological domain as prayers are. For a householder sponsoring a feast, it is of prime importance that *shomaj* members are invited. Locally termed "feeding people" (*manshi khawai*), hospitality (*otithia*) is the foremost form of patronage. It is charged with ambiguous messages aiming as much at the achievement of equality (equal dependence on God) as at the achievement of rank and domination. The former is sought in the act of sharing food boiled in the same pot (*ek harite*), the latter is expressed in the intricate game of dependence/subordination guided by the standard rules of comportment between guest and host. This includes the sitting order that reveals the status of each guest. In all commensal feasts food is always served boiled (rice in water, meat in oil), meat should be included, and women, although largely responsible for cooking and serving, are excluded from the gathering around the meal. At circumcisions or memorials which are the feasts explicitly concerned with the assertion of the host-*gushti*'s membership in *shomaj* and of agnatic unity the cooking is done by a male crew. Women are only allowed to pound spices[19].

Food is also a prototype of the charitable gift (Murphy 1986). Given in charity, it should be unprocessed—unboiled rice or raw meat—or as leftovers, the form depending on the occasion: rice is given to beggars on their Friday (now-

---

[19] Ordinarily, involvement in the process of food preparation and cooking is graded according to the status of each woman in the family. Accordingly, meat and *torkari* is prepared by the mother-in-law (head of the team), rice by the daughter-in-law and spices are pounded by a "new wife" or a servant.

adays extended to daily) rounds; raw meat distribution follows sacrificial slaughters; leftovers (*jutho*) are distributed in connection with large commensal feasts like weddings. Because beggars are in most cases anonymous outsiders unable to reciprocate, almsgiving is one of the ways the *shomaj* asserts its cohesion to the outside, unspecified Islamic world, its boundlessness.

What is served in the context of ostentatious hospitality (*otithia*)—"guest food"—is distinguished from alms and ordinary food. I shall elaborate on the wider *dhormic* context of the items which constitutes this category.
It will be shown that each derives its divine connection from different cosmological domains. The universal Bengali staple-rice comes, from a female deity of Hindu origin, while meat, that marks a meal as extraordinary—has as its source a male deity representative of Islam.

Rice (*bhat*)—superfood

In Gameranga, *bhat* is used synonymously with food. "Have you eaten rice?" (*Bhat khaechen*) is a greeting or a welcoming phrase meant to inquire whether a person has had her meal. The positive answer prompts further questioning as to what was added to the rice "*Bhat ki dia khaechen?*". It is only in this question and the answer to it that the word "*bhat*" acquires a culinary specific sense of "rice", opposable to the other items in the dish. Then it tells something definite about the composition of the meal. "*Bhat*" thus has a generic meaning—"food", independent of the form of transformation and it has a specific meaning "boiled rice"—denoting the basic component of a Bengali dish. In Gameranga, as in most South Asian communities, "food is held to be imbued with moral qualities which affect the mind and disposition of the eater" and it is believed that in sharing cooked (i.e. converted, culturally processed) food, these qualities, habits and character are transmitted and internalized by those who eat it (Cantlie 1981:43). Cooked rice (*bhat*) which is considered "the food" par excellence, is particularly conductive to the transmission of spiritual and affective states, even *dhormo* in case of inter-*jat* commensality. Offering a plate of boiled rice is one way of integrating strangers who come to stay for an unspecified period of time. So, a passing beggar, unlike an anthropologist, is given just a handful of raw rice (*chaul*). The emotional load of offering cooked food is accentuated by the risk that it can always be declined as polluting, while unprocessed food items—rice-grains, meat cuts from a slaughtered goat, unboiled egg, coconut, banana—are unambiguously clean and therefore acceptable.

The distinction between qualities of rice are locally important, not only agronomically with respect to botanical varieties growing at different seasons and soils, but according to the forms into which it is processed and the culinary purposes it serves. The main distinction is between *dhan*, which is the generic name for paddy (as a plant, grains, stalks, flowers), *chaul*—husked and parboiled grain—and *bhat*—boiled rice to be served as a meal.

An answer to the question as to what was added to rice at a particular meal is also meant to reveal the eater's status or the standing of the household where she is a guest. Or just her disposition at the moment following a meal. This can range from just salt or juice of squeezed lemon, to *phuti mach* (low status fish) and vegetable *torkari*. Meat is always associated with feasting or being a guest[20].

Food intake is considered a proper meal provided it consists of boiled rice. There is a large variety of adjectives to distinguish between tastes of rice from various regions, harvests, etc. Most Bengalis believe that the rice of their natal land is the sweetest in Bangladesh, sweetness being the attribute of the most superior of tastes. The quality of paddy is believed to be determined by the soil and climatic conditions in each region as well as by the skill and character of those who cultivate it. A region's (*desher*) identity is consubstantiated with other substances in the soil and by extention with the staple grain it yields. Because the preservation of paddy-seeds from harvest to sowing is exclusively a housewife's responsibility—women partake by implication in the process of creating and re-creating the identity of the region (*desh*)[21].

A person's psychological well-being is directly and unequivocally related to her intake of rice. Whenever my face betrayed sadness, the women asked me if I missed my mother or if my host's servant did not give me enough rice. Emotional and bodily disposition (largely depending on the intake of food) are mutually related aspects of a person's well-being. Being able to fill one's stomach with *bhat* is also an indicator of belongingness, intimacy and comfort. This multiple association is implied in the doubts expressed by a village housekeeper in Dhaka. The *memsaheb* to whom I confessed the acute loneliness I felt during various periods of my fieldwork, reported that her Bengali servant to whom she had translated that passage of my letter, reacted with surprise, "Does not she eat rice with them? Gopalpur is famous for sweet quality!".

In its life-sustaining, strength-giving, cooling, aesthetic and emotional qualities, lack of rice cannot be compensated for by any other food. Not eating rice equals hunger, loneliness and suffering. In Bengali, both conditions are conveyed in one word—*khuda*.

Landless villagers articulate their attachment to and nostalgia for rice at pre-harvest time when they have to eat subsidized wheat instead. This particular month of the year is associated with suffering as expressed in calendar-folklore: "If March is difficult, because peasants have no work, April is worse—everyone eats wheat"—(*Badur mashe, kostho, kishan chole na, shotir mashe beshi koshto, shobai atta khae*). The destitute women who cooked and

---

[20] Though a large fatty fish has the same association.
[21] For further circumstances supporting this assertion, see "Spatial distance between affinal *gushtis* and provenance of wife", chapter 15.

took their meals at the government subsidized *etim khana* (feeding center set up on the ground of my landlord) during meagre times, complained of hunger after eating a plateful of wheat-porridge which they had cooked themselves. An affluent, educated landowner who had been sentenced to four-years' imprisonment after the liberation war, used to compare his experience of prison with my life in Gameranga. Whenever he wished to express empathy at being parted from "the things of my home", he pointed to food as a critical factor— "I know how you feel eating rice twice a day—in jail they used to punish us by serving wheat bread unceasingly for four months. I thought then, I would die".

As a plant, paddy (*dhan*) is paralleled with human life when estimating the age of marriageable girls: the names of two crop varieties which ripen at different periods are used as metaphors for various stages of ripeness for marriage. In its unprocessed state, paddy is the foremost indicator of wealth (land, gold, sari, money are other standard convertibles). Paddy is considered sacred and rice eating a pious act. Its sacredness is derived from association with deity Lokhi (Bengali rendering of Laksmi) who has been imported into Muslim Bengal from the cosmological universe of North India (Greenough 1983, Wadley 1980) to symbolize the proliferation of life and general well-being. It is a sign of auspiciousness (*shubida*) in subsistence management[22]. The villagers in Gameranga ascribe the ultimate responsibility for the providing of food to Lokhi and Allah who each represent the sovereign deity (and the two *dhorm*ic traditions within which peasants operate). At the onset of the ploughing season, a householder may invite a *moulana* for a meal to secure his blessing, but during harvests, the approaching boats ladden with paddy sheaves are announced with screams "Lokhi is coming to our house!" (*Lokhi ghore ashche*). In the neighbouring Indian state, Orissa, the festival of Laksmi is celebrated in the month of *Augrahayan*, the time of year which coincides with the rice harvest and with weddings (Marglin 1981). A chain of folkloric associations between Lokhi, universal fertility (of land, vegetation and women) and a perfect wife (*bou*) is widely documented in poetry and historical studies from South Asia (Blanchet 1984, Chaudhuri 1965:204, Greenough 1983, Majupuria 1978:77, Wadley 1980).

In Bangladesh, a family's prosperity as well as a person's well-being is indicated by a granary full of paddy or a stomach filled with rice. However, in these days of scarcity one hears more often of the absence of Lokhi—failed harvest, bad luck with fishing, cow that does not give milk, increasing debts, stolen oxen are all evidence of this (Greenough ibid.). Lokhi in her various embodiments is acknowledged in a range of contexts. Once, a landless neighbour received a small chicken from his well-married sister against the slack period to come. His wife and daughter spent considerable energy to searching for crumbs and scraps to feed the only inhabitant of the coop (*murgir ghor*). As it grew, they hoped for a large meal to come. After a month a predator flew

[22] Cf. chapter 17.

away with the chicken. "*Olokhi*" (misfortune), sadly remarked the wife. Later, the husband returned from a day-employment in the fields with a large fish. "*Lokhi dieche*" (Lokhi gave it), said he, and explained that a flying bird dropped it just in the spot where he worked.

When a man from Gameranga, settled in town, talked of his sudden but steadily increasing profit from his transport business, his younger brother explained later on: "It started after his marriage", and added, "His wife is a Lokhi". When still single, men tend to ascribe even a success beyond the domestic sphere, e.g. school examination success, to their mothers, who are then assimilated to Lokhi. The sacredness of rice, its association with a female deity and with life itself, finds further expression in elaborate rules of grain processing. The notable cautiousness is revealed in the strictness with which children are reproved for playing with rice grains.

Meat (*mangsho*)—the extraordinary

As noted earlier, to consider the category rice as a generalised representative of food is a matter of context. When food (*bhat*) is opposed to non-food (non-edible plants or animals), meat (*mangsho*) is included under *bhat*. However, in the realm of political achievement, rice, albeit indispensable, is opposable and subordinated to meat. As a specified category of food, even meat carries multiple and contradictory meanings; in a secular context it qualifies social distinction, as an item prominently linked to Islamic ritual calendar and almsgiving[23], meat consumption is aimed at transcending hierarchy to promote a sense of equality among the co-eaters. At a level of animal classification beef (*gorur mangsho*) constitutes a specified category of meat in that its consumption as will be shown, marks the *jat* boundary vis à vis Hindus.

The inclusion of meat in the menu makes any meal in Gameranga extraordinary. Life-cycle ritual, commemoration of a dead *gushti* member, *Id* and *Roja*, recovery from cholera or an electoral campaign provide occasions for the host household to slay an edible domestic animal. Also notice of an approaching guest, provided she or he is a respectable outsider (urbanized relative, even an anthropologist) prompts a frenetic search in a well-off home for a chicken suitable for a meal. Meat is not only valued because of its high cost and assumed strength-giving quality; apart from its obvious link with hospitality, it has a prominent place in the domain of sacrifice where it translates into the politics of exchange expressed in the code of honour (*ijjat*) and social obligation.

---

[23] Although both unboiled rice and meat are alms-giving items aimed at specific recipients, distribution of raw meat is more densely marked as it presuposes ritual slaughter of a prestigious animal.

Text

Meat is the main focus of Islamic dietery rules. Flesh, like other substances and behaviours, is subject to a five-point classificatory scale of obedience, ranging from that which is obligatory to that which is forbidden (between are acts which are desirable, optional or objectionable). Among things explicitly forbidden are incest, consumption of alcohol, or meat of animals that "die other than by human hand, the flesh of swine and the fluid blood of slaughtered animals" (Tapper 1986). In Gameranga, any piece of meat intended for human consumption is always preceded by a ritual slaughter, as "no flesh is permitted unless the name of God has been invoked at the killing" (ibid.).

Procedure: slaughter and distribution

The slaughter itself is a minutely regulated procedure. Pure intention, physical and spritual purity while executing the rite are essential to all actions intended to please God. Thorough ablution and a prayer by all present precedes the act. It is also important that the animal is free from any defect, that its face is directed toward Mecca and that the executor sacrifices by repeating *Bismillah* while cutting the throat. All blood must be let out. Animal slaughters are further guided by rules regarding participation. In Gameranga the status gradation of edible species—uncastrated bull, castrated goat, chicken, fish (which does not count as meat but an item for daily consumption) corresponds to the degree of inclusiveness of those who carry out the slaughter. A cow requires at least two *moulana*s, but one religious functionary is sufficient when a goat is killed; women are excluded even as an audience. A chicken can be killed by a layman and rules are often relaxed to allow the housewife to assist him. Women alone are permitted to kill fish (*mach*) which does not count ritually as meat (*mangsho*).

As I said, the slaughter of the most prestigious of all animals—a cow (*goru*)—requires the presence of two *moulana*s to officiate at the rite. Though in speech the generic term "cow" (*goru*) is applied, the bovine to be sacrificed is an uncastrated bull (*shar* or *ariya*) which has been particularly well fed and well cared for beforehand. The importance of the animal being "brought up" with care in the sacrificing household (*nijer palche*) (as contrary to a plain purchase) derives from the idea of sacrifice as giving part of the self (so as to invoke the resemblance with Abraham's willingness to offer his son, as one informant learned in Islam told me).

Once Zobeda vowed over her young dying son to offer the household's best cow if his life was saved[24]. As no sacrifice materialized half a year after the boy recovered, I

[24] In a sense, it was a rhetorical proclamation, because women are never involved in the event itself; in another sense, within the household precints, cows are always reared and pampered by housewives, thus becoming "a part of them". Nevertheless Zobeda was old and respected enough to make such a vow and then persuade her husband and sons to effect it.

questioned the seriousness of her vow. She explained that the best cow of her stock was just a calf when the promise was given and therefore needed time to be fed and petted, as bigger merit (*suab*) accrues from sacrificing the best member of the stock. Besides, she had to await the arrival of her adult son (settled in a town) to materialise the slaughter.

Ritual calendar

Meat-eating and sacrifice has its place in the ritual calendar. Both senses are epitomized in one of the Islamic feasts (*Id*). Although all slaughter has sacrificial attributes, villagers particularly associate the sacrificial aspect of a slaughter and meat-eating with the *Korbani*—the Feast of Sacrifice (denoted also as Id-ul-azha, Bakra Id or Id-ul-kabir), which is celebrated by the most conspicuous and massive slaughter of cows (and goats as a substitute) throughout Bangladesh. It is held on the 10th day of the ultimate month (Zil-haj), of the Muslim calendar to commemorate Abraham's willingness to sacrifice his son Isaac. It is celebrated by visiting and charitable gift-giving[25].

Rules of distribution: sacrifice and alms

It is required that the meat from an animal sacrificed either on *korbani* or independently (as a fulfillment of a vow (*manot*) at the time when things go well again after some misfortune)[26], is dissected and that the pieces are scrupulously divided into three equal portions, each placed on a banana leaf. The householder who supervises the dissection sees to it that the portions are equal not only in quantity, but with respect to the quality of meat. He usually moves desirable pieces of meat several times from one portion to another before securing "a perfect equality". In fact, beyond the experience of congregational prayers, it is here, in connection with sacrificial practice, that the *dhormic* emphasis on equality (of all Muslims) is explicitly given expression.

On *korbani*, one portion is kept by the sacrificing household, one is given to relatives and the rest to beggars. Once a woman agnatically related to the household where I was a guest came to return the portion of the goat that had been allotted to her; she was upset, claiming that the share included the worst cuts, "good for beggars, but we (own brother's household) do not need to eat bones" and left. Because meat distributed on fulfillment of a vow (*mana kora*) is meant as pure charity, no piece of it should be consumed by the sacrificer.

---

[25] Clothes are often given to the poor on Korbani. A group of not-so-poor widows from Uttor Para used to travel to Khulna and return with second-hand saris they acquired as alms on Bakra Id.

[26] When her son had recovered from cholera Zobeda vowed "I shall slay a cow" in front of her neighbours; or a man at the time of his wife's second still-birth, promised a sacrifice "if the next issue be a living son". Another villager slaughtered a goat as he had promised on the occasion of his daughter's difficult delivery—"if she should survive". These examples of vows aimed at securing survival elucidate the way villagers view sacrifice: part of the self (substantiated in the household's pet) is to be offered in order to save another self.

The best pieces may go to *madrasa* to be cooked and eaten by teachers and students, the rest to needy families or beggars.

By distributing raw meat, emphasis is made on securing God's blessing by merit-making (*suap*) that ensues from charity, rather than on political claims or on securing recognition by the *shomaj*. However, as the demeaning allusion to beggars (*bikhuk, fokir*) in the above quote reveals, the anticipated content of the charity portion to the poor (and to dependent relatives) may not necessarily correspond with the equality of the discourse. As Murphy (1986) also observed, the emphasis on charity by the middle class Sunni Muslims in Delhi (whose food transactions he studied), is in itself recognition and institutionalization of inequality—an ambivalence inherent in the dialectics between piety and honour[27].

By distributing cooked meat at commensal feasts (like weddings or circumcisions), the sponsor honours his guests and substantiates communal solidarity and equality through the sharing of culturally processed substance—meat and rice. This will hopefully be reciprocated by a counter-invitation by his equals or by services from his inferiors. It is not customary to thank the host because the food is given by God (*Allah dieche*) and, as my informants said, it is a duty to invite the *shomaj* as well as to accept the invitation. Alms to beggars (raw meat or rice) imply no expectation of reciprocity. As Pitt-Rivers (1979) remarks (in the context of modes of consubstantiation), to give to someone who cannot reciprocate is to humiliate and not to honour. In towns children from *ijjat* aspiring families learn this early. "Are you a beggar?" a father reproved his daughter's covetous glances at me while I was unpacking fruit purchased at *bajar* .

In Gameranga, beggars seal their inferior status not only by accepting on the basis of non-reciprocity but as recipients of left-overs (*jutho*) from the plates of guests at commensal feasts. The givers confirm the existence of beggars by deliberately leaving remnants on their plates (and by stressing the importance of doing so to an anthropologist who might have chosen to throw the bones to the dogs instead[28]. It should be noted here that the beggars passing Uttor Para are outsiders not only geographically, but also in a social sense, in that they are placed outside the reciprocal network that underlies social interaction within the *shomaj*. Conversely, those people in Uttor Para who earned their livelihood by begging, made their rounds beyond their home *para*. A beggar's insignia—a long thin walking stick—and manner of walking—dragging the feets—carries the idea of not being of here as well as of being physi-

---

[27] The model of food transactions and the inbuilt conflict between the domain of piety and honour that Murphy (1986) noted among Sunni Muslims in Delhi is compatible with the ideology and praxis of food exchanges in Gameranga.

[28] On weddings (as other commensal events), the whole dining area is encircled by beggars and dogs, awaiting leftovers. The presence of the former is encouraged as it gives an opportunity to each guest, and indirectly to the host, to fulfill the obligations of charity. Therefore at feasts, a couple of men are appointed and equipped with bamboo sticks to chase the dogs off.

cally fatigued of by walking, and hence entitled to receive support. In combination these attributes constitute a metaphor for a form of earning a livelihood[29].

Giving food (the prototype of charity) to beggars is one of those gestures that carries two contradictory messages as to its moral significance (Pitt-Rivers ibid.): framed within the social–secular network of taking–giving it is to dishonour; viewed cosmologically, it materializes the highest form of piety (dispossession for the sake of God's acceptance).

In terms of my ongoing argument that extrahousehold commensality serves to assert *shomaj*-belonging, beggars, (i.e. *shomaj* members getting food beyond *shomaj*), seem to be transcending these boundaries; they materialize the idea of reaching a wider universe; the same expansiveness that an ordinary householders attains in prayers, a beggar materializes by actually walking (dragging the legs to suggest emaciation and invoke pity) across the boundaries of *shomaj* and taking food wherever it happens to be given. The same concern (with crossing of the boundaries while begging), yet on a larger, national scale is clearly expressed by Rolt's (1991:18) informant: " Beggars ... that is what this government is making us into. We are all learning to be beggars because the government wants it. The more beggars there are the more money the government gets from your country, the USA, Sweden and all the others ...".

Beyond charity: sharing with equals and "feeding people"

As I said, slaying an animal for meat is an act of thanksgiving which implies sharing. More than other food items, meat is linked to extrahousehold communication—not only with God in sacrifice and alms-giving as described above but with those who are able of some form of reciprocity[30]. Household celebrations, notably circumcision and post-funeral feast but also weddings, make invitation of *shomaj* members compulsory "It is for *shomaj* we do it", complain not-so-well-off householders for whom even a simple feast results in indebtedness. Others wait for years to accumulate the necessary capital for the circumcission of sons when the *shomaj* is invited to a feast. Feasts sponsored by

---

[29] It seems that apart from divine credit, beggars' "outsideness" contributes to fostering the image of the indispensability of this professional category. Whenever I suggested to the better-off housewives whether a servant-job could not be arranged for one of the healthier and younger beggars who happened to ask for alms in their households, it was brushed aside as "outside people are unfit to be employed for food only". *Shomaj* membership makes it possible for a patron to employ landless dependent non-kinsmen (within the *shomaj*) with food as the sole remuneration; however, no man would work today just for food for a non-*shomaj* employer, I have been told.

[30] Food exchange is customary among agnatic relatives. The appearance of a chicken on the menu obligates the housewife to send a small portion to immediate *gushti* neighbours "to avoid envy"; clandestine cooking late at night is a way housewives in Gameranga evade this duty. It is only possible to give meat to some relatives selectively by cutting a path through the jungle in the dead of night.

politically ambitious patrons or candidates at electoral campaigns are celebrations of political ambitions that transcend *shomaj* boundaries.

Meat tops the list of items considered "guest food". It is inextricably linked to the code of hospitality (*otithia*) and respect (*ijjat*). Plenty to the point of wastefulness, recurrent coaxing to "take more", and multiple serving mark the event of hospitality. The way food is forced on a guest (cf. Carstairs 1957:50, Murphy 1986), and the exorbitant quantity served raises doubts as to whether the aim is the well-being of the guest or that of the host. Commensal feasts aimed unequivocally at raising the host's rank or promoting some sort of secular power like solicitation of votes, are referred to as *dawat* or *khawai* — "giving" or "feeding", thus depicting the straightforward instrumentality of this kind of interaction. "Beef"—usually substituted by mutton—cooked in clarified butter or oil and curried, is the most valuable addition to rice. It is significant, that the preparation of meat dishes for a large meal that involves a *shomaj* gathering is carried out by a male cooking team. Rice may be boiled by women who however, never eat in the company of outside men. On many occasions of extrahousehold commensality, women are just relegated to spice-pounders.

Being myself occasionally in the position of guest of honour, my affluent hosts would ostentatiously command a wife or a servant to collect the best of the chickens or ducks. When I protested, my host replied—with implied assertion of the *shomaj*—"It is to show you that not all of us are beggars in Bangladesh". God would also be invoked in case of a clear self-promoting sharing. Unable to stop my host putting additional portions of meat on my plate by pleading a full stomach, I would point out the contrast between the prevalent undernourishment and the sumptuousness of the meal before me. My host would insist that, after all, "All food is given by Allah", thus disclaiming his self-assertive (and *ijjat* making) interest in the name of submitting to God.

I hasten to add, that the mood and mode of sharing in households, where there was not much *ijjat* to defend, and where I happened to pay casual visits on my rounds was different. Depending on the season, housewives would rush to fill a plate with anything available as a snack: puffed rice, broken-and-roasted rice, boiled egg. Children were particularly outgoing, offering unripe fruit in various forms and mixtures, habitually sprinkled or crushed with salt and chillies. In the homes where I used to be a regular visitor, the housewives invited me for a meal on several occasions. Rated as "poor man's (*goriber khabar*) food", they always expressed worries as to whether I could eat "what we usually eat": miniature fish (*phuti mach*), rice boiled-and-fried with lentils (*kichuri*), fried and curried broken rice (*khut*), fried banana flower (*mocha*). After such a meal, female hosts would present me to an occasional visitor (brother or husband's sister, coming from outside) as—"she ate with us" and enumerate proudly the number of times.

It seems that the ultimate rationale of feasting for the sake of *shomaj* (be it epitome for Uttor Para or "we, Bangladeshis") is the idea that what promotes togetherness of the *shomaj* pleases God (Murphy 1986). Clearly, self-assertive, coercive "feeding" and wastefulness intrinsic to *ijjat*-bound hospitality denies the basic assumptions of piety—submission to God's will. The conjunction between self-aggrandisement (ostentatious waste) and self-denial (charity) is possible through meat. Apart from the sacredness imputed to the provenance of all food ("of God"), meat's prestigiousness lies in its association with animal sacrifice which is an indispensable precedent of all meat consumption. Thus the affluent and ambitious can convert political self-interest into an act of piety. On the other hand, casual hospitality extended to a neighbouring anthropologist may bring an outsider closer inwards.

Beyond piety and honour

At another level of discourse—*dhorm*ic belonging—the villagers elaborate the Koranic emphasis on meat by singling out beef as the most valuable. It is always a cow (*goru*) people recall in vows, although a goat substitutes for it on actual sacrificial occasions. Men and women stress their preference for beef, although it enters their daily diet only very exceptionally and when it does it seldom reaches women's plates. As if the most important criterion of common humanity was to be able to eat the same food (Pitt-Rivers 1977) a foreigner, adopted into the village, is repeatedly questioned as to the quantity of rice she can eat and about her taste for beef. It is also a way of securing information and re-confirmation of the status of her *dhorm*ic affiliation. A taste for rice and beef also indicates the degree of an outsider's absorption into the category "We Bengali Muslims". A negative answer with respect to beef-eating places her automatically in the category of pig-eaters (*shuorer mangsho khae*) or vegetarians, i.e. persons of an alien, inferior and less civilized *jat*, "like a Hindu" (*Hindur motto*). Cow is a prominent symbol of Hindus, who are not only the immediate neighbouring non-Muslims but, as an urban informant claimed, "probably our predecessors of 400 years ago". Hence the extolled prestigiousness and healthiness of a beef diet is a marker of distinct Bengali Muslim identity.

Like all Muslims in the subcontinent, people in Gameranga identify themselves in opposition to Hindus by concentrating on the symbolic destruction of their symbols, when the situation calls for collective self-assertion. Among those symbols the cow is the most prominent. It is a phenomenon to which Gaborieu (1985) refers as a "ritual of provocation" in the Indian context. He writes: "The members of each community see the other's religion as diametrically opposed to their own, as an inverted religion, ulta dharma. Actual features of each religion or even made up symbols are picked up to show that no conciliation is possible …" .

PART THREE

Agnation and Affinity

CHAPTER 11

Representation of gender in the notions of patriline

As I showed in the previous chapter, *shomaj* is a territorial unit embracing families who live within its boundaries. For its residents, *shomaj* is an embodiment of social control, formally secured through *matubors* who are the spokesmen for agnatically related groups—*gushti*s. For *matubors* themselves, *shomaj* provides an arena of influence beyond their kin group. Social control and influence is attained through *bichar*s, whereby the distinction between *dhormo* and *odhormo* as well as the authority to make the distinction is publicly vouched for and enacted. At another level, *shomaj* supplies an idiom of Islamic solidarity and equality, aspirations affirmed by collective worship which marks the daily cycle and by funerals which mark the life-cycle. Togetherness is then consubstantiated by sharing ritual work and food. The communal values of solidarity and equality often neglected in daily praxis and economic pursuits are thus attained through rituals in which *shomaj* and *dhormo* are merged and objectified. The minutely followed processual regulations of *shomaj*-promoting activities are informed by Islamic texts whereby women are absent or relegated backstage.

I shall now move inwards from the community boundary to the kinship units which constitute *shomaj*. The previous enumeration of these units[1]—expanding circles—evades the question of how the ties of belonging within each circle and across the boundary are maintained. Following Strathern (1979) I assume that, in order to understand the cultural categories in social use, we have first to be concerned with building up an idea of what "the 'descent constructs'are and how they logically relate to other constructs". The fact that the patriline in Bangladesh is a non-corporate unit[2], that the genealogical memory is shallow and that there is a lack of marriage prescriptions with respect to *gushti*'s endogamy or exogamy, invites a series of questions regarding the function of the *gushti*.

Where are we to look for its meaning? How does a *gushti* express itself and how is the sense of agnatic identity achieved? When property is divided, forefathers forgotten, marriages arranged strategically, we may ask: what recalls and maintains the line and for what purpose?

---

[1] See chapter 4.
[2] According to Keesing (1975:17), corporate group embraces five attributes. These are—acting as a single legal individual, collectively held title to land, co-operative labour, unified political form (e.g. dealing with litigation) and continuation of the group after a member's death.

In what follows I shall attempt to elaborate on the local terms denoting the patrilineal unit and the wider cultural contexts they cover. These terms and their extensions may give an indication of the ideas that hinge on the consciousness of belonging which distinguishes "one's own people" and "others".

The term *gushti* and *bongsho* which are synonymously used in anthropological literature to denote the Bengali agnatic unit are known to the villagers, but admitted only after the most direct of questioning. They appear rather as thought-of units. *Bongsho*, however, is used spontaneously in the context of explicit ranking such as is occasioned by marriage inquiries and negotiations and, in that case, it refers to the patronymic title. Whenever a reference is made to the patriline as a social unit, its collectiveness and duties of loyalty, villagers speak of "brothers" (*bhaiera*) or "blood relatives" (*rokter attio*), when distinction is sought from non-blood relatives[3]. A branch of a patriline is called *shori*. All these terms are invoked in genealogical abstraction—*gushti*. In non-marital contexts of ranking, as in the case of feuding, villagers speak of strong (*shokti*) or weak (*norom*) *gushti* or its "strong branch" (*shoktoshori*) when estimating each other's numerical and moral strength.

Patriline defined botanically—*bongsho*

As noted earlier, *bongsho* is a term which points to the quality of a patriline rather than the group (*gushti*) and, as an inheritable and shared attribute, it is the most explicit marker of a person's belonging. It also refers, as some authors claim, to the particular bodily substance of males—semen (Inden 1977: 5). A closer look at the origin of the word and its shifting reference may uncover some of the meaning coded into the Bengali notion of lineal descent. Etymologically, *bongsho* (*vamsa*) also means "bamboo" (Bertocci 1984, Inden ibid.,) which is a treelike grass growing in clusters. Each trunk is a series of continuously linked and rapidly growing hollow stems. It is a reed species easy to bend but hard to break. The new shoots appear from the joints of underground roots at some distance from the central trunk. The circumference of the main stem decreases with each newly-grown node; the younger, top stems are narrower, weaker, greener and more elastic than the older ones.

Bamboo appears to me as an arbor vitae, a graphic representation of lineality and mutual relations within a patriline, specific to a peasant community in Bangladesh. Lineally jointed nodes which form an elastic yet unbreakable trunk, suggest the agnatic lineality of Bengali descent. The way the process of vertical growth is marked by decrease in volume invites an association of seniority with strength and its superiority over the weakness of recently grown junior nodes. In this way the plant draws attention to birth-order on which the

---

[3] Affines are just *attio* or *bier attio*.

principle of male rank is based. The plant's reproductive pace and direction—
rapid vertical and horizontal proliferation—suggest qualities associated with
the Bengali notion of auspiciousness—intrinsic increase, addition, expansion.
In my Dhaka residence prior to fieldwork, my gardener dissuaded me from
planting bamboo in my garden saying, "It is like a happy family—once you
plant it, it never stops growing". How the ideas of descent intertwine with the
ideas about co-residence, is graphically expressed in the manner the new
shoots of bamboo spring out from the prominent root. Their underground linking represents the horizontal jointness of *gushti*'s households established by
co-residence and shared bodily substance. These particular features make a
botanical species a convenient image to think about society in general.

   This plant homology, invoked earlier[4] in the analogy I drew between the social units and "layers of an onion" has precedents in South-Asian botanical
folklore, where trees and plants are considered to be animate, and in even
more generalized folk cosmology, which has it that "there is nothing in the
world where life does not exist" (Upadhyaya 1964–65). It is also consistent
with the stress we find in Bengali modes of thought on the intrinsic unity of
spirit, matter and duty, recalled in previous discussion of *jat, dhormo* and
shomaj. Bamboo in particular holds a prominent place in Indian botanical
folklore. Its status of sanctity is largely documented in Bengali poetry, where
god is depicted as playing melodies on bamboo flute to charm *gopis*[5]—"His
flute took my heart—his flute, a thin bamboo trap enclosing me—… that hollow, simple stick …" (In Praise 1967:30). Here the hollowness of the stem is
instrumental in producing a tonal preludium to sexual union between male
deity and female devotee. Instrumental music (in contrast to music produced
by the radio) is banned from the expressive repertoire of Muslim villagers today. The exclusion of musical instruments is due to the claim by local fundamentalists that all non-orthodox cultural expressions must be of Hindu origin.
However, when I asked a villager to specify the events of a wedding ceremony (*bie*), he lifted his fingers to the lips in a gesture suggestive of blowing
of a flute. Like other elements of Bengali folk culture, flute persists, albeit
muted, in the consciousness of Muslims where it is associated with the most
important ritual of fertility—the wedding.

   Still today in the local language, *bashi* (bamboo flute) is one of the euphemisms used to denote the sex organ of a pre-adolescent boy (Aziz 1985:42).
The reference to male sexual anatomy and fluid implied in *bongsho* is thus
clear. It is the quality of holowness as a metaphor of the passage of life-re-cre-
ating substance produced by males, that points to the male aspect of fertility.
Timber sellers in Gameranga use to say "bamboo is as strong as a man"

---

[4] See chapter 5.
[5] In the lyric poetry of Bengal, *gopis* are village cowshed girls. At the time they were in love with
the god Krishna, they were the wives of others—"They leave their homes and families and husbands and honor—as it is called by men—and go to him. Their love for him is deeper than their
fear of dishonor" (Praise of Krishna 1967:vii).

(*basher shokti purusher moto*). Elsewhere in the subcontinent, an extended version of this analogy has it that "bamboo is as strong as a man, as yielding as a woman, as simple as a child" (Godden 1972:132). The inclusion of additional social persons (mother–child unit) here averts attention from the exclusiveness of agnatic ascendancy to the actual social unit where the line is generated—recall the gardener's analogy above. In Gameranga, agnatic groups are classified as strong or weak, depending on the number of male members. This in turn depends on the sexual potential and auspicious fertility of the family unit. An impotent man is said to be lacking in strength (*kono shokti nei*). The quality of strength recalled in the bamboo trunk is thus replicated in thinking of a line's physical as well as reproductive capacity.

Bamboo as noted earlier also has an important place in burials. The platform where the dead body is laid for washing and later carried to the grave is made of bamboo. The sides and the cover of the grave are laid with newly cut bamboo[6] and when, after the burial, the grave is covered with earth, new bamboo is planted on the top. In Gameranga, bamboo planted on slightly elevated ground, is the only topographical marker of graves (*khobor*)[7]. When asked about a recently deceased person, people point to the sky and may add, "Allah took her" (*Allah nie geche*). This inquiry about the same person made a few months after death had occurred, is responded to by indicating the bamboo grove where the deceased was burried. This shift in direction from the cosmic route of the soul to the terrestial locus of corpse disposal indicates the manner in which ancestors are memorized and invoked over a span of time. Walking through a jungle my escorts never failed to bring my attention to a particular bamboo cluster and identify it as a grave. Names were not usually remembered but lineal affiliation could be, as families bury their dead on their own or, in the case of the landless, on a relative's land. In a temporal perspective however, bamboo provides the only tangible reminder of a gushti's ancestry. Its ever-growing stems which mark the graves represent an extension of memory at the point where the actual remembrance (of a corpse's identity) ceases. Bamboo is an emblem of patriline which continues to grow in spite of the loss of a member. It is that which survives (human) death.

I have shown how the botanical symbol, its physical attributes and ritual use condenses thinking about the nature of descent existence, representing both its maleness and its continuity. The analogy drawn here between the qualities of a plant and a social group (*gushti*) is situated within the opposite domains of human existence—the proliferation and disappearance of life. In this sense, bamboo also draws attention to the very contingency of the world of meaning, where meaning:non-meaning invites the association with being: non-being.

---

[6] In this way bamboo makes a "ceiling" which is one of the derived lexical meanings of the term *bongsho*.

[7] There are two areas where bamboo is generally grown: patches of jungle (*jongol*) which are interspersed with the fields (*danga*) and bamboo groves at the back of the houses (*bagan*). Both places serve as graveyards, latrines and disposal areas for dead animals.

As regards gender, bamboo also reifies the ambiguous presence of diversity of which women are the source. As it appears visually, in its shape, spatiality and (smooth) surface, a bamboo trunk suggests the absoluteness and perfection of lineal jointness, diachronic nature (i.e. continutity) and self-sufficiency of the male presence in the world. Bamboo thus imparts the features of all dominant representations (ideologies and rhetorics). The underground root system, by means of which proliferation is accomplished, vegetatively resembles the way biological reproduction is dealt with in the secular context. Because pregnancy is rendered as shameful and giving birth polluting, this exclusive domain of female knowledge and practice is relegated to the backstage of the agnatic space (*bari*). Birth also, is the most muted of the rites of passage among the Muslims in Gameranga. The negation of bodily involvement in procreation expressed in the vegetable idiom bears a resemblance to the mythological elaboration the same preoccupation receives among ethnographic neighbours. Campbell's (1976:140) comment on the Hindu descent model prevalent in Northern parts of India poignantly illustrates this:

"… the patriline's ideal self-image could best be represented by an unbroken line of celibate holy men, such as found in the mythological lineages of North Indian Nath cults. There, as elsewhere in Hindu mythology, male offspring are produced by a series of miracles instead of by normal sexual intercourse between men and women. Fertility, and thus continuity, is achieved without the loss of purity entailed by the householder's involvement with women" (Campbell ibid., quoted in Bennett 1983:126).

Common to both forms of imagery is the interest in constituting a perfect definition in which all signs of diversity are suppressed[8].

In Gameranga, the illusion of continuity while excluding women is further enacted in the initiation of boys (*musulmani*). A boy's entry into adult manhood is marked by removal of the superfluous part of his sexual anatomy (cf. the perfection of the bamboo trunk) whereby the initiant is also separated from his mother[9], i.e. from the world of women, the dividers of *gushti*. There is no corresponding rite of passage into adulthood for girls (e.g. ritual of menstruation), except marriage.

The absoluteness of the bamboo's visible structure appears to me to be replicated in a concern with muting of the representations of deformities and divisions which are part of ordinary experience. While women's vital contribution to the continuity of *gushti* is abstracted as underground root reproduction (and outward extension), the visible part of the bamboo suggests absolute perfection intended for the authorization of order and dominance in public dis-

---

[8] Writing of the official systems of imagery (versus the grotesque folk tradition of marketplace and carnival) Bakhtin notes the same concern in dealing with bodily processes: "Anything that protrudes, bulges, sprouts, or branches off is eliminated, hidden, moderated" (Clark, Holmquist 1984:320), not only with regard to the management of human body but language as well. In Gameranga, anything linked to fecundation, pregnancy and childbirth is uttered in a reticent, evasive manner and only in the absence of authoritative "others"—men and older matrons.

[9] Mothers do not participate in the operation to console their frightened sons, neither do they attend the wound when it gets infected. This care is relegated to other female relative.

course. From this abstraction comes the eminent concern to mute even the divisions and "deformities" through which the very existence of the agnatic group is made possible.

Patriline defined biogenetically—*rokto*

The shared substance which provides a model of relatedness (Schneider 1980: 24, Keesing 1975:127) in Bengali culture may be borrowed from various semantic domains—spiritual-emotional, (such as prayer), biological (blood, womb), linguistic (shared name), nutritional (boiled rice), botanical (bamboo). Thus the genealogical idiom is expressed through brotherhood, blood and bamboo, i.e. symbols with a distinct semantic provenance.

In Gameranga, the biological component of agnatic relatedness is made explicit in the term "blood relative"—*rokter attio*[10] which points to the sharing of an organic, red fluid substance by a particular category of people related to self.

Blood (*rokto*) as a polysemic symbol[11] par excellence (Turner 1967:51–57) means different things in different contexts and for each gender in medical belief in Gameranga. A clear distinction is made between female and male blood. The former is represented by menstrual blood and the blood of parturition, both extremely polluting; the latter includes blood shed by men in feuding which is linked with the honour of a patriline and the blood of circumcision marking the birth of a Muslim and more importantly a boy's removal from the mother-child unit and his integration into the world of agnatic eternity. In the most general sense, blood is viewed as a basic bodily substance, one from which all other vital fluids, such as sperm (*bij*) or mother's milk (*dudh*), are derived. Therefore, the loss of a mere drop of blood (as well as semen) is associated with wastage and dramatically feared[12].

---

[10] *Rokto*—blood, *atta*—self or soul, i.e. "that which survives death" (Fruzzetti 1976a), *attio*—own people. Generic term for "relative", an ego-based group. Synonymous with *rokter attio* is the application of a modifier *apon*, which specifies a particular relative, e.g. *apon bhai*, as "true" or one "having relations with self" (Fruzzetti ibid.). *Apon* is mainly used to denote a distinction between a close and *emni attio* (just so, not real, fictive relative or *dur attio*) distant relative.

[11] A single symbol that gains a wide spectrum of meanings in different contexts (Turner 1967:50). Blood obtains a range of meanings depending on whether one refers to menstrual blood, blood shed in feuding, blood as genetic substance or blood spat out by a TB infected patient.

[12] In the village hospital where I also carried out fieldwork, there was a rule never to mention in the waiting room the event of bleeding which might have accompanied minor surgery or tubectomies, as such uncaution had led on many previous occasions to the frantic flight of waiting patients.

Bengalis are also reluctant blood-donors (even when the recipients are blood relatives) and medical researchers attest to the unwillingness of Bengalis to participate in blood tests. See also chapter 12.

That loss of semen also causes great anxiety, is evident from the vast range of semen-improving medicines and aphrodisiacs sold all around Bangladesh and also from the fact that sexual insatiability classes some women as "husband killers" (Aziz, Maloney 1985:47). The fear stems from the belief that blood and its transformed state, sperm, are contained in the body in a very limited quantity and is hard to replenish.

Within the domain of human fertility blood is critically bound to other substances. From the frequent conversations among the villagers on the subject of bodily well-being, a pattern of casual relationship can be traced between food, blood, semen and quality of offspring (i.e. *gushti*). It is generally believed that particular foods are blood-producing[13] and hence conductive to good semen which in turn determines the quality of the line.

With respect to kin classification in Bengal, Fruzzetti (1976a) writes: "Blood is something one shares with the persons of one's line, one's brothers and those related through 'brotherhood'. These people are linked together by a blood relationship ... The members of *bhayat* are distinguished according to blood (*rokto*) which is passed from father to son and blood shared among brothers".

In Gameranga, a person speaks about "blood" relatives only when directly questioned or pressed by the anthropologist to explain the category "own people" (*attio*). In this explanatory context *rokter attio*—"those who have the same blood", or relatives by birth—conveys sameness structured by the principle of blood passed through male descendants and such denotation implies a distinction from relatives through marriage—*bier attio* or just *attio* (Fruzzetti ibid.). Blood thus bears the structurally defining property of *gushti* membership.

Spontaneously, a reference to bodily substance is often made when a person justifies an emotion as emanating from a part of the physical body. In this case the maleness of *gushti* is de-emphasised by the inclusion of sisters, daughters and mothers. While the critical substance in constituting brotherhood (i.e. *gushti*) is blood, the brother/sister tie is established by the "shared womb" (*ek peter bhai/bon*)—brother or sister of the same belly. Reference to this kind of consubstantiation averts attention from agnatic reckoning, because the mother's blood or womb counts as nourishment and nest, and as such it "is fully devoid of any structural property" in Bengali kinship (Khare 1975). The following summary of an excerpt from my fieldnotes illustrates the point:

One week before her death, Jahanara, a young divorced woman, complained bitterly about her brother's refusal to provide medicine or hospitalization which would cure

---

[13] Universally, throughout South Asia, one of the criteria for food classification is the consideration of the blood-producing capacity of the food item in question. In the daily diet this alleged property is ascribed to fish species, believed to "have blood", an asset alleged to be manifested in their resistance after being caught, their ability to stay alive in a small quantity of water (and some times even without). This particular vigour is ascribed to the species *koy mach* (*anabas scandens*) which, in addition, has spines by which it manages to pull itself up out of a container. This is considered by my informants as an indicator of supereme strength. Other strong species are fish of the carp family (*rui* and *katla*) but also *magaur* and *shingi*. All of these sorts rate highest as prestige (or "guest") and convalescence food. In contrast, cray-fish (*chingri mach*), although appreciated for its taste, is considered nutritiously inferior because of the absence of blood. The underlying logic behind such classification is that strength and persistency (even sexual) inhere in blood—the main elements in the construction of *gushti*—therefore, the presence of it in locally valued food is believed to induce the same qualities in the human body (see Rizvi 1979:154). Widespread anaemia for example, is explained in this context and also tuberculosis.

her advanced TB. Emaciated, she kept lamenting *"ek peter bhai, ek peter bhai ..."* (brother of the same womb). Responding to the accusation, Jahangir blamed Jahanara for having opened a legal case against him some years before in spite of being his "true sister" (*ek peter bon*).

Both siblings thus voiced their hurt feelings at mutually failed solidarity by pointing to the once shared, procreative substance—their mother's womb.

Also the parent–child ties are frequently recalled by reference to blood, which is then implicitly paralleled with an "unalterable genetic substance" (Schneider 1980:25). The genetic emphasis is implicitly assumed in the belief held throughout Bangladesh that children take after their parents—in physical constitution, pigmentation as well as temperament, moral and other personal traits[14]. For instance, petty thefts by children at the age they are supposed "to understand" (i.e. *balyakal*) invite comments like 'thief like his father' (*babar moto chor*); or when a student, the brain of the local school and a boarder in the ex-headmaster's home, stole twenty Taka from the anthropologist's handbag, some villagers promptly remembered and explained that even his father, who had died ten years before, was a notorious thief; or Nargiz, the local beauty who did not object to receiving sweets offered by young men on market days, invited comments from older women "like her mother, she is a whore". These illustrations show how disapproved behaviour of younger people, inclination to stealing or immodesty, is first of all explained in relational deterministic terms, as signs confirming common biological identity with their parents.

The consanguinal ethos (Khare 1975) which pervades the Bengali descent system (Fruzzetti 1976a) is replicated in the villagers' heightened concern with the ideology of pure blood. This finds expression in the reluctance to solve sterility by adoption[15]. In my sample of 193 families, out of six sterile couples, only one adopted a boy after the husband's repeated failure to impregnate his first wife and all subsequent wives brought to his household for that purpose. The adopted child (*palong chele*) was however, the husband's brother's son, i.e. a male who shared blood with his foster father. As evidence

---

[14] In a wider existential context, it is believed that a person's fate is designed and inscribed on the forehead by Allah during the first few days after birth. Mothers and grandmothers attempt to affect it by placing various objects around the newborn infant's head which are believed to invoke desired properties. The asssortment ranges from a talisman (*tabiz*) tied around the baby's neck, a piece of iron, a match-box, a pencil or blue bangles placed under the pillow. Such measures are taken to affect in a positive direction what has been pre-destined by God or to direct a person's path in general terms—such as happiness, prosperity, a "good husband", a "good head" for passing exames, etc. A person's temperament and proclivities in the management of daily life are to a large extent interpreted in terms of genetics however.

[15] Adoption, and fostering slot into the category of problems of adding outsiders to "one's own people". The variety of statuses of such outsiders (wives, officers, anthropologists, construction workers, servants from other villagers, students in local *madrasa*—a merit-bringing tenant) corresponds to a range of solutions whereby some are culturally standardized, as in the integration of inmarried women, and others are ad hoc solutions as in the case of putting up with an anthropologist (see Kotalová 1986).

against my repeated suggestions to another childless couple[16] to adopt an or-phaned child, the husband, backed by his relatives, pointed to the case of a foster son Kaiser, which was widely debated during my stay in Gameranga. Kaiser was brought to the household of a rich landlord, when some villagers had found him, according to folklore, as a "baby floating on the lotus leaf in the canal" about fifteen years before. The landlord, although he himself had fathered a large number of progeny, agreed to keep the foundling and rele-gated him to the care of female servants adjacent to his household[17]. From childhood, Kaiser manifested features, which made him difficult to socialize into a village stereotype. His blackness and facial negroid features, wild tem-perament, uncontrollable and unpredictable shifts of mood and attacks of rage, but also a great deal of charm and imagination expressed in poetic language in his better periods, combined with his rebellion against schooling and Islamic tenets, earned him the reputation of a *bolot* (fool)[18]. Kaiser's eccentricity was tolerated with amused nods of the head; at times it enraged those who shared the house with him, but it was always attributed to his assumed Bede origin[19]. When Kaiser was about fifteen he ran away; nobody heard of him for months and when he re-appeared, it was as a labourer in another rich peasant's farm in a neighbouring *para*. Kaiser's escapade was widely discussed. "It is in his blood", commented villagers, thus pointing to the alleged vagrant way of Bede life. The closest neighbours attested to lack of food K. experienced in time of his stepfather's absence and also to the promised inheritance of a piece of land which Kaiser kept recalling but which was left without consider-ation[20]. Both factors could well have been taken as a serious motive for Kai-ser's decision to leave, however, the local interpreters chose to view the esca-pade as additional evidence of the local axiom that a person's true nature is in-herent in the substance one inherits from parents and that substance is an en-during, persistent link conceptualized as blood. Kaiser's unorthodox physiognomy, proclivity and final decision to run away from where he had a

[16] Sterility in an agnatically oriented society as Bangladesh is the most inauspicious event and a childless wife—*bajja*—is an object of regret. It is always she who is held responsible for the ste-rility of the couple. In the *gushti* where I was based and apropriated during my fieldwork, I man-aged to persuade a childless couple who had been married for 12 years to undergo a medical ex-amination. When the topic was brought into conversation, the wife continued to blame herself even after the test showed clearly and the doctor diagnosed her husband's sterility. The husband however, refrained from his plan to bring in a co-wife.

[17] He was a case of an absentee landowner with his wife and other children settled in town. The household was practically run by quickly alternating female servants.

[18] Lacking in the degree of understanding expected at a particular stage of a person's maturation.

[19] Bede or Baydia are allegedly Muslims, albeit of an inferior caste, as they do not intermarry or eat together with agriculturists. "They are different *jat*," women explained when a female Bede glass-bangle seller appeared in our courtyard and I wondered how it came that she moved so unin-hibitedly. The fact that Bede do not keep their womanfolk in *purdah*, is the most conspicuous and provoking feature of their life style in the Muslim agriculturists' view. A group of Bede men, women and children came to Gameranga from time to time as performers of itinerant occupations like snake charming, tooth healing, blood letting. Nobody knew from where they came.

[20] Kaiser's stepfather found his claim unreasonable and untimely at such a young age.

relatively secure position, was an expression of his father's blood. All this was recalled as an argument by the childless householder against adoption. "Do you understand that Kaiser could not have been made either a 'true son' or a 'true Muslim'?" My informants thus elaborated on the dilemma of fostering a child of "others" by stressing the unalterability of one's biogenetic make-up.

Patriline defined lexically—*bhai*

To speak of brothers in Gameranga, is another way of talking about a patriline. However, compared with other agnatic denotations, "*bhai*" (brother) or "*bhaiera*" (pl.) in daily use is the most frequent kinship term and the most inclusive term with respect to the distance from "ones own people". This suggests, that the hoped for quality of the brotherly relationship extends into a wide range of social relationships. *Bhai* thus denotes and proposes a moral stance.

Bengali kinship terminology is derived from the North-Indian lexicon, where *bhai* dominates as the central category (Dumont 1966). According to the logic derived from this lexicon, a brother is "a man of my generation with whom I have one ascendant in common" (Kolenda 1982), i.e. the father in the nearest case and a remote ancestor in the furthest. Therefore, as a man of the same generation but also a descendant of the same father, a *bhai* embodies a sibling line, which is emphasised, as well as male lineal succession, which is implied. In Gameranga, *bhaiera* refers mainly to living persons, those who keep *gushti* in working order. It is the latter link with a man's father's other sons, which is in focus when considering household and *gushti* organisation. This relationship—between "father's sons"—is central in the social structure among Bengali Muslims. The relationship is based in the idea of birth succession whereby seniority of agnatic males ranks over (i.e. encompasses) juniors, experience over inexperience, strength over weakness. Ancestry seems to be de-emphasised in the notion of *gushti*; on the ground that male succession and continuity is conveyed in the praxis of the youngest brother's duty to care for his old parents, rather than memorizing dead ancestors in genealogical records or in preserving conspicuously decorated graveyards. The force of ideological cohesion between brothers is embodied in the image of the bamboo plant and the fluid biological substance they share and transfer, as well as in combats for a collectively shared moral substance—*ijjat*.

Like so many Bengali (kinship) terms, *bhai* has a shifting reference. The term does not only refer to a son of ego's parents. *Bhai* is as Dumont (1966) stresses, the most collectivizing of kin terms. This attribute is evident from the practice of addressing unknown men (occasionally even women) throughout Bangladesh. In daily transactions, if the intention is cordial, virtually any male (with certain reservations of age and status) can be called *bhai*. The male members of one's current social unit (be it a *para*, *gushti*, school, team on a

wrestling ground) are preferentially introduced to outsiders as *bhai*. Genealogical distance (the degree to which blood is shared) and even religious and
ethnic distance, is not specified for outsiders at the initial encounter. Confrontation with the total strangeness of a non-Bengali anthropologist at the beginning of fieldwork makes all Bangladeshis—even female—think of themselves
and present themselves as *bhai* ("We are all brothers here"), i.e. in terms of
the dominant male structure. In encounters with non-Bangladeshi audience
this collectivizing praxis is so extreme as to excede the otherwise sharply
maintained boundary of religious belonging. It was then, (at that stage of my
acquaintance with villagers) that a young man introduced me to his Hindu
teacher colleague as "*amar bhai*" (my brother); only later the same man was
to explain the difference between Muslim *para*s and the only Hindu *para*
(Napit Para) in Gameranga by pointing to the filthiness and treacherousness of
the latter[21]. This example clearly shows that the boundary drawing and refractions within nominal categories are relational and contingent (Cohen 1985:
115). Here the inclusiveness and refraction within category *bhai* is generated
vis à vis an ouside interlocutor, a situation which prompts the need to assert
and re-create a collective self-image—the self for others, which is the "self"
motivated by aspiration to abolish genealogically derived determinancy. *Bhai*
is the very category to fulfill the purpose. "Here we are all brothers", even
women would say. The degree of inclusiveness depends on the assessment of
the outsider's difference[22].

The placement of a boundary around a relational category is accomplished
through a scale of reductions. The greater the difference a villager perceives
between himself and the visitor, the more inclusive the category is: for a non-
Bengali person the boundary around *bhai* is drawn round "Bangladesh"—the
land of Bengalis; however, facing a person from within his own district, the
boundary of brotherhood was drawn around Gameranga. Very early after my
arrival, during the introductory lessons on official discourse, male informants
would draw the widest circle of brotherhood to include all Muslims. In so far
as "all men are sons of Adam", as a religious layman in Gameranga claimed,

---

[21] The boundary-drawing by which a villager in Gameranga specifies her or his unit of belongingness (i.e. "the same as myself" or "among us" category) is motivated by events which place her on
the boundary. The need to delineate the bounds of similarity is prompted by encounters with an
'outside' audience (a non-self), which make the interlocutors to realise the difference and their respective belonging at the same time. Where exactly the boundary is drawn depends largely on the
cultural-geographic identity of the interlocutors and the length of their acquaintance. In the course
of a year's interaction the equations of brotherhood in self-presentations ranged from Bengalis,
Bangladeshis, people from the villages surrounding Gameranga, people of Uttor Para until in the
end only *gushti* members, i.e. blood brothers passed as "brothers". The identity of those presented
to me then, was specified in more complex terms like *chachato bhai* (FaYBrSo), *khalato bhai*
(MoSiSo), *apa* (ESi), *dulabhai* (ESiHu). For gender refraction of kinship belonging, see chapter
10, note 1 and chapter 12.

[22] The other kinship terms frequently used for bringing non-related people terminologically closer
are "sister" and "mother". In the field, people who knew some English and even some who did
not, called me "sister"; passing beggars approached me with "mother".

all Bengli Muslims comprise an endogamous group. In this wide generic sense of endogamy, brotherhood is an expression of Islamic belonging in the universal community based on shared faith. A year-long familiarity with my presence made my neighbours reduce the application even to the exclusion of cousins, in other words, the term would be used only to refer to one's parents' other sons and for cousins a modifier *chachato* or *mamato* was added. Even among themselves, Bengalis exploit this linguistic possibility to increase or diminish distance, provoke compassion or aloofness. A mother, to dissuade her small daughter from scratching the face of her cousin, rebuked her, "He is your brother, true brother!"—*apun bhai*—she stressed, thus converting her brother's son at this very situation into her own.

Patriline defined morally—*ijjat*

As I stressed earlier, patriline in Gameranga is not a unit of labour or appropriation. On the ground a *gushti* may accommodate households with very different access to resources and economic interests. Thus the household of an affluent landlord may be surrounded by the houses of a palm-tree tapper, a beggar, the widow of a day-labourer as well as a teacher. They all compose a *bari*—the localized patriline, without much regular economic or labour co-operation[23]. Poor families may enter a client relationship with their better-off kinsmen but they can also withdraw and choose patrons beyond their *gushti* or even the village. Patronage is always established on an individual basis and is of a very shifting nature. The asymmetry of patron–client relationship is concealed behind kinship terminology, yet both clients and patrons are aware of where they stand in relation to each other. This awareness is upheld through a range of strategic exchanges. Nevertheless, the relationship between a client and his patron may turn within a short time from mutual dependency to total alienation.

As other observers of Bangladesh peasant culture have noted, group efforts are "perennially vitiated by conflict and competition among individuals" (Bertocci 1977, Maloney 1985), a mode of interaction geared, according to the villagers, by evil human forces, like *hingsha* (envy, lack of trust), *kharap drishti* (evil eye), by the fact that "everybody wishes to be a *matubor* (i.e. leader)" or by general proclivity to greediness and cunning (*chalak, lubi*). Corporateness, however, is achieved and dramatically manifested whenever a dispute with a member of another *gushti* escalates into an armed fight (*judho, maramari, golmal*). Then, all able bodied men in the *gushti* go together, and fight in defence of *nam* (reputation) or *ijjat* (honour, prestige), even if the concrete piece of

[23] The interest from money loaned to an agnatic kinsman is lower than that from external loans and a meal as the only payment for labour is only acceptable among *gushti* members. A widow may pay a lower rent for a house to her deceased husband's brother, than other people would.

disputed property belongs to only one of them. Inter-*gushti* fights erupt less frequently and less abruptly than household disputes (*jhogra*) and their revenges are subject to scheming and careful timing. Nevertheless, householders are always on their guard—each house is equipped with at least one strong and well-used bamboo stick (*lathi, shorki*) specially manufactured for the purpose. The event thus transforms each householder into a fighter (*lathiel*) and the village ground—usually at the *para* boundary—or a particular piece of disputed land, into a battlefield.

Combats are particularly associated with the ploughing season, because it is then that it usually comes out, that a particular piece of land had been sold to more than one buyer[24]. Land disputes constitute a distinct category—*jomir golmal*. At that time of the year, the male ward of the village hospital where I also did my fieldwork, was overcrowded with patients injured in the combats, so that a single bed might be shared by up to three patients. This annual emergency (recorded in hospital journals as "multiple injury") was anticipated and planned for by the hospital's administrator, who would not admit patients other than injured victims of these seasonal fights. There was also political pressure from various local factions on the doctor to act as a witness in the court, a task which consumed much of his time as it involved long boat journeys to the court in the district town.

Also the housewives in Gameranga feared these events and lamented, "A lot of blood will be shed" (*onek rokto hobe*). My neighbour Rupia, whose husband was known as a fierce fighter, was particularly worried for his life, as the couple had no children and his death would surely worsen her position in the *gushti*.

Agnatic integrity, involved here and represented by the image of the interlocked parts of a bamboo stick is further defined by *ijjat*—a moral virtue I intend to elaborate on. *Ijjat* is a moral substance, which apart from blood and patronym, is shared by all *gushti members,* but which, unlike the other substances, is a standard of moral excellence and distinction and therefore has to be gained and defended. As a form of subjective sentiment and behavioural propriety, *ijjat* is generally ascribed to men, but as an objective attribute, through which the hierarchy of *gushti*s is established, *ijjat* is genderwise a mutual concern. As such, it applies in numerous contexts to distinguish persons, households and *gushti*s. As a mark of distinction among people who share the same *dhormo*, it pertains to the domain of moral discourse but, unlike failure to behave in accordance with one's disposition (*dhormo*), lacking in *ijjat* does not make a person accountable to *shomaj* or any other jural body[25]. The values involved in both concepts are similar, however, *ijjat* (like patronym) is an attribute and hence more critically bound to the interaction. As such it generates (and confirms) self-assertion and self-agrandizement through hospitality,

---

[24] The reasons for land disputes are more complex than that, but I will not go into details here.
[25] A man who does not profer *ijjat*, because he is unaware of the rules or is lacking dignity is degraded but is not accountable for it.

physical defence, verbal conquest, i.e. potentially wasteful behaviour (Murphy 1986) inconsistent with the tenets of piety (Islam—"submission to God").

It is clear that *dhormo* incorporates multiple ideologies and that there are contradictions within each of them. Within Islam the highly valued discourse of honour coexists with equally valued discourse of piety. As Muslims in New Delhi studied by Murphy (ibid.), people in Gameranga tend to rationalize this discordance between secular interests and piety (assertion of *gushti* versus submission to God) on the claim that any positive committment to society (be it a *gushti*, a *para* or Bangladesh) is ultimately "good for God".

With respect to *ijjat*, as with most Bengali concepts, informants could not supply an unequivocal, concise definition, but presented a couple of inter-related, overlapping terms, suggesting there are several qualities and aspects to respectability. A man of respect is known as a *manna gonno*—somebody, everyone pays attention and listens to (*shobae mane*), who in turn is careful to maintain his own esteem (*nijer shonman rakha kore*). Because showing off self-esteem increases respect, he radiates resoluteness (*pashan*) and readiness to defend himself, i.e. the attributes that increase his image of respectability (and so diminish the actual need to resort to the physical means like bamboo stick)[26].

To my question whether men cry when stricken by sorrow, women used to say "no, men lack *maya* (affection), they are hard" (*purusher kono maya ney, pashan hoy*), thus pointing to the fact, that the physical expression of the sense of self-esteem, in posture and tone of voice not only marks the distinction between those who have *ijjat* and those who do not, but also, that the sense of moral virtue is externalized differently by women and men[27].

Care for one's appearance is an important indicator of a person's self-regard. In this respect, the head receives most attention in grooming—oiled hair parted in the center over the forehead, tied and twisted into a knot in the case of women and well-trimmed beard or moustache of the men denote that sense. Typically, madness which is associated with the lack of self-regard (but may also be a voluntary withdrawal from "society"—a prominent form of women's dissidence) is marked by exemption from grooming and oiling one's hair. It is, however, not sufficient to dress, talk and speak in a respectable manner. Unless it is recognized by others, a person's moral worthiness remains within the precincts of subjectivity, even an object of mockery. The consensus with regard to a person's respectability is formed on the basis of a collective memory of good deeds (*gorbhot*). *Gorbhot* is a collection of secular credits and deeds or gains (not quite like *upokar*—a religious merit), such as having a good wife (Lokhi), money, plenty of fertile land, a daughter well-placed in marriage or a son's successfully passed exam. All these are the means to acquire respect but none in itself is sufficient for the attainment of *ij-*

---

[26] If need be *ijjat* of those whose position is also sealed off by *bongsho* is defended by those whose deference their respectability compels.
[27] Cf. chapter 8.

jat. Informants claimed that insufficient *gorbhot* still does not preclude *ijjat* as the latter subsumes both *shonman* and *gorbhot*. In terms of transiency, *gorbhot* is the most temporary aspect of respectability, *ijjat* the most permanent. The latter emanates from a vast number of sources, of which one's duties toward kinsmen and *shomaj* seem to be the core value.

Unlike the merits of *gorbhot*, *ijjat* once lost can hardly be re-gained. The loser, however, can live on the *ijjat* once lost for quite a time, before he and his family drop completely from a prestigious position. The villagers were more explicit and straightforward in defining the attributes of men who lack *ijjat*. Accumulation of wives either by chain monogamy or polygyny, lying (*mithuk, "tar kotha thik nei"*), delayed paying off debts (*"shomoy motto pauna dai na"*), notorious wife-beating (*bou mara*)[28], womanizing (*magibaj, dharaner purush*), being a thief (*chor*), or constantly scheming to get things or advantages from others without one's own effort, were listed and provided with a name of a *gushti* where a person who had gained a reputation for such behaviour belonged. A young man, now settled in town, related the case of his father as an example of lost *ijjat*:

"My grandfather Roshon, apart from having plenty of land (*jomi wallah*) possessed a lot of *ijjat*, so that the whole *para* was named after him—Roshoner Para. As a young man, his son—my father—who gained a B.A. at the Islamic College in Calcutta, wished to follow his example. Like a zamindar inspired by Gandhi's ideals (Gandhibadhi) he founded a high school which used to attract students from far away, led a simple lifestyle, wore simple dress, ate food like others, refused to drink tubewell water, opened an orphanage (*etim khana*) and gained access to the relief goods regularly distributed among the poor. He was never short of new ideas of how to bring betterment to this area, particularly to his *para*. People found him a bit strange but held him in respect. As a food inspector, after the partition, he came into a lot of money, converted it into land, some of which he distributed among his brothers and cousins. Lacking his skills and determination they missmanaged what they had gained and lost everything. The oldest of them, Iqbal, the *matubor*, is a disgrace to all *gushti*. He sleeps a lot, always stays in the house, does not watch over his property and sons and so everything escapes from him. Seeing this, my father now allocates all surplus resources towards preventing his brothers from total decline, instead of, as previously, directing his duties for the good of all *shomaj*. He initiated a regular weekly market in the school grounds, but in the meantime, the school has declined and as you see, he has lost all his supporters".

On another occasion, the same man told me that what made *ijjat* definitely disappear from the *gushti* was Iqbal's (the *matubor*'s) decision to bring home (at his age—over 60) a young concubine, the day after his deceased wife's funeral; the sexiness of a man over his "sexual age" and the lack of piety with respect to mourning was the point of definite retreat from respectability. The people who were due rations of relief oil and biscuits, re-named his father's "orphanage"—*etim khana* as *bhaiera khana* ("feeding brothers"), thus pointing critically to the actual direction the food was chanelled.

---

[28] Although wife-beating is universally approved and practised in Bangladesh, husbands who batter their wives too often and without apparent reason are condemned.

As an example of gained *ijjat*, the same informant mentioned Sayen Ali—the schoolmaster "who has gained a lot of *ijjat* by now, despite his deplorable background. Now, he is a new-honourable in the village (*gorib theke boro hoye geche*), has plenty of land, speaks well and supports his poor relatives". An interesting point in this example of acquired respectability is that the schoolmaster was the first man in the village to let his wife (after giving birth to three children) be sterilized. For this he was declared persona non grata in the mosque for a time and even banned from *shomaj*, but apparently, this scandal did not affect his honour permanently. His title "schoolmaster" points to his merit as the founder of the first girls' school in the area. As I came to the village the *moulana* asked him for his daughter as a wife for his son.

Hospitality (*otithia*) is another expression of collectively shared *ijjat*. For children, as they grow up learning to be social is to learn first of all how to take care of a guest. Socialisation in hospitality entails skills such as accurate assessment of a person's social status and knowledge of the items to be provided and presented to the visitor accordingly. This association between objects, body posture and social standing of a person, which children learn so early is most clearly expressed in seating arrangements. Offering an appropriate seat is precisely the form of social exchange whereby the pattern of body use is correlated with the idea of social hierarchy and where awareness of rules (of hierarchy and *ijjat*) is simultaneously performed and socialized (see Jackson 1983b, Toren 1983). Aziz's (1979:44–45) observation on this point in the Matlab area corresponds to my experience of visiting in most places in Bangladesh:

"type of seat offered to a visitor or fellow villager is an indicator of the status of the latter. From higher to lower status, the offerings might be: (1) chair, (2) round wooden or cane stool, (3) low wooden stool or *chhota chauki* or (4) *pidi* or plank seat. In most families, many of these items must be borrowed … A mat is also a common and popular sitting device … a mat of fine texture is considered more appropriate for a person of higher socioeconomic status rather than a coarse *hogla*. From such a person the individual with lower socioeconomic status maintains a certain level of physical distance as a mark of respect".

Seating furniture for the guest is the first thing children are despatched to get and it is a housewife's or a servant's task to serve first *pan-shupari* and then, depending on the guest's status and season, other food items. After I happened to enter the courtyard of even a poor household for the first time, a bustle arose backstage to get hold of some kind of refreshment, a glass of water, even a boiled egg or at harvest-time puffed rice or seasonal fruit. The more nutritious items and prestigious china or glass, even a spoon, were gathered from the better-off households. Fanning a guest's head in the hot season and de-lousing are other services pertaining to the repertoire of guest-care.

In my attic room, my own sitting or drinking would be interrupted at any time, just because a new respectable or respect-demanding guest (e.g. an "officer") happened to visit a neighbouring home. Children would come and claim anxiously the chair on which I was sitting or a cup from which I sipped tea, because a "guest has arrived" (*otith ashche*). Then I myself was re-defined as long-time guest. Once, as I myself visited a rich, well-reputed home in the neighbouring village, the landlord commanded his servant to select the best of the chickens roaming in the courtyard to be slaughtered and prepared for me. He turned to me saying, "So that you do not think all Bengalis are beggars". It seemed as if he took the opportunity to defend *ijjat* of all Bangla *desh*[29] and thus to extend his claim to honour beyond his immediate group. In fact, his *gushti* included a few families who would have had to resort to begging were they not fed by my host. It was his sense of piety, including care for dependant agnates as well as a couple of non-agnates, vigorous praying evidenced by a mark on his forehead[30], plenty of land and profits from his shop in Khulna, which gave his household a high prestige. "He does not let his wife work or leave the house and his daughter was withdrawn from school just in time before her first menstruation" the doctor's wife remarked admiringly to confirm general opinion that Noab Mia is a real *bhodrolok*[31].

While hospitality on behalf of *gushti* is taken as an unquestionable collective duty, there are other individual strategies to enhance one's honour. In addition to usurious money-lending to dependant peasants, there is a wide-spread habit among well-off householders of borrowing money from various sources and thus of building up an image of credibility. Whenever I myself was approached in this respect, (this could amount to several times a week), the claimant would drop the names of a few of his previous creditors or name the kinship link to my landlord (to justify the claim) and then ask for a sum of Taka. Although I never succumbed to such claims, news was occasionally spread with my name included among the creditors. Provided their *ijjat* was recognized, such men would go to the market (*hat*) without a *paisha* and still buy anything they needed. Here the resemblance to Kabylian ethnography is striking. Bourdieu (1986:185) writes about "drawing on the credit and the capital of trust which come as much from reputation for honour as from a reputation for wealth. It is said of such a man that 'he could come back with the whole market even if he left home with nothing in his pockets'. Men whose reputation is known to all are predisposed to play the part of guarantors—either for the seller, who vouches for the quality of his animal in their presence, or for the buyer, who, if he is not paying in cash, promises that he will repay his debt promptly. The trust in which they are held, and the connections which they can mobilize, enable them to 'go to the market with only their faces, their names, and their honour for money'". With respect to the *ijjat* of a "market man" it applies also in

---

[29] Although I was not important to my guest personally, killing of an animal as a show of honour was based on the assumption that I represent the whole foreign *jat* as well as, and more importantly on that occasion, my host family in Uttor Para. Food served to me was taken as an index of esteem paid to the *gushti* that adopted me (cf. Abu Lughod 1986: 66).

[30] Apart from *tupi*, beard and verbal assertions (declarations of faith), the undisputable sign of a man's piety is a blue mark which appears on his forehead as a result of regular praying—"*namaj porte, porte, mathae dag pore gieche*".

[31] See chapter 13.

Gameranga that "strictly personal qualities, 'which cannot be borrowed or lent' count at least as much as wealth solvency" (ibid.).

I shall now return to the actual enactment of *ijjat* whereby a *gushti* is united for the purpose of its defence. Fighting is an important event in the context of gender rhetoric because informants used it to justify their preference for sons. In actual fact, it is precisely at this point of physical assertion that male and female share in *ijjat* interlinks. As I said at the beginning, *ijjat* appears in two ways: on the one hand, it refers to the sacred quality conferred on a virtuous man, on the other hand, it points to his ability to defend what bestows it, i.e. what is most precious to him. "Honour", as Bourdieu (1986:61) notes, "has a meaning and function only in a man for whom there exist things worth of being defended". In other words, only a man who has something to lose, can be put to shame[32].

As noted earlier (pp. 109,129–130), the aspect of defence and hospitality loads the ethos of *ijjat* with ambiguity, because its various sources convey values not coherent with Islamic piety (charity, protection and care, submission to God): conspicuous commensality concurs with wastefullness and defence with dominance based on the use of physical violence.

For people in Gameranga, even the landless, land is the most precious resource. As a man's self-esteem derives largely from being a good cultivator[33], an encroachment on land he owns and identifies with, is not merely an attack on his source of livelihood but on the *ijjat* of its owner and by extension on the *ijjat* of his *gushti*'s physical force. In this context, the difference made by villagers, between strong and weak *gushti*, refers first of all to its numeric strength. The number of able-bodied men a *gushti* comprises indicates as well its reproductive capital (Bourdieu 1986:61–62, 214), which includes not only the successful birth rate of sons but the circumstance that promote their survival and their acquisition of the physical strength of fighters. All this pertains to the domain of women's responsibilities and is critically linked to the sustenance skills, protective and healing powers of women. The sons are thus valued not only as a labour force ("cannot you see now why a son is indispensable to us?" an old man pointed out to me, as strong young men kept unloading boats full of harvested paddy) but as *lathiel*—fighters, ready to defend what pertains to *ijjat*. The word *lathiel* derives from *lathi*—bamboo stick, thus conveying the means of fighting[34].

---

[32] See the case of Zahera in chapter 9.

[33] This gains recognition as a distinctive collective feature attributed to Bengali Muslims settled in the neighbouring states. From Assam, Cantlie (1988) reports that Bengali Muslim cultivators distinguish themselves by being able to yield three rice harvests a year, the skill that also shows in the surface appearance of their fields—"one can tell the land belonging to Bengali Muslims."

[34] It should be noted that *ijjat* related violence is not limited to large-scale public combats. In fact, hidden violence seems to be more frequent than the enactment of honour in front of others. Patrilines involved in prolonged feuds may resort to hired murder; other strategies include attack from ambush and lethal injuries or leg fractures inflicted on a son just on his way to or from the final school examination (*gushti*'s cultural capital) or in the case of women, rape or acid thrown in a nubile daughter's face. I happened to encounter many of the victims of inter-*gushti* conflicts during my research in nearby hospitals.

The bamboo rod (*lathi*), apart from visually representing agnation and "legitimate force" (*danda*) (Dumont 1980:302), also serves non-metaphorically, as a means of doing things. As "a concept covering important political phenomena" (ibid.), and taken for granted in the ordinary flow of life,"it is activated and given literal value" (Jackson 1983b) whenever the *gushti*'s boundary is to be reinforced.

Although the number of fighters and sticks alone would not win a combat without an authoritative leader, (one who has the skill to mobilize all the *gushti*'s capital), it should be remembered that the reputation of belonging to a strong patriline suffices to keep potential offenders at bay and in case of married women it provides protection from maltreatment in their affinal home ("she has plenty of brothers to rely on").

As a subjective feeling and behavioral style, *ijjat* is a male emotion and as such it is expressed differently from *lojja*, which is a corresponding female virtue. However, as a collective attribute of a *gushti*'s worthiness, *ijjat* is both a male and female concern. The responsibility for the management of the *gushti's* reproductive capital falls entirely on women. Wives are the sole agents to be blamed when fertility fails and those who perform the role of curator of family health. The management of births, feeding, prevention of death and protection of anything at the stage of growth is women's exclusive concern. It is also women who inscribe in their childrens' bodies "in abreviated and practical form ... the fundamental principles ..." (Bourdieu 1986:94) and strategies of honour (*ijjat* as well as *lojja*). Women have a stake in honour in still another important way. Their sexual modesty (*lojja*) as regards purdah is the paramount criterion by which a family's and a *gushti*'s *ijjat* is evaluated. It is in the idiom of purda where *ijjat* and *lojja* interlinks. Lapses from feminine etiquette, particularly too frequent and open transgressions of the household's boundary or even a more critical *para* boundary are signs of sexual laxness and invite warnings like "*ijjat cholie jabe*" (*ijjat* will disappear) or "*ijjat ei barite thakbe na*" (*ijjat* will not stay in this home). A man's ability to keep women inside and immobile (like Noab Mia mentioned above) depends not only on his authority to control them. He needs resources to provide bathing facilities, servants to fetch water and run errands. For most housewives in Uttor Para, though none of them would ever work in the fields, moving in the open in connection with providing a livelihood is a regrettable necessity. It is always done surreptitiously. An interesting inversion occurs on the day of the election to Union Parishad (local government). On that day, paths and school grounds in the area are flooded with women who are brought to the ballot box to vote. The wives from prestigious and pious *bari*s consider this a regrettable duty and a sin; many have to be forced by and literally dragged behind their male relatives for whom any single vote they can secure to support their patron or patron's candidate, is a matter of political competition.

Summary

This chapter was introduced by two questions concerning the ways a birth group is thought about and what purpose it serves. By way of conclusion I shall recapitulate what seems to be central. A birth group, or descent among Muslims in Gameranga is defined by the idea of sharing among its members of distinct elements or substances which comprise a number of semantic domains and which are transformations of each other: food, blood, semen, honour. This idea is further supported by the image of the botanical species bamboo (*bash* or its derivative *bongsho*) and its lexical metaphor "brothers" (*bhaiera*) which both invoke the attributes and the moral of an ideal agnatic relationship. The core value suggested in these representations is the unbreakable and eternal cohesion of agnates, the strength and the precedence vested in seniority and the continuity of the patriline beyond the death of an individual member.

Given the fact that there is no way for a person in Gameranga of establishing his/her credentials other than in terms of belonging and that is effected by reference to the most prominent agnatic kin group or other male authority, agnation is critical to the objectification of a person's belonging. On the basis of this *gushti* appears to constitute an idiom of relatedness as well as personhood[35]. The strong identification with one's patriline manifests itself in three senses. First, a person perceives herself as being physically, morally and emotionally i.e. through blood, honour and *dhormo*, inseparable from her or his bloodgroup. This mode of metaphoric relatedness blurrs the strict Western distinction between a person's subjective and objective mood and shifts emphasis onto the flux between these two aspects of personal self. Consequently, an action of a person affects the whole group and a groups's reputation affects the prospects of each member[36]. This fusion between self—non-self is secured by the employment of metaphors of diverse semantic origins—biogenetic, vegetative, human, moral—which nevertheless flow into each other. Shared blood means closeness in space, shared childhood experience and memories; the commonality marked by blood intersects with verticality visualised as bamboo.

Both are translated into shared concern for honour as manifested in corporate armed action or homicide in times of crisis. Further, the wide range of meanings attached to "blood", "bamboo", "brotherhood" and "honour", provides for flexible interpretation and hence it permits subjective as well as objective identification. This aggregation of various meanings assigned to *gushti* serves to transform "the reality of difference into the appearance of similarity with such efficacy that people can still invest [*gushti*] with ideological integ-

[35] See chapter 10, note 1 for women's perspective on *gushti* belonging.
[36] For example, upward marriage or the acquisition of a prestigious job is beneficial to the reputation of the whole *gushti*, while a daughter's elopement has detrimental consequences for the daughters of other families in a patriline.

rity" (Cohen 1985:21). It is this very imprecision that bears out the effectivity of a symbol or a metaphor (Cohen ibid., Jackson 1983b)[37].

The second context in which the oneness with *gushti* comes into play is in communication with various others with whom one shares neither blood nor *dhormo* or territory. A person always presents himself with reference to his group of origin, and vice versa, people are always percieved by outsiders as belonging to and representing an agnatic group. Here *gushti* provides people with an idiom of distinction, a sense of oneself and themselves vis à vis others. As Cohen (ibid.,58) reminds us, idiomatic boundaries are relational: *gushti* marks a birth group in relation to other birth groups. Although a representation (bamboo, blood, brotherhood) is never completely coincidental with the meaning of what is represented (*gushti* in this case), the dialogue would not be possible without it. In the encounters with non-members within its ambits of comparison, a reference to the *gushti*'s name sets a frame for interlocution at the same time as it becomes the motive for assertiveness. In Gameranga the sense of conceiving oneself in terms of *gushti* is actualised whenever the Other is perceived as posing a threat to the boundary surrounding it. Social interaction either in combats (where bamboo is at once a metaphor of unbreakable unity and an actual means of assertion) or verbal exchanges maintain the moral unity and the sense of belonging to a *gushti* in working order.

The third sense, in which *gushti* gains importance is that through its various representations, agnation becomes generalised to constitute a preferential perspective in all cultural domains and practices. Being valued as a positive social quality agnation serves as an idiom of prestigiousness and so a predominant way of reckoning in Bangladesh. The division of space, property, concerns and roles within a household, is set up on the agnatic principle. Prestigious knowledge and the style of speaking takes on the qualities of bamboo; assertion of moral dominance and preferential cosmology is coached in terms of its lineality and strength: authority and power are literally pursued by means of a bamboo rod. Dwelling on its emblematic characteristics, agnation imposes "principle on the construction and division of reality" (Moore 1986: 170); as a result, all dominant social values are defined in agnatic terms. Notably, this applies in official discourse, during the initial periods in encounters with outsiders, when schematic reality is explicitly recognized.

The problem is that the unbreakable agnatic unity, the exclusiveness of the Fa-So-Br tie and the unproblematic reproduction of the agnatic group as objectified in multiple metaphors is in conflict with lived reality. There is a substantial economic differentiation within agnatic groups, but even where brothers happen to be equal in terms of resources, there seems always to be a reason

---

[37] From a different perspective Jackson (1983b) posits metaphor as a force transforming various domains into one image. It is this unificatory function he claims, that facilitates the movement between all the domains of Being—personal, social, natural—and from one context to another.

for fraternal competition. As among other agnatically organised groups, "the closest genealogical relations—that between brothers—is also the point of greatest tension" (Bourdieu 1986:39, Davis 1983:116–124). Among Muslims in Gameranga this tension is further underpinned by the convention of kinship etiquette which prescribes avoidance between brothers. Not only is fraternal cohesion contradicted at the level of kinship ettiquete, by facts of biological reproduction and economic interests; unilineality itself is challanged by the practice of including matrilateral kin into *gushti*, the strength of the mother–son tie (that survives *musulmani*), by the load of married women's affection for their brothers (and vice versa) and by sentiments that even men nurture towards their mother's side. In the management of daily life, the completeness of male domination is further strained by a range of covert activities by women.

With regard to material representation, the unilineal monolithic perspective visually conveyed by arbor vitae is further muddled by objects and tasks structuring daily experience. The implements and movements employed in daily processing activities (when women lift and let fall a pestle of *dekhi* as they grind rice grains, or roll *shil* over *pata* when pounding spices) are shaped and activated in a way that intermingles both phallic and uterine shapes and dispositions. At practical level of subsistence women thus co-ordinate maleness with femaleness.

Returning to the question posed earlier, I hope to have shown that *gushti* fulfills three interrelated functions. As an idiom of personhood and belongingness *gushti* sustains the self, the self with respect to others and the objectified and objectifying self. In this latter regard, as a principle locus of objectification, *gushti* shares its properties with all symbolic representations in that it is capable of sustaining incoherences which exist both within the dominant structure and between its representation and practice in social action. Cohen helps me to see this as he recalls the truism, that "the very nature of symbolism itself contains not merely the competence of [condensation and] discrimination but the sense of negation, … that the very rationale of symbols [be it kinship terms, substances or gestures] is that they are different in some way from the entities they symbolize" (Cohen 1985:58 referring to Babcock 1978 and Boon 1987). So, in view of its multireferential, multivocal capacity and in view of the contradictions and imprecisions, the metaphors of agnatic hegemony are able to accommodate, I would support Cohen's (1985:21) view and claim that the main efficacy and significance of *gushti* lies in its competence as an "ideal media through which people can speak a "common" language, behave in apparently similar ways, without subordinating themselves to the tyranny of orthodoxy".

CHAPTER 12

Women, patriline and affinity

Though the vertical directness of bamboo does not invite much association with femaleness, those extensions which are vital for the group's survival are mediated by women—sisters or wives to the *gushti*. The kinship ties that extend across the boundary of a *gushti* are materialised through marriages.

Before dealing with marriage transactions I shall attempt to explore the formal position of women vis-à-vis the *gushti*.

I shall begin with a consideration of the patrilocal principle according to which women are detachable from their natal group. This will be shown by presenting the reversed case of uxorilocal marriages which give rise to the ridiculed category "man of the house". I shall further focus on the factors that underline the indeterminated nature of women's structural position: the depersonalising form of address, circumvention of the law in regard to sister's inheritance of immovable property and easiness of divorce.

The second part concerns the institutionalised visitations (*nayor*) paid by wives to their natal homes. In contrast to the rather static emblems of agnation, *nayor* is both a metaphor and event through which plurality of meaning may be created, sustained and manipulated. As I will show, the journeying wife, apart from drawing a link between the two patrilines which she structurally represents, also moves towards recognition of a unity between the two poles and contexts of her life and so to a realisation of alternative realities.

After I detail the event of walking and the metamorphosis a wife undergoes in the course of journey, I turn to the metacommunicative and reflexive function of journeying. The event of walking between two homes through which the wife realises the idea of distance, affords and outside (i.e. critical) vision. This is a position she shares with the fieldworking anthropologist.

Sisters in Bengal are members of their fathers' *gushti* but only their brothers can pass on their blood and name to their children (Fruzzetti 1976a). Unlike Hindus (Davis 1983:66), married Muslim women retain membership in their father's *gushti* after marriage at the same time as they acquire membership in their husband's *gushti*. The position of sisters thus seems to entail a paradox which I shall develop by focusing on the residential principle (another instance of shared substance). The culturally constructed maleness of the *gushti*, which I elaborated earlier, is further reinforced by the principle of detachability of women, according to which daughters leave their fathers' home and join the families of their husbands after marriage. The reverse situation, epito-mized in the ostracized category of *ghor jamai* (resident son-in-law or "son-in-law of the house"), does occur, but is a solution of necessity, for example of a man without sons. *Ghor jamai* is universally look down upon in South Asia (Bertocci 1974, Cantlie 1984:110, Kolenda 1982). In Gameranga, the *ghor ja-mai* solution belongs to the category "poor-people's-marriages". His awk-wardness is implied in the attribute "of the house" which alludes to the un-manliness of staying where women should be. The few *ghor jamai*s I knew of were involved in peripatetic occupations like travelling business or in some other way practically absent from the village—busdriver in town, daily la-bourer in another district or shopkeeper in the *thana*-village—an ingenious so-lution according to Bourdieu (1986:51), which enables the son-in-law to keep the profits of his labour while removing him from the embarassing situation in his family. Loyalty of *ghor jamai* in inter-*gushti* conflicts is not to be counted on. His "outsideness" is explicitly manifested in exclusion from the *shomaj*, i.e. from public decision making, which is another condition he shares with an in-married woman. So strong is the feeling against uxorilocal residence, that the *ghor jamai*'s status affects negatively that of his children at the time of marriage negotiations and it takes a few generations before his dependents can re-gain *gushti* status, a process which can be speeded up by the family's econ-omic growth.

Daughters are temporary members of their natal homes; it is this fact that reduces considerably their salience in "thinking about *gushti*". Instead, their value is articulated in connection with marriage exchange. The importance of their being exchanged and detached is reflected in the rule according to which an adult man cannot marry before his sisters of marriageable age. In other words, the failure to give away one's nubile sister (or daughter) in marriage impedes the continuity of the *gushti* and seriously affects its prestige (*ijjat*). A sister's contribution to her father's line is her detachment from it, while her own achievement of completeness can only be attained in the *gushti* of stran-gers. A marriage, among other things, also means a transfer of guardianship over the bride from her father to her husband. Thus, permission for further education, employment, hospitalization or any other disposal of a married woman's time outside her conjugal residence, is to be sought from her hus-band, this even in the case of her temporal stay in her father's house. Blanchet (1984:78) gives the example of a young wife who came, according to the cus-tom, to give birth to her first child in her father's home but when the delivery proved complicated and her life was threatened, the parents had to seek her husband's permission, first to let a doctor see her and again when it became necessary to take her to hospital. This caused a further delay in a 3-day de-livery and cost the infant's life. I witnessed a similar case in a missionary hos-pital where a young wife about to give birth to twins came accompanied by her parents. The foreign doctor decided on a Caesarian section but could not perform the surgery before a messenger was dispatched to fetch her husband from a far away village. The doctor told me that one of her female patients had bled to death while her in-laws hesitated to give permission for an operation which involved the transfusion and donation of blood. The question of guardianship is tricky in cases of uxorilocal marriage: in two cases of female employment, permission was sought from the woman's father and not from the husband.

A woman's membership, however is not resolved by marriage. In each gushti a clear distinction is made between daughters (*meye*) and wives *(bou)*. Accordingly, a man's sisters and daughters are included in the former category and are addressed by their names, while his mother and wife, belonging to the latter, are called *ma* or *bou* respectively. After marriage a woman does not change her name, instead, she adds to her former name Begum which means Mrs. Even her parents-in-law refer to their son's wife as "*amar bou*"— my wife. After she bears a child, she is refered to as "so-and-so's mother" (e.g. Rohimer *ma*). The names of in-married women are often forgotten. When I carried out a family census and insisted on obtaining the names of housewives who were temporarily absent, a number of elders had to be consulted to obtain the correct name. Married women themselves are extremely reluctant to disclose their name "because of shyness" (*nijer nam bolte lojja kore*). A woman's membership in her husband's *gushti* is perceived mainly as a claim on her offspring, work, deference and loyalty. Paternal kin have jural right to all chidren born to wives of the *gushti*. Both men and women in Gameranga consider it not only right but natural—"the pull of blood", though after divorce, a mother takes her unweaned child with her for a period of time. As soon as it is weaned, however, the child has to be returned where it belongs[1].

A wife's actual integration is a gradual process, the success and speed of which depends on her powers of reproduction, the sex of her first child, her adaptive skill and personal temperament, and also on such factors as the size of her dowry, whether her mother-in-law is still alive, availability of the husband's younger brother, with whom she may enter into a joking relationship and thus alleviate her feelings of alienation.

The degree of separation from the father's patriline varies in South Asia. For other patrilineal groups like Hindus, birth group (*gotro, kul*) exogamy is so total that women can marry again into their kin group only after several generations[2] (Aziz 1979:101, Fruzzetti 1976b). Under the patrilineal ethos there is no legal or de facto obligation on the part of kinsmen to support their married sisters and Hindu women are not entitled to inherit patrimonial property. Writing on Brahman Chetri in Nepal, Bennett (1983:314) maintains that "once their marriage expenses have been paid, these women have no further

---

[1] There are cases of children residing with maternal relatives while growing up, after their parents' divorce or father's death; such arrangements are considered irregular and temporary solutions.

[2] According to Aziz (1979:101), among Hindus in Matlab the tabu of endogamous marriage extends up to 7 generations on the paternal side and up to 5 on the maternal side.

claims to the ancestral property of their natal lineage", a fact that according to the author accounts for the voluntary nature ("selflessness" and "nobility") of brotherly love. Bennett adopts the term "filifocal" for relationships which celebrate the value of affection and personal choice between siblings and opposes them to the "patrifocal" values of duty implied in conjugal love (ibid.). In addition, divorce in Hindu theory and also actual praxis is not as easily attainable as among Muslims, and so there should not arise a need for Hindu kinsmen to support their sisters economically after marriage[3]. By contrast, marriage does not separate a Muslim woman from her natal *gushti* as definitely as is the case with a Hindu wife. There are various cultural provisions and practical circumventions which secure the continuity of the filifocal link and indicate the transience of daughters' membership. For example, the absence of restriction on endogamy among Muslims (unlike the Hindu rule which prohibits marriage between people who can trace common descent in prescribed degrees) means that cousin marriages are licensed and practised[4]. In Uttor Para, 64 out of 200 wives were married within the *para*, which means that the category of kin and affines potentially overlap[5], a factor which additionally blurs the wife's *gushti* membership and fuses maternal and paternal ties.

By transferring guardianship to another man at marriage, the concern for a daughter's well-being does not cease. It is then of a protective, rather than a regulative nature, and this sort of responsibility is passed from the father to the brother. Women often pitied me for not having a brother as "it is only a brother who can protect you from your husband". Because fathers are prohibited from visiting their daughters in their conjugal home (except in cases of lethal injury or disease), a brother is the most frequent visitor and donor of small gifts. Behind his concern, there may be a realisation that his care will preclude any claim to her share of the patrimony. It is believed that patrimonial land is only claimed by women whose brothers did not show any concern for them after marriage (Abdullah 1974:27).

Directly linked to the question of the wife's membership are considerations of inheritance and divorce brought into focus at the time of marriage negotiations. Unlike Hindu Dyabhaga[6] Muslim law entitles daughters to inherit one

---

[3] Van der Veen (1972:83 n.10) reports on Anavil Brahmans in India that one possible way for a man to re-marry is to drive his wife to suicide.

[4] For demaracation of endogamy among Hindus in Matlab described by Aziz (1979:101)—see note 2 above. Among Hindus in West Bengal, the cutting of the blood link for a bride is so complete, that only a woman of the third generation, i.e. wife's DaDa can return as a bride to her MoMo *gotro* (Fruzzetti 1976a).

[5] The survey I carried out on for different purposes, indicates the wives' natal home's locality — "within *para*", "beyond *para*", "beyond *gram* (village)"—and not the kinship link with her husband. From casual information I gathered, it was clear that "within *para*" marriages include a number of conjugal ties between cousins. The only kinship monograph on Bangladesh by Aziz (1979) indicates that out of 1719 couples in Matlab area, 84 were cross-cousins and 62 parallel cousins.

[6] According to Hindu law wives stand fourth and daughters fifth in the line of property succession (Bertocci 1974).

half of their brothers' portion ("two daughters equal one son"), but, as Bertocci and others note for Bangladesh, the law is "honoured more in breach than in practice" (Bertocci 1974, van Schendel 1981:136). In Gameranga, most of the wives who came from landed families did not claim their portion of patrimony from their brothers, thus following the pattern common in Bangladesh (cf. Bertocci 1974, Schaffer 1986, van Schendel 1981). However, what outside observers attribute to the smallness of the pieces of landed property and explain as a measure against further fragmentation, brothers tend to attribute to "the love their sisters have for them" or to the distance between the father's and husband's home. Indeed, women may complain about unfulfilled dowry, but not about their exclusion from inheriting land. Whenever I brought up the topic, informants would refrain from speaking in terms of breaches of law; rather, like their brothers, they expressed their failure to claim in emotional terms—"out of love for my brother" or "for my brother's happiness".

There is no doubt about the strong emotional attachment between brothers and sisters, a sentiment cemented by shared womb and childhood experience. In addition, the brittle nature of the conjugal relationship, where a wife is easily replaceable, makes it reasonable to assume, that, as Bertocci (1974) writes:

"A wife must maintain some security against the possibility that she will be widowed or divorced and should either of these misfortunes befall her she has little resource but to return to her childhood home. If she has not taken property which is due her under law, it is likely that her brothers will take her back with greater willingness and grace than would be the case if she had angered them by taking her share of inheritance".

A sister's disclaimer is usually not recorded legally, but it is tacitly understood that her portion of land is being exchanged for the right of asylum with her natal *gushti* (Ellickson 1972:26). Similarly, the concern of brothers for a married sister's well-being is based on the expectation that she will not claim her share. It is, however, important to stress that even women from landless families think of their natal homes as the ultimate resort in time of marital split and many do return even to their landless brothers' homes when their parents are dead. A woman's farther's home (*babar bari*) is always linked with the hope of protection in the time of crisis. It is a brother's duty to arrange for a second marriage if his sister has been repudiated by the husband.

The points I have considered above can be further demonstrated by referring to the case of Jahanara:

After being divorced and emaciated by a long spell of tuberculosis, Jahanara returned with her small daughter to her paternal *gushti* in Uttor Para where she hoped to receive help from her brother. Her brother rejected her, referring to the successful claim she made to her portion of land some years before, when she, encouraged by her husband's family, brought a case against him. Although still young, Jahanara was not in physical condition to be re-married. She found shelter with an older widow in the *gushti* just before she died.

Jahanara is a case of a woman who asserted her legal rights "succesfully" (in the end the piece of land she won was lost to her husband's *gushti* whence she was expelled together with her small daughter), but in so doing she forfeited her brother's love and thus cut the most vital link with her natal home. There were other cases, like that of two settled urban matrons, daughters of Game-ranga, who got their share of land, because, "then, land was plentiful, but not men" (i.e. brothers who could cultivate it in their case). They came regularly, twice a year to supervise the rice processing at harvest and ultimately to look after the product.

So far I have named the rigid categorization and depersonalisation of wives, lack of rules of marriage exogamy and the custom among women of renouncing their share of landed inheritance in favour of their brothers as factors contributing to the maintenance of double membership with respect to *gushti*. Furthermore, a wife's link to her natal home is kept alive by regular visits, called *nayor din*[7]. Unlike the membership maintained through unclaimed rights to land, *nayor din* is often given legal recognition in the marriage contract (*kabin*), which specifies how often a bride may return home. *Nayor din* is also ritually enacted in the sequence of wedding rituals, when the transfer of the bride to her conjugal home is followed by a two and a half days' "return" to her father's home (*babar bari*), where she is supposed to communicate whether things are going well in her new home, particularly with respect to the sexual adequacy of her husband.

After the wedding, *nayor din* is maintained by a journey the wife makes to her natal house at least once a year. During the first years of marriage, young wives (*notun bou*) are particularly eager to go *nayor*. These visits are timed so as to coincide with the post-harvest winter season or rather with the monsoon (*borsha kal*) when fruit, particularly mango (*am*), is ripe and abundant. Back in their homes, daughters are indulged as welcome guests and it is therefore important that their visits fall on abundant months. In Gameranga, the guest food particularly associated with *nayor* are rice cakes soaked in boiled date tree sap (*bhija pitha*), or ripe mango served with milk and boiled rice (*paka am duth bhat*). The husband, if he accompanies his wife should be served the head of a big fatty fish together with rice or any other prestigious food and sweetmeats. The rice harvest, followed by palm tapping in winter—a time of the year refered to as "the time of cakes" (*pithar kal, khejurer rosh din*)—and the mango season are particularly auspicious for going *nayor* (*nayor jawa*). The husband (*jamai*) should always be formally invited to visit his father-in-law's home with his wife. From his point of view, his wife's house is a "home of others" (*porer bari*) and it is therefore expected that the *jamai* be treated as a guest of honour. This is expressed through the food served. As also Aziz (1979:105) observed in Matlab, "without the inclusion of chicken curry in the menu, *jamai adar* or affection to the son-in-law is not fully expressed". The fuss made of the son-in-law is done in the knowledge that on his return he will

---

[7] *Nayor*—"married woman's father's home"; *din*—"day".

invariably be asked about the food served at his father-in-law's[8]. A daughter's children are also pampered in their mother's natal home and many of my male informants remembered these visits fondly. The mother's home is always associated with warmth and affection and many insisted on my visiting with them their *mamar* (MoBr) or *nanar bari* (MoFa). It should be added that for a married couple, the wife's *babar bari* (father's home) is the only "public" place where the visiting couple can be relaxed with each other—not in the sense of expressing overt affection, but at least talking and sometimes even laughing together. The length of *nayor din* depends on various circumstances, such as the wife's life stage, or whether there is another woman to cook for her husband while she is away. In one case a daughter of Uttor Para was never to return from her visit as her husband brought home a new wife during her absence. A daughter's visit can also be interrupted abruptly, if a suitable escort turns up suddenly who can take her back. Before departure, the daughter is always given a gift to be taken back to her conjugal home. It may be fruit, vegetable or sweets (*lau, pepe, murgi, dim*)—always home produce of her *gushti*'s garden or kitchen, i.e. what imparts her home's substance. Albeit less sumptuous than the volume of gifts reported from other parts of South Asia (van der Veen 1972:80), they still represent the cultural paradigm of gift-giving and the standard expectations of a daughter's situation in her conjugal *gushti*. They are tokens to be exchanged for their daughter's good treatment in a place which is assumed to be hostile. In the husband's *gushti*, whatever gift the wife brings with her is perceived as a duty of her family, not a kindness to be reciprocated. Van der Veen's (ibid.) observation among Anavil Brahmans in the Deccan applies equally to the affinal gift-giving situation in Bangladesh: "The manner in which these presents are received is striking. Giving is not regarded as kindness of the giver, but as a duty. The practice is to make disparaging remarks about the value and quality of the presents". As I said before, a husband, although always formally invited, joins his wife only exceptionally. A wife's absence thus provides an opportunity to pursue illicit liaisons, in some cases even to bring an additional woman for a more permanent cohabitation. The onset of polygynous households tends to be associated with the wife's illness or *nayor din*, i. e. physical absence or inability to provide domestic and sexual services.

In a commentary on "female identity" in patrilocal cultures, Fortes points out its most salient structural feature:

"Women move—they might move only across the road; they might move to a house they know intimately, having been in and out of it a lot; but they move, and at that move they stop being daughters and become wives and mothers" (Fortes 1983).

The reality of a woman's position vis à vis social structure in Gameranga could not be expressed better. Throughout my thesis I treat wives as outsiders

---

[8] We may recall that a marriage is an alliance of two *gushti*s and at *nayor*, the *jamai* represents all his patriline.

and implicitly parallel this aspect of their position with that of the fieldworking anthropologist (i.e. somebody from "outside")[9]. In fact, 32 per cent of wives in my sample were married within the precincts of their natal Uttor Para, i.e. across a path, bamboo grove or canal and 27 per cent within the village, i.e. across the *para* boundary. Genuine outsiders amounted to 37,5 per cent[10]. Apart from its effect on the system of cousin marriages (overlapping of agnates and affines), *nayor din* must be a much less exciting experience for girls whose *babar bari* "can be seen and heard" from behind a bush. Yet, "daughters-of-*para*"-wives are not free to visit their kinsmen at will. When they go, they do so stealthily, always risking reprimands from their in-laws[11]. The element of moving away and a process of cutting ties with the natal home is thus ever-present, irrespective of the actual physical distance.

The idea of distance appears in the wedding ceremony, which itself consists of several journeys between the bride's and groom's homes: when the actual residences are too close for movement between them to qualify as a "journey", the procession meanders by a circuitous route in order to make affinity seem more like what it should be—a proper distance. *Nayor din* is the revitalization of this distance. If a wife's *bari* is in another place (about 65 per cent of Uttor Para wives), her visit means crossing the boundary which constitutes the limit of her in-married mobility as well as the marker of her double belonging. Wifehood implies an emotional journey and *nayor din* is a recurrent reminder of this. I give some details of the actual journey as these illuminate the nature of belongingness and of purda.

Each journey is preceded by the soliciting and granting of permission, which in itself involves a complex strategic negotiation between mother-in-law (or her deputy) and the travelling wife. Without going into detail it should be noted that in her day-to-day behaviour a woman is always mindful of the

---

[9] I maintain that the skills and knowledge critical to the gradual adaptation from new to old wifehood are concomitant with the method and theory that imparts anthropological learning. Both bride and fieldworker move abruptly from one context to another and in both cases the transformation has ramifications beyond spatial movement, as it is linked to ideas which refer simultaneously to the body, sentiments and conceptualization of self (cf. Moore 1986:73, Jackson 1983b).

[10] Referring to Ruzicka and Chowdhury (1978:25) Aziz (1985:61) presents comparable data for Matlab, where out of 2795 marriges in 1975, 2.1 per cent of partners were from the same *bari*, 8.1 per cent from the same *gram*, 10.8 per cent from the same union, 40.9 per cent of cases from the same *upazila* (or *thana*) and in 47.9 per cent of marriages a bride was brought from outside the *upazila* .

[11] The extent to which in-laws are restrictive of a *bou*'s ucontrolled visits to her native home is clear from the case of a young wife in Uttor Para, married just across a pond from her parents' home. Once, while chatting with her husband's sisters, cooking and breastfeeding her baby, a young woman noticed heavy smoke and soon even flames in the direction of her birthplace; she grabbed her baby and ran over to it. The sight of her father's house in flames, as she approached it, overwhelmed her with sorrow and she fainted. Her sisters-in-law arrived a little later to join the crowd of on-lookers. One of them lifted the crying baby and when the young mother recovered from her faint, all the sisters-in-law reproached her for being neglectful, pushed the child into her lap and commanded her to return "where she now belonged".

consequences of her actions in terms of obtaining permission from her mother-in-law (*shashuri*) to go *nayor*. A woman, who is about to embark on her journey, puts on *burkha*, which is a black enclosing cape that covers her body from head to the toes. The top part is a sort of a hood with latticework over the eyes and mouth. From within her veil, she can see but herself can be seen merely as a social category, a representation, not as a particular person. *Burkha* is the travel garment par excellence and those who cannot afford one, put on their best sari and fashion its decorated end (*achol*) in a way that obscures a woman's features but permits her at the same time a limited vision. A recent fashion that substitutes for the expensive garment is a patchwork of second-hand-USA-imported-stuff—pieces of nylon lace underwear (slips and bras) in pink or blueish colours sewn together by the local tailor (*dorji*) and sold as a cheap substitute for *burkha*. A woman's travelling kit also includes an umbrella, in some cases sun-glasses and other paraphernalia meant to protect her and, more importantly, to communicate to the passers-by that she is a married woman and that, although she has trespassed into male precincts, she is not violating the principle of purda. *Burkha* is a married woman's garment, capable of expressing even more conspicuously than a sari (in its traditional design *burkha* is the only black garment to be seen in populated spaces), her "anonymity" and feeling of *lojja* and, because of its high cost, she also conveys the status of her husband's family. *Burkha* is unanimously considered a prestigious and beautiful dress and women in Gameranga thought my inability to share their appreciation strange.

Unless a woman goes *nayor* accompanied by her husband, and in that case she walks a few yards behind, she should be escorted (and even carried) by another person. At the beginning of their marriage, wives are usually fetched by a male relative, often an unmarried brother. As soon as she becomes a mother, the company of her child, either on her hip or holding her hand, may suffice. For well-off wives it is considered inappropriate to walk. Touching the ground with one's feet is considered as declassing (improper at best), and the effort of walking is associated with hardship (*koshto*), particularly for women. Therefore, the wives and daughters of respectable families (*bhodrolok*) are always provided with some means of transport to save them from physical effort. For that purpose, a boat (*dinghi*) covered with a hood or a palanquin (*palki*) is hired. After a week in Gameranga, when I announced my intention of going to the post office in the next village, about 2 kilometers away, the older men in the *gushti* where I was adopted considered the matter and insisted on providing me with an escort. After a boy of 15 or so, adopted in one of the households, was persuaded to go with me, somebody remembered that I should have an umbrella. In my initial innocence, I protested by pointing to the spotlessly clear sky, to which my landlord said, "For a woman of your standing, it is not sufficient to cover the head with sari, when you walk so far"[12].

---

[12] In fact, Bengali women of "my standing" would never walk at all—boat or *palki* were the means of transport for those who could pay.

Accompanying me proved problematic—not only was I not used to walking over shaky bamboo bridges (*char*) which constitute the extensions of walkable paths over the canals, but my interest in surroundings, manifested in frequent halting, expressions of astonishment and questions, proved a nuisance to my escort. My recreational, "unfocused", exploring manner of moving in the world contravened the boy's idea of decency and all he had to say during the trip were commands, "Hurry up!", "Come!", "Go on!", "Will you come or what?". Needless to say, he never again volunteered for the task. As I was allotted to the provisional category, "new wife", at that stage, it was not difficult to imagine how completely a genuine new wife, newly-married into the community, is at the mercy of her in-laws, and how different a vision a girl acquires by marriage. Like myself, new wives who come from afar cannot even orient themselves spatially in a foreign land; unless one walks at night, there is no way to pass unnoticed, so if ever they were tempted to run away, they would probably get lost. Later on several occasions, when I myself was accompanying a number of married women to their parental homes, I could in each case observe an interesting metamorphosis which occurred along the path of the journey. As mentioned previously, women depart from their affinal homes overdressed, with their eyes focused on the path, "not seeing, not hearing". My occasional pauses to view a picturesque scene, a tree or a bird or my responses to the curious gaze of passing-by travellers were again met with an irritated reprimand from the woman in my custody to go on. At a certain point, however, Azia ("the wife") herself slowed down, folded her umbrella, took off her sun-glasses and lifted the veil from her face. Occasionally she could greet a man passing by and exchange a phrase of recognition. To my astonished, "What are you doing?", answers would range from "Am I not among brothers here?", "Is it not my father's home?" to "Everybody knows me here", or she simply pointed to a cluster of houses emerging in the greenery. The vision of *babar bari* in the horizon was a sufficient answer.

Here I would like to pause and recapitulate the salient points related to the problem raised in the introduction, namely the position of sisters in relation to the *gushti* (as a way of approaching the nature of affinity). By way of conclusion I will connect affinity, as enacted in *nayor* journeying, to reflexivity.

Given the type of marriage regulations (lack of enforcement of permanent *gushti* endogamy or exogamy), the praxis of inheritance and the distinctions between *babar bari—shashur bari* (Fa-in-law's home), we can speak of a married sister's double membership or at least of a lack of fixed and permanent membership. This dual attachment is strongest during the first years of marriage, the stage of "new wifehood". Then the young wife is emotionally still of her *babar bari* (Fa's home), a membership underlined by freshness of memories and forfeited rights to landed inheritance. Politically, as she is aware, her interests lie in the *gushti* of her husband. Only on the land of her in-laws can she reach full womanhood through a successful alliance with her husband and later her son and even exercise some kind of effective power, an aspiration consistently curbed by various forms of purdah (cf. Bennet 1983: 165, Sharma 1978).

Structurally, marriage is an exchange between two lines, or households forming two branches of a *gushti*, where sisters, translated as wives, become links rather than authorized members of either patriline. This linking is given cultural recognition in *nayor* ("a happening in a wife's father's home") when a wife moves in regular intervals, physically and mentally, between two points of her life orientation—patrifocality and filifocality[13].

Nayor jawa is, however, more than a graphic enactment of a sister's structural position, and a wife's going and coming (*asha—jawa*) does more than represent and communicate social facts. It seems that young women, who are in any case excluded from the formal arrangements (negotiations of legal and material transactions) of their marriage, experience the problem of belonging emotionally rather than formally in terms of legal membership. I wish therefore to point to the experiential features of belonging in so far as they contain meta-messages suggestive of an alternative epistemology to the dominant, agnatic ethos. Writing on *dhormo* I have elaborated on embodiment as a form of cultural learning. Here my primary concern is distance embodied in walking away from óne house and one state of mind to another house and another state of mind and then back. Distance is intrinsic to the process of going and coming (*asha, jawa*) and to the process of learning to know. Distance is also the circumstance a new wife shares to a certain degree with the anthropologist.

On *nayor* a wife goes away and acquires a temporal and spatial distance from the conjugal world characterized by sexuality, submission, strategizing, from the world where she is objectified as a wife (*bou*) or a mother (*ma*). She moves towards the world associated with non-sexual intimacy, knowability of the familiar, sweet food and indulgence. In this world, she is known as Jahanara, Rohima, Mahinia, Alinor ... i.e. somebody's daughter or sister. Within the space of a day's journey, these principles are brought into focus and into contrast, thus providing a wife with insight into the double aspect of her reality. As for an anthropologist, so for a travelling wife, "the illusion of total truth is amended by the revealed discrepancies" (E. Ardener 1982).

This, as I have shown, is experienced and expressed through her body which she re-arranges at a certain point during the trip while undergoing a metamorphosis. By discarding her "veils" she not only reveals the discrepant nature of her position in the two homes, but provides a commentary on the transient nature of her belonging, i.e. her self. The light-heartedness prompted by the sight of her natal home opens her body and speech, and simultaneously evokes a special kind of expectancy, a receptivity to indulgence. The journey thus becomes both a physical movement and a change of being. Quite apart from the difference between the point of departure and the point of arrival, there are features in the process of going back and forth (*nayor*) that sensitize

13 See Bennett 1983.

the wife to an awareness of being both an outsider and insider vis à vis the home of her past and also the home of her present life. In moving from one to the other, a woman becomes aware of the different aspects of herself. The critical moment of the journey—unveiling—suggests a process of moving between two positions, as if the traveller claims and disclaims her social, i.e. objective identity, saying simultaneously "I am a wife" and "I am not a wife". The paradox she produces by discarding her veil is the paradox of reflexivity, which in Turner's (1984) words is an act that implies "an agent's action upon [herself] indicating the identity of subject and object". Other scholars write of meta-situation or meta-commentary when they deal with a boundless range of techniques by which "we reflect ourselves to ourselves" (Gorfain 1986). Common to these devices is the capacity to refract and deconstruct the whole or at least to acknowledge the dilemma (Bruner 1986, cf. Caton 1987, Gorfain 1986, Kapferer 1984,1986, MacAloon 1984). It is from this perspective that I see a Bengali Muslim wife traversing the landscape between the world where she is a wife and the world where she is a daughter and I maintain that the process of transformation she undergoes extends beyond *nayor din* into ordinary life.

The capacity of *nayor jawa*, and indeed of the affinal situation generally, to raise self-awareness lies in the paradox which Hastrup (1987) associates with the temporal distancing that also occurs in fieldwork, particularly in cross-cultural communication. She claims that the "paradox consists in the subject [i.e. anthropologist] experiencing herself as object, and then perceiving the object as subject in the next instance". Like the newly-arrived anthropologist (assimilated to the category of "new wife"), the new wife in her conjugal home in Gameranga comes "to see herself as 'object' in a discourse made by others", after which she, in common with the anthropologist, begins acting as a new kind of subject corresponding to her status as object (Hastrup ibid.). Like the anthropologist of whom Hastrup writes, she becomes (or may become) an other to her self, which is exactly the process through which one learns either how to be "a wife" or how to be "an anthropologist" or any cultural role.

For Bangladeshis, the inability to maintain a link with one's blood relatives and birthplace is considered a great misfortune. For women, the father's home is the only place they visit and in spite of journeying, particularly for women, being considered an extreme inconvenience, *nayor din* is much looked forward to[14]. I believe that, apart from enjoying the privileges of guest status on *nayor*, the main reason for this "love of travelling" is the opportunity it affords for attaining and reviving that outward view which clarifies the meaning of her life. Irrespective of the point of departure and the purpose, the processual details intrinsic to travelling favour a contemplative mood in which self-re-

---

[14] In fact any journey (moving away) is valued by women in Gameranga, as became apparent from the range of excuses given by some of my widowed or destitute female informants to take a walk "abroad". A need "to accompany" the anthropologist, "to borrow" something elsewhere, was the most usual excuse given to their guardians.

flection can occur. For Bengali Muslim women in particular, while traversing a landscape, the gradual distancing from the overcrowded, overdemanding quotidian existence, provides a rare occasion to relax, shut out the world and retreat into thoughts—a condition facilitated by *burkha*[15]. In these terms, *nayor* can be considered a voyage of world-discovery as well as self-discovery (Crapanzano 1987)—a voyage outside which is also a voyage inside. Invoking the journey as a chain of metaphors of affinity and knowing, and including within it the accompanying anthropologist, we can add an additional meaning to *nayor din*—as an intersection of the "identities of the interlocutors in a cultural dialogue" (Hastrup 1987:104)[16]

In view of this and in view of the points made on previous pages I contend that *nayor jawa*, and more generally affinal links in a patrilineal, patrilocal society, afford Bengali Muslim women an external vantage point (Bourdieu 1986:1, Crapanzano 1987, Rosaldo 1983) that permits a reflexive and critical vision of the world and the self[17]. It turns the objective category "new wife" into a positioned, questioning subject and uncovers the reflexive portion of the self. As going and returning is normally a children's and a male prerogative, I would also claim that a *nayor* trip may promote a sense, of what it is to be an adult man and a reminder of what it was like to be a young girl. In short, the experience of *nayor* points to the shifting ground of the dominant agnatic ethos—in fact of any knowledge (Crapanzano ibid.).

[15] The veil, as I claim elsewhere, is the instrument of paradox par excellence (see chapter 18).
[16] *Nayor* appears to have shared my experience of first coming to the community and subsequent occasional commuting between Gameranga and the domains dominated by Westerners. It was in their homes, hospitals and other facilities I could recover my health and the sense of my "former self" during fieldwork.
[17] I have borrowed and paraphrased here Crapanzano's (1987) view of anthropology and propose *nayor* as a metaphor of the "epistemological dilemma of any reflexive undertaking", be it the affinal situation, fieldwork or writing about it.

PART FOUR

Production and Reproduction of Hierarchy

CHAPTER 13

Categories of social distinction

There is a great and persistent concern among rural Bengalis with categorization and ranking people, events and phenomena. Every individual knows and is quick to estimate who is above and who is below him. Indication of rank is displayed in casual conversations and official inquiries, whereby persons are specified by references to skin colour, size of salary, academic degrees, birth order within the family. Also explanations of events, willingness to do certain jobs and attempts to predict each other's intentions, manifest a predilection for categorical hierarchization. Van Schendel (1981:242) depicts the poignancy of the impression management ritual as he re-calls (in a slightly different context) his observations of two countrymen—relative strangers— who met on a village path:

"their greeting usually led to a rapid verbal status display on both sides. Unless one of the two quickly concluded that he was inferior in status and signalled it by acting deferentially, this could lead to a true 'barking contest', an escalation of status claims and counter-claims".

Upon meeting a genuine foreigner, questions regarding her identity center around the topics which have precedence in the villagers' classificatory paradigm of hierarchy. From the answers the villagers attempt to establish a category for the outside person in order to place her as accurately as possible in the local hierarchy (Kotalová 1986). At a more generalised level the villagers view "the rural" (*gramer*) as opposed and morally superior to "the urban" (*shohorer*). As a representation of outsideness (*bidesh*), *shohor* and urbanites are associated with chaos: sexual temptations, insidious scheming and cunning, but also with an elegant lifestyle, affluence, luxury goods, a diet consisting of tea and biscuits, superior knowledge and permissiveness. *Shorkar* ("government" equated with carelessness and theft as well as a depository of relief goods), *dakait* (bandit), even prostitution and cannibalism[1], suggest the range of associations which things urban invoke. By contrast, villagers and being of a village excell as pure, trustworthy, innocent victims of outside manipulations. Villagers experienced in both life-styles pointed out to me that the many manifestations of uncontroled sexuality, like prostitution or romantic love

---

[1] A rumour went round Uttor Para, spread by a *ghor jamai* who earned his living as a rickshaw-*wallah* that in Dhaka, where he worked, several restaurants used human flesh in their food and that pieces of dissected infant bodies were found there laid in ice for a week-consumption. Several women approached me and asked whether I myself had experienced something similar. My attempts to qualify the rumour as *khali kotha* (empty talk) was not taken seriously.

which are carried on surreptitiously (*gopone*) in Gameranga are openly fostered in towns. Language, dressing style, diet are subject to the same distinction.

In explicit comments on each other's standing in the community, brought about by marriage evaluations or the anthropologist's inquiry, the villagers resort to a vocabulary of distinction, quite different from categories of agnation (*bhaiera, bongsho, gushti, rokter attio*) or habitation (*gram/shohor*) mentioned above. While property is a major factor here it is never divorced from the virtues of moral and ascribed status[2].

Among the villagers, the poorest (but also the richest) tend to present a clearcut dichotomous model of social stratification, in which the peasant *jat* in general bestows upon "us" and "others", corresponding to *gorib* (poor), *choto lok* (lesser people) or *murkhu* (ignorant) on one side and *dhoni* (opulently rich), *mahajon* (money lenders), *boro lok* (big shots) or *bhodrolok* (gentle people) on the other (van Schendel 1981)[3]. Although the denotations of each stratum bear reference to different dimensions of prestige, the first category basically includes the landless, who have to earn their living as labourers on others' land (*kishan*) and those who have a piece of land but have to till it themselves. They usually eat only one meal a day and during meager months have to eat wheat flour (*atta*)—"*gorib manushto, atta kheae*" (being poor, one has to eat wheat flour porridge, or unleavened bread). As van Schendel (ibid.) points out men from these families may be tolerated at *shomaj* sessions as listeners. They are sometimes referred to as *kishan* (labourer) and when they are unable to work they drop further in social esteem to the category of *bhikuk* or *fokir* (a beggar, indigent).

Apart from the difference in wealth and access to public decision making (manner of participation in *shomaj* gatherings), ranking in Gameranga includes assessment of mental skills, involvement with physical labour and various aspects of lifestyle. Accordingly, *choto lok* are said to lack the initiative, diligence and skill required for successful management of all available capital. Neither can a *gorib* householder afford to keep his wife idle and secluded, nor provide her with essential supplies like a number of saris, jewellery and hair oil. She and her children are ordered about by the housewives of their patrons and they accept working for the patron of the same *gushti* for food as their only remuneration, i.e. as a *jonghodar*.

Wealthier members of prestigious *gushti*s generally distance themselves from the *gorib* cousins claiming, "We share the name and place (i.e. court-

---

[2] According to the consensus of the villagers in the neighbourhood, Uttor Para where I lived, was known as the poorest and also the least reputable section of the village. This provides a context in which the categories of social hierarchy and subsequent classification were generated.

[3] Because the denotations used in Gameranga correspond exactly to the vocabulary of social distinction recorded by van Schendel (1981:92–93, 174–175, 243) in other districts I draw heavily on his translations as well as classification by access to productive resources and manner of participation in *shomaj* gatherings, as indicators of effective power.

yard) but as you can see, we are different"[4]. The difference indeed, is conveyed architecturally—the size and degree of dilapidation of the houses and the impenetrability of seclusion fences betray the social position of their dwellers even to an occasional visitor.

The well-off villagers (as well as urbanites) explain their poor cousins' condition by the lack of intelligence (*budh nei*), traits of laxity and carelessness— "they let wealth run away". This indicates, how a personal achievement or rather non-achievement can invert the rank of a patriline and hence the collective mark of a person's identity. Although individuals frequently justify doing things or behaving in a certain way by reference to the collective—"does not everybody do so?" or "… think that way?"—there do exist cultural domains (other than material achievement) in which individuals are subject of social ranking apart from their membership in a particular birth group (Davis 1983: 104, van Schendel ibid., 92)[5].

In an economic sense, the "other" from the point of view of *chotolok* are big or respectable people (*borolok* or *bhodrolok*), a designation pointing as much to landownership, effective power, distinctive life style as well as to some immanent quality of nobility derived from an unspecified past[6]. For example, the old men in the now declining and splitting Sikhdar *bari* (altogether 24 households), remember nostalgically its founder, their grandfather, for politically shrewd decisions, the ability to persuade people, land accumulation and generous distribution among low-caste (*napit* and *dai*) Hindus, whom he had invited from other district to settle down in Gameranga.

Borolok are said to eat well ("two to three cooked meals a day and tea-biscuits in between")[7]. Transistor radios and digital watches are modern yet indispensable gadgets attached to this class, at least in the eyes of those who try hard to emulate their style. As elsewhere in Bangladesh communities, *borolok*

---

[4] Consistent with this is the lack of appreciation Bengalis show of architectural uniformity, displayed universally in modern housing schemes. Two young men from the area of my research who visited Scandinavia on different occasions, commented with indignation on suburban housing style, where large areas are dotted with chains of houses of the same size, form and colour. Reading this aspect of Western material (and political) culture sociologically, they found the lack of social differentiation (or rather reluctance to differentiate expressly) reproduced in spacial arrangements, utterly disturbing and anti-social. According to Bengali standards, social differentiation should be displayed as tightly and graphically as possible, so that rich dwellings should always be surrounded by poor, who, in village rhetoric "need the protection".

[5] For men achievement in competitive games, efficacy of medical remedies of a *kobiraj*, reliability of a fortune-teller accrues considerable status (apart from the discourse of honour). Van Schendel's (ibid.) informants named wisdom and artisan skill as a mark of positive distinction.

[6] Bertocci (1972) specifies qualities as association with landed aristocracy, position in colonial administration, military service, revenue collecting system in pre-independent Bengal. In similar vein, van Schendel argues that in the absence of anything resembling a true aristocracy in Bangladesh, the term (used by elite), as well as the *gushti* titles refer to the achieved statuses of any people thought to be rich, cultured and of "good families" (van Schendel 1981:243).

[7] Prior to fieldwork, in my Dhaka residence, the *baburchi* gave recognition to my allegedly higher status by insisting on supplying my household with white bread and refined cane sugar, while himself used *ghur* (brown sweetener of boiled date palm sap) and *atta* (wheat brown flour) for baking his *ruti*.

is expected to entertain visitors to the community, make loans, give donations, grant reasonable favours to *chotolok*, act as go-between or a judge in disputes (cf. Bangladesh 1980:41). In short, *para's* honour rests on their shoulders (Bertocci 1972). After being a guest in a rich man's home for a time I commented on my host in my diary:

"Although the landlord's power in the community seems to be in decline his residence remains the focus of beggars, destitute women, an anthropologist, his allies, officials and constructions workers (the builders of the first water sealed latrine to appear in Gameranga), who all find their refuge here during their sojourn in the village. Lodging and food are provided for outsiders of appropriate status even in the landlord's absence. Besides, its location next to the school, *hat* (market) ground and a huge *pukur* (water tank), all of which the landlord founded after the Liberation war, make his *gushti's* precincts the focus of social and economic activities. December 1982".

Material wealth does not automatically endow wealthy people with the kind of prominence which emanates from *bhodrolok* or *shikhito*. Davis' notes on the connotations of this status in West Bengal apply equally to Bangladesh:

"... cultured and restrained of manners, civilized, learned, of superior quality and cultivated taste. It is applied to those individuals who have sufficient wealth ... plus sufficient taste and manners to live in a comfortable dwelling, to lead a relaxed, regulated life, to use polished language, to wear fine clothes, to be knowing of civil manners and to be properly educated as a good ... [Muslim]" (Davis 1983:1034).

Clearly, to *bhodrolok* are ascribed the qualities of lifestyle achieved through generations; these are inscribed in the body and thought (Bourdieu 1986:218).

In Gameranga, the self-importance of the new wealthy, unsustained by reputation (*bhalo nam*), i.e. history of accumulated merits, is ridiculed. People are quick to distinguish between new rich, upwardly moving upstarts from genuine *bhodrolok*. Also the recently-graduated, unemployed sons from low-prestige families, who emulate the style of *shikhito* in order to command respect, draw sarcastic comments, "*saheb hoye geche*" (he has now become a saheb).

The clues to my understanding of local distinctions between genuine and less accomplished aspirations to power-holding, were provided by the wife of the doctor in charge of the local hospital. Being herself an outsider to the area and to village style in general (of which she was utterly contemptuous), she was nevertheless in acute need of social orientation. She thought it of utmost importance to estimate correctly the status of those of her husband's patients, who could afford to attend his private evening clinic. Apart from payments in cash, the influential clientele, coming from all surrounding villages, could offer various services and exchanges to alleviate alleged hardship the family suffered in such a backward place[8]. In the end, the wife's sociological explorations led to a classification of the villagers according to the advantageous-

[8] The insight into the socio-logic of the area was also indispensable for working out under-the-counter deals concerning pharmaceutical drugs, in which all the hospital personnel is inevitably involved and which yield no small profits.

ness of keeping them close or at a distance. Once, when I inquired about a group of men in the waiting room and used the word *bhodrolok*, the doctor's wife corrected me emphatically, saying that in spite of being rich—"masters of a lot of money" (*onek takar malik*)—not all of those peasants are worthy of respect. To illustrate the point, she compared Noab Mia (who, besides having plenty of land, a profitable cloth-shop in Khulna, piety inscribed on his fore-head[9], originates from a family with *uchho bongsho*, feeds many people[10], keeps his wife from productive work and daughter from school) with Abu Seikh—the most affluent man in Gameranga. According to her, Abu cannot be considered *bhodro*, as he came to his riches in a matter of only two years, by dubious amassing in connection with Partition and recently by grabbing land from Hindus. "No, it is not a good family, his wife is abusive to her serv-ants, who never stay for long, and one of his daughters, people say, had a ro-mance (*bhalo basha chilo*) when she went to school, so he had to withdraw her and hastily arrange a marriage".

Distinction between *gushti*s

So far, I have dealt with a two-fold imagery of stratification of society at large. In a more narrow and concrete sense of village stratification, what really counts is a person's land and symbolic capital (pedigree). The poorest and the rich tended to present village society as a "dichotomy based on landowner-ship" (van Schendel ibid.,243), where land goes with prominent position while landlessness with passive participation in village decision-making. Two self-sufficient, moderately well-off peasants with some formal schooling and interest in national party-politics, who assisted in the evaluation of my family survey data, divided[11] households into the following categories: landlord (1), rich peasants (7), middle peasants (70), small peasants (34) and poor peasants (90). Their criteria were purely economic (i.e. land and salaried income).

---

[9] Reference is made to the blue mark which comes out on the forehead of a person who prays five times a day, as a result of vigorously pressing one's forehead to the ground. High moral prestige is attached to this sign of piety.

[10] Local reference to protective (as contrary to usurious), patronage.

[11] To clarify the authorship, it should be mentioned that the suggestion of this classification, based on Arens and van Beurden's (1977) framework came from myself. In a debate I overheard on fac-tional-political issues, these two men casually made a distinction between urban-settled land-owners, middle peasants and those who work on others' land. Following this, I suggested to them a five strata division and presented the socioeconomic data I had collected on the households of their community; on becoming my occasional assistants the same men correlated the five-strata scale with my survey data and their local knowledge without great discord, though, the hierarchi-cal position of a few families was disputed and had to be reshuffled several times.

Distinction by titles

At this point I should mention "name" (*nam*) as an important inter-*gushti* criteria of ranking. In this context of distinction *nam* refers to a term by which a patriline is commonly known in the community, and less to "reputation" (although both concepts are closely linked). As noted previously, one of the denotations of patriline, its title (*bongsho*) is mainly heard in connection with marriage negotiations. Having *bongsho* does not tell us that a man has brothers—such information would be superfluous—but point to the distinctive quality of a person's blood connection, originating in the past. *Bongsho* thus carries hierarchical social value and serves in gaining status. Titled households are ranked as belonging to *uchho* (high), *modhyo* (middle) or *nicho* (low) *bongsho*, which is a vertical distinction based on an assumed value of their title, rather than on the *gushti*'s cohesive strength or quality of leadership (as conveyed in prefixes *boro* or *shokti*). The emphasis on ascribed status is frequently made by those informants from titled *gushti*s whose own household has become impoverished.

Most households in Gameranga are associated with an appelative, however, not all of them are patronyms. For instance, the names of many *gushti*s are derived from the practice of Islam, like Khazi *bari*, Mullah *bari*, which may indicate an hereditary occupation but not an actual source of livelihood. A few families of these *gushti*s actually have a member with documented religious merits, or one who is recognized as an authority on religious matters. This gains moral dignity for the birth group and a degree of respectability but does not in itself grant high status. Families without title may be those in the process of forming a patriline. It is said, that it takes four generations to build-up a patriline and so a family at the second-generation stage since its foundation, is "just so" (*emni*), a mere category of people; they may posses respect, landholding and adhere fastidiously to Islamic piety but such families are extremely vulnerable in situations of theft, dacoity and other calamities and they count very low in the marriage market. In emergencies, they seek patronage from well-established, titled *gushti*s. "They are nothing, in spite of having everything", my landlord commented on their lack of belongingness. Playing with the literalization of the metaphor of "bamboo", another informant added to the nature of *emni* families' marginality in *shomaj*:"Lacking *bongsho* they have to resort to the use of *shorki* [synonym for bamboo stick] against dacoits", meaning that in the absence of symbolic capital, patronym in this case, the families have to use tangible means of violence to defend their homes against robbers[12].

---

[12] I.e. bandits of foreign provenance, who represent no little threat to household possessions, particularly in topographically marginal settlements. However, in spite of a very concrete threat, defence against external raiders is not loaded with same *ijjat* values like inter-*gushti* violence and is not therefore accorded the same merit in the village discourse of honour. Suggested by this condescending statement is that a prestigious belonging provides a person with an imaginary power—a protective force that makes the use of actual physical violence, i.e. actual working of bamboo rod, unnecessary.

In their respective studies of social stratifiction in rural Bangladesh, Bertocci (1972) and van Schendel (1981) put a slightly different emphasis on economic factors (i.e. material ownership) in determinating a person's status in the community. For villagers studied by van Schendel (ibid.,243), the non-economic factors had become secondary in importance, with an important reservation, however, that "wealth could not entirely take away the stigma of titlelessness" (in the same way as "poverty could not totally undo a prestigious family title"). On the same point, Bertocci claims for the peasants in Comilla that "property and status tend to coincide," but as he says, status, derived from title, continues long after the economic base has gone (Bertocci 1972). I would stress, that the time factor—dropping off-period—is important in the context of marriages. A long time after the onset of impoverishment, the title-derived prestige is perpetuated and can still be (collectively) considered as an asset to be counted on and converted advantageously. This is because the exercise and maintenance of power presupposes a symbolic mastery i.e. non-economic forms of dominance. This competence (which is embodied) makes it possible for a man who has lost materially (all his land and even the roof above his head) to manipulate the collective definition of his situation in such a way as to keep him within the category of the "owner" (*malik*) long after it is not economically (or morally) substantiated (Bourdieu 1986:190). Temporariness is a further dynamic force. Bertocci (1974) stresses the creation and re-creation of social structure in village Bangladesh by pointing to yet another aspect of the temporal dimension in the apparent fixity of status positions. He argues, that given the factors like population size, partible inheritance, monsoon climate and riverine delta behaviour (i.e. exterior objective forces) "it is unlikely that a family can maintain superior wealth over a long period without some difficulty". He views the status of the patriline as moving periodically between rise–fall stages of a family's history, "the decline of wealth for some and increase for others, in a process which probably evinces a 3 to 4 generation periodicity".

Strategies

Mobility stressed (from different theoretical perspectives) by both authors as an essential feature of social hierarchy in Bangladesh also implies that the "relation of domination and dependence are products of continuous creation" (Bourdieu 1986:237). Bourdieu writes of "social magic" or "enchantment" when he points to the endless daily activities aimed at transformation of economic capital to symbolic capital, a process in which dominant as well as dominating party are equally involved (ibid.,195).

My experience, over a year, of my neighbours' in Gameranga rising to and falling from material positions at which I met them on my entry to the field, added to endless searching for new patronage and leaving the old, corroborates this. However, an apparent restraint to structural re-definition is a systematic reinforcement by multiple symbolic means of the existing structure (of encompassment) in all cultural domains. Bourdieu (ibid.,87) points to the overdetermination and simultaneity of means which speak of and reproduce a person's place in a hierarchy[13]. Refering to Kabylian peasant he writes "His rising or falling trajectory" is contained simultaneously in her/his body—strength, beauty, stigma—as well as verbal products, like sayings, maxims, songs (ibid.,20,82,88). On the other hand, a dominant position—prestige and respect—invoked by wealth (access to land, cash, education) cannot endure unless socially and supernaturally recognized. Recognition in turn presupposes incessant manifestation of the virtues attributed to the rank category to which a person aspires[14].

In Gameranga, social recognition involves dispossession of wealth by those who have and of labour, gratitude and loyalty by those who do not have. Dispossesion is the core strategy in power negotiations and a basic and explicit principle of the patron–client relationship. I shall exemplify this by showing how the strategy is operationalised in the effort to integrate an outsider.

Making social distinction, people in Gameranga never totally separate the social and the moral from the economic domain. Virtually all financial dealings, monetary requests and compensations, employment contracts and remunerations always imply deep and intricate social and emotional involvement[15].

My own endless effort to eliminate what I considered disturbing, professionally and personally, to my own modus vivendi and operandi, was constantly combated by those I shared my life with. Recurrent requests for money were not only a matter of taking advantage of a well-off outsider (my intitial rage was ocassioned by this simplified assumption), or a habitual way of opening a personal relationship. In the words of a schoolboy, a native of a different village and a lodger in the same house as myself, "people are testing whether you are good or bad". It was clearly a test of my preparedness to legitimate the authority of my possessions (symbolic and material) by dispossession and also an attempt to explore my willingness to establish a creditor/patron relationship with potential debtors–clients. My refusal to dispossess myself was taken as a disclaimer of legitimate authority and prestige, because,

---

[13] The case in point here is the principle of habitus or "the system of dispositions—a past which survives in the present and tends to perpetuate itself into the future by making itself present in practices structured according to its principles" (Bourdieu 1986:82).

[14] To be socially recognized as an owner and authority, demands skill and time to create and re-create daily social ties with clients. It is an activity referred to by Bourdieu (1986:190) as "weaving the ethical and affective, as well as economic, bonds ... which may durably tie his clients to him". Supernatural recognition (never totally separated from the former) presumes repeated daily communication with God, manifested in prayers, charity and the magical creation of increase (*borkot*). Because possession in itself is critically linked to the benevolence of supernatural providers—Allah and Lokhi—the chain of disposessions starts with them.

[15] The loss of money (Taka 200) motivated, according to my informants, the suicide of a young man at the time of my fieldwork. Maloney (1985a) corroborates this single observation in a comment on money-management in Bangladesh.

as Bourdieu (1986:195) reminds us, all dominance and authority derives from an economic basis, yet "the only recognized, legitimate form of possession is that achieved by dispossessing oneself". This, in the Gameranga context, constitutes the basis for an assymetrical relationship whereby a patron holds his debtors in moral obligation, gratitude and loyalty. (To secure some kind of modus operandi for anthropological fieldwork, other ways of binding offered by the village cultural repertoire had to be exploited; sharing women's experiences proved to be less prestigious but an emotionally a more satisfying solution).

The possession of wealth as a source of social distinction does not only entail a supernaturally sanctioned moral obligation to share with poor relatives and clients. Legitimate, profit-yielding landownership involves moral ties to metaphysical providers ("It was given by Allah", "Lokhi is coming") and know-how, not only of agriculture but also of marriage politics ("His wife is a pure Lokhi"—*Tar bou Lokhi*). The material–cum–metaphysical source of wealth is constantly overmessaged in various socially recognizable forms. "He is a true patron" was an explanation given to my inquiry about a blue spot on the forehead of a rich landlord. He was known as feeding many people and the *dag* indicates the frequency and ferocity of his communication with God at the same time as it tacitly communicates his place in the hierarchy. The attributes of *bhodrolok* correspond more or less to the moral values of *ijjat*[16]. In both cases, the values are embodied.

At this point I bring up the theme which has been introduced previously in connection with acquisition of *dhormo*. Here embodiment is focused at as a process of generating social status. In this context, body serves as a metaphor mediating between the personal experience and the objectification of a person's place in hierarchy. Ethnography collected beyond Gameranga may help us to understand this[17]. Dealing with the multidimensional aspects of households' status in various communities in Bangladesh, van Schendel (ibid.,243) inadvertently draws attention to the link his informants make between social categories and how these are experienced through the physical body. In a Comilla village, the richest farmers, who produced a surplus were known as ones who had "power in their body and money in their pockets" (*gae zor ar taka*) and in Bogra a villager from the household which wholly depends upon labour expressed his place in hierarchy by claiming that "all we have in the way of possessions are our bodies" (ibid.,265)[18].

In the first case, money is transformed as matter internal to the body of its owner and in turn manifested "in the form of manly prowess" (Bourdieu 1986:

---

[16] It is sometimes said in Gameranga, *chotholok* lack *ijjat*.

[17] Cf. chapter 11.

[18] The embodiedness of social position consists in the fact that those in Gameranga, who o n l y possess their bodies, wrap it at least in lungi, which is not provided with a pocket (although the knot through which the lungi is tied often contains coins for an emergency); money can only be carried properly in a pocketed *kurta*—a shirt which many of my informants could not afford to wear.

87). We recognize here the realm of *ijjat*, where to have "power in body" is to communicate not only what one has in the way of possessions (i.e. money or land) but also one's preparedness to defend it. The latter quote points to body strength when used in actual involvement with productive work, thus betraying the lack of material possessions to be converted and to be defended (and which would make it possible to relegate manual work to others).

A wider question focused in the creation and re-creation of distinction is one of embeddedness of actual economic capital and its symbolic articulation. It seems to be the point in question made by those who "have", when to their dismay, those, who "have not" let all they happen to have had, disappear. Indeed, land and money do not stay with an owner (*malik*) who fails to perform as such (Bourdieu ibid.,58,67). As much as *dhormo* is not upheld merely by *bichar* and overt coercion, but a range of precepts and recommendations, so the status derived from tangible resources cannot endure unless reinforced by a particular form of rationalization. I have elaborated on the dispossession of wealth as a strategy of domination. I have also pointed to the embodiment of virtues attributed to a particular position as a way of experiencing and objectifying one's place in the hierarchy. Other forms may be assumed to invoke a person's rank, e.g. the sartorial style of those who have money and therefore also pockets to keep it in, the visual memory of their gait, the body posture, the way of speaking which makes it entirely possible for those who temporarily fall from a materially sustained position, to do marketing even if their pockets have been empty for some time (cf. Bourdieu ibid., 20,89).

CHAPTER 14

Recreation of hierarchy through marriage exchanges

In connection with marriages, the dynamic nature of status categorization comes into focus in still other ways.

First. In the current marriage market a dominance ensues from bringing home a wife for a son. The status of negotiating parties thus seems to be culturally fixed in that wife-givers are subordinated to wife-takers. However, provided the negotiating families have children of both sexes, the apparent fixity is dissolved and dominance is inverted when the sister is due to be given away in marriage.

Second. The ups and downs in dominance are relatated to the ad-hoc character of marriage exchanges in which new considerations come into the picture with each new exchange. Not only are the matching qualities of the partners to be re-considered at each marriage; but as I shall detail in the next chapter each negotiation is a process of attaining equality between the parties by recognition, affirmation but also convertability of status components attached to the candidates.

Although title and landholding are still the most important indicators of a family's position, the present prestige structure in Gameranga also admits education, earning capacity, commercial success and urban connections. The ideal is still a family background, where a respectable patronym (*bongsho*) is sustained by landed property and nowadays also some prestige-giving modern amenities like a digital watch, bicycle or transistor radio. Only very few people in Gameranga attain this ideal. However, the absence of some of the prestigious indicators or lack of accomplishment of some sort, is negotiable and convertible during the process of matching. For example, a decline in economic prosperity—a widespread experience—may be substituted for by a prestigious title, or the education of one of the sons may in the future be converted into salaried income, expansion of landholdings and ultimately marriage to a daughter from household of good standing. In addition to structural qualities which male and female marriage candidates may share, the endowments of women include physical attributes such as chastity, colour of complexion and length of hair. (Also tone of voice and way of walking count but are less vital than the former characteristics).

Commentators on Muslim and other cultures (Vieille 1978, Lindenbaum 1975, Douglas 1970:178) argue that women in marriage are valued as exchange goods or as currency; or, as Lévi-Strauss (1967:60, 1969:496) claims, women, like words are exchanged and communicated (i.e. spoken about) but unlike words, they also speak. In Gameranga, the "speaking" of women does not take place during marriage negotiations or rituals. They may spoil the game, but usually they do not. As scarce and genuine "consumption goods" to be exchanged advantageously, girls after menstruation have to be kept out of public sight, trained in modesty and the maintenance of bodily purity. Having several brothers is suggestive of a strong likelihood of protecting these virtues and counts therefore as an asset. If a girl has been the object of another marriage alliance previously, i.e. if a bride's sexuality has been bound to another man, she is not considered pure and scarce any more and is forever eliminated from the desirable category of "exclusive goods" (Lindenbaum 1975). In fact, any physical imperfection (i.e. that what spoils the imagery of agnatic perfection), be it a broken hymen, a limp, frizzy hair or over-dark skin, necessitates compensation. If a dark marriageable woman is a rich father's daughter, her colour may be compensated for by proper education. A dark female medical doctor I knew in Dhaka was the only one of several sisters who received prolonged education because "my parents thought I was too dark" and the family of a dark-skinned girl in Uttor Para had to produce a gift of a transistor radio to compensate her suitor for the defect. The Bengali wedding ceremony does not entail any spectacular ritual where proof of the bride's virginity is publically exhibited as is the case in some Muslim cultures. The value placed on an intact hymen becomes clear from the counter-gifts claimed for divorced women and widows on the occasion of their second or third marriage. The case of Hosnara, a divorced–cum–widowed woman of 25 illustrates this point.

Hosnara had been married a few years before to a man from far away. A token dowry but no groom price was claimed at that time—fair-skinned, round-faced, with waist-length hair, she affirmed the image of a pretty girl. Her family could live on their own rice for the whole year and the lack of *bongsho* did not matter in a long-distance alliance situation. After her husband committed a serious crime and was imprisoned, she was betrothed to his brother. After some time, her second husband committed suicide and then she returned to her father's home in Uttor Para. When her brother and parents (middle range peasants) started again to look for a third husband for Hosnara, the following items were promised to a marriage candidate: a cow, a piece of land, the timber from a bamboo grove, a transistor radio and a pair of spectacles (both novel symbols in the prestige structure). Not many virgins among her peers were provided with such a lucrative dowry–cum–groom price. Such a large amount in Gameranga standards would be neceesaary for parents aiming at hypergamic marriage. Poor households in the neighbourhood were particularly alert to the opportunity and eventually, the choice was between two young men—a day-labourer (*kishan*) and a fisherman (*jele*). Both were landless, without even a plot on which to build a hut (*jomi nei, jaiga nei*—no field, no parcel). The sister of the fisherman discussed widely the prospect of having Hosnara's as sister-in-law and named as a drawback that she had already known two men (i.e. had been married twice), and that she might not be willing to obey their commands as her brother lived so near. After some consideration, Hosnara's brother's choice fell on the first candidate, because fishing on a permanent basis, although more profitable, after all, is a low-caste occupation.

I have given examples of women's physical attributes (among other "units of equivalence")—failed beauty and failed virginity—to point out the flexibility and negotiability of family status at the moment when it is most acutely at stake. Virginity among Muslims in Bangladesh does not merely refer to the bodily state of a woman. Unlike skin colour, it speaks of woman's self-control, a virtue on which male and the whole family's *ijjat* largely depends. Intactness of a nubile female body is an asset, a form of symbolic capital readily convertible into economic capital (Bourdieu ibid.; e.g. amount of dowry or groom price). Once a woman is spoiled in pre-marital sexual laxness, she cannot be exchanged on the same premise as an intact object (Lindenbaum ibid.). To fall short of beauty, although a secondary consideration, is regrettable but much less surrounded by anxiety, as it is not caused by an action on a woman's body as is a broken hymen. Education is the conventional form of compensation for a deficit in anatomy and physiognomy. For a male marriage candidate the depreciation entailed by previous marriage—of a divorcee or widower—or physical drawback—old age, blackness—is insignificant, compared to women in a similar situation.

PART FIVE

Reproduction of Patriline and Hierarchy in Marriages

CHAPTER 15

Arranging marriage

In this section I shall deal with the way that belonging and gender is expressed through marriage exchanges. After delineating some general rules for establishing marriage alliance (between two patrilines) I shall consider what makes a person matchable "in a given state of matrimonial market" (Bourdieu 1986: 71). I begin with the objective factors that affect the choices—intra-family authority in marriage arrangements and consideration of spatial distance of the *gushti*s. I then turn to the personal attributes of groom and bride and conclude by analysis of the ritual display of these assets at *bou dekha*. Throughout the exposition I will thus move from the structure to experience.

Matching the *gushti*s

The good name (*bhalo nam*) of the *gushti* is a collective concern and, as Aziz (1979:42) observed in Matlab, "there is a continuous desire and effort on the part of a kin to raise the position of his *gushti* members". Exchange of women in marriage is its foremost expression, because marriage in Bangladesh rather than a personal adventure, is a core rank-generating transaction between two groups. Marriage thus provides the unique moment on which the various components of social status—*bongsho*, wealth, education and physical–cum–moral endowements of women are focused. Psychological factors, such as suitability of personalities, are beyond consideration; a marriage based on romantic love disrupts the complex pattern of reciprocities and can only be effected by elopement of both partners. Such a choice however, endangers the marital prospects of the bride's female siblings. Attempted suicide is a very common solution to the dilemma between *gushti* and personal interests in the choice of mate.

Apart from incest regulations which for a Muslim woman eliminates as a marriage partner her "brother, father's brother, mother's brother, mother's father, father's father, brother's son or sister's son and ... [for a man] his sister, mother's sister, father's sister, mother's mother, father's mother, brother's daughter and sister's daughter" (Aziz 1979:59)[1], there are no proscriptions nor prescriptive rules regarding patrilineal endogamy or direction of exogamy.

---

[1] The disregard of the incest tabu, results in expulsion from *shomaj* (Aziz 1979:59) or elopement (Blanchet 1986).

The open-endedness which is characteristic of Bengali marriage exchanges means that a new pattern of considerations and manipulations is to be set up with each exchange (Fruzzetti 1976b).

People in Gameranga may marry their cousins and they often do. They also wish and many strive to marry their daughters up-wards. However, the cousin unions which occur with some frequency among the poorest and the rich, are not guided by a genealogical rule. Neither are hypergamic desires elaborated sufficiently to constitute a regularized pattern. The absence of a concrete, enduring group of takers does not yield a hypergamy in the Northern Indian sense (Fruzzetti 1976b). Neither in theory nor in practice do any of existing marriage forms take on sufficient significance or function to be considered within the realm of marriage rules or elementary structures (Bourdieu 1986: 46,70). It follows that women in Gameranga are exchanged not for other women according to a fixed pattern in terms of direction or repetitiveness of exchanges, as much as for political advantage (Pitt-Rivers 1977:186). It is a case of culture where, as Pitt-Rivers (ibid.) put it, the prospect of gaining a political alliance seems to be the basic principle and current status of the parties involved is the main factor in negotiations. Fruzzetti (ibid.) speaks of the "matching of the lines" (with the aim of maintaining the equality and status of the respective families) as she characterizes the main feature of West Bengali marriage transactions. Parents in Gameranga maintain as well that their children should be exchanged with the equals, though, speaking of daughters, they add "or to a superior". The emphasis on the process of attaining an equal position which Fruzzetti (1976a,b, 1982) recognizes for West Bengal marriage alliances applies equally to Gameranga. She writes:

"Marriage establishes units of equivalence, hence it is preferred that the statuses of the contradicting lines and houses should be as close as possible. Alliance in Bengal is therefore the conclusion of marriages that would create similarities among different lines and houses ... Status, ... and equivalence has to be calculated for each new alliance ... (therefore) each new marriage brings new criteria and new factors into the alliance system. In turn new possibilities for future marriage are opened up by each marriage exchange" (Fruzzetti 1975:119,129).

The ad hoc quality of negotiations and the influence of past transactions for future marriages that Fruzzetti noted in West Bengal, concurs with the practice of marriage exchanges among Bangladeshi peasants. The situational emphasis means that it is difficult to construct the variables which determine the relationship between the families and even to establish "the whole balance sheet" of exchanges in a single family, in terms of capital available, domestic power structure and the stage of the household's life cycle at the time of negotiations (Bourdieu 1986:67,70). This is not to claim however, that the choice of a man who wishes to find a spouse for his daughter or a son is entirely deliberate.

Participation in marital projects, division of concerns

The news that a family member is ready for marriage attracts counter-announcements of available grooms or brides in other families and other places. The guardian of a person available for marriage may receive suggestions from relatives, patrons, people encountered at the market. Although each case is eagerly discussed and commented upon by all *gushti* members (adult comments came often to my ears repeated by children), participation in procedures follows the same gender and seniority principle as any collective project. While mothers, grown-up sisters or paternal aunts may play an active role in spreading the information and undertaking preliminary investigations, the matrimonial negotiations and deals are conducted exclusively by male relatives. The objects of marital exchange—prospective bride and groom—are excluded from the process of selection altogether. However, there is a slight asymmetry in that grooms, though not taking an active role in the search, retain more freedom than their sisters to reject the choice (Bennett 1983:71) made for them by others. The bride's assumed passivity is evident from the fact that even my attempts to elicit from informants' memories the details of arrangements that preceded weddings were considered offensive by the women I asked. This was because knowledge about their marital future would have suggested a lack of modesty, misplaced curiosity, even blasphemy (Sharma 1986:164–165)[2]. The answer to "Why did just he become your husband?"[3] if attempted, would equate the respondent with the worst of sinners, namely with one who questions or appears to have doubts about the existence of the supreme power of God. Young girls on the verge of marriageability address their prayers for a husband to Allah. (Men hope for a woman-Lokhi). When married, women claim a particular man—be he a thief, a womanizer or a spender of any sort—has been predetermined by fate to become their husband. Some specify the process as a kind of predetermination that had been "written on their forehead at the moment of birth" (*kopale lekheche*). Therefore, any attempt to alter the pre-determined order of marital destiny either by searching for the motives behind parental choice or by voicing a preference for a particular candidate (grounded on personal attraction), is considered to be a sin. Suicide or elopement is one way a young woman or man may voice an opinion on their marital future. This is, however exceptional; usually the bride and groom do not take part in the decision-making process, and those young girls who dared to express dislike for the groom their father has chosen, are usually coaxed into submission[4]. A mother or an elder sister may sometimes succeed in dissuad-

---

[2] In general, any question which suggests that the interlocutor has forbidden knowledge is taken as an insinuation of her participation in sinful knowledge and hence acting.

[3] A question attempting to elicit the background of some of the most blatantly incompatible marriages.

[4] It follows that the collection of comparable data on marriages is difficult not only because matrimonial strategies of Bengali Muslims aim at so many social goals, or because the variables determining each choice are defined anew with each project (and therefore subject to constant fluctua-

ing the father from choices which they deem entirely unsuitable, but on the whole women have the least to say. In the case of a daughter's marriage, the mother is concerned with her well-being in the affinal household, in a son's case it is the prospect of dominance over a future daughter-in-law which guides a mother's preference. Generally, it seems that when a family faces the situation of a child's marriage, female and male concerns differ: women are more sensitive to the practical and political needs of the household, while men tend to pursue the political interests of the agnatic group.

While knowledge of those marital manoeuvres which are pursued in the name of *gushti*'s collective interests is lacking, mothers and even brides themselves can usually list the items of marriage wealth which followed them to their conjugal households. Those whose marriages were contracted during the last twenty years may even know the amount of Taka (*muharana*) formally agreed to be paid by the groom's family to the bride.

Whether it is reinforcement of agnatic cohesion or the need for extended networks of alliance, men always seek to contribute to the growth of the *gushti's* prestige or at least to its maintenance (at the lowest level of expectations) (Bourdieu 1986:60). As a result, men in Gameranga tend to seek macro-level information about the whole *gushti*—its *bongsho*, number of males as an indication of strength, their integration, the history of capital acquisition, current network of alliances and enemies, while women seek to know personal characteristics and family situation: age, marital history of the prospective bride/groom and that of the siblings (whether there was an elopement, divorce, madness, suicide). In the upwardly moving or semi-urbanized families, who are apprehensive of the new trends in marital exchanges and where women have a bit more to say in household matters, mothers tend to prefer a daughter-in-law who brings a large dowry or a son-in-law with productive capital (e.g. salaried income), whereas fathers tend to emphasise education. In other words, women seem to be less concerned with symbolic or collective gains than with the practical functioning of the household, and therefore attach more importance to personal qualities of new members and to the acquisition of consumer durables for household use (cf.Bourdieu 1986:213).

Spatial distance between affinal groups (gushtis)— provenance of the wife

Bi-weekly markets (*hat*) provide a suitable place for pursuing marriage inquiries as they attract peasants from areas which correspond to the range within which marriage exchanges are open for consideration. Locality, as I showed in previous chapters is an important domain in establishing a person's

tions in economic and human capital of the *gushti* and to marriage market trends), but because those to be married may genuinely not know why a particular spouse has been selected (Sharma 1986:165).

belonging, patriline as well as marriage alliance. It affects marriage ideology in three senses: first, with respect to *para/gram* endogamy[5]; second, locality is important with respect to exogamous marriages where the "outside" (*bidesh*) as a field of matrimonial alliances is subdivided according to the cultural closeness of its areas in relation to one's own community; third, locality is considered with regard to closeness/remoteness of two affinally related households.

Spatial endogamy implied in intra-*para* or intra-*gram* marriages, as well as the import of wives from far away places, attracts both rich and poor wife-takers, each for different reasons. The former category enters cousin marriages as a way of keeping patrimony intact, while the most vulnerable families marry their neighbours (and hence patrilateral cousins) to consolidate spatial closeness with blood link in the acquisition of helpful protectors. The political interests of the poor do not usually expand beyond the *para* boundary; if they move beyond the commuity, it is mainly in search of employment and so there is nothing to motivate a desire for exotic women—"Nothing brings me out, why should I look for an outside wife?" The taste for "the different" among wealthy peasants is the mark of the educated among them, those who can afford the risk of taking wives from culturally and geographically insecure places. The category of the poor who resort to outside marriages are the landless-turned-itinerant-businessmen or those whose choice is determined solely by considerations of an instant economic gain.

Like in Assam studied by Cantlie (1984:82), "marriage is often spoken of as the passage of women between villages[6]. It will be asked of a daughter 'To where have you given her?' or of a daughter-in-law, 'From where have you brought her?'". In Gameranga also, a wife's provenance is an important factor in a man's choice of a spouse, not only with respect to logistics but from the point of view of cultural adaptability. Apart from the indigenous territorial units—*gushti, shomaj, para,*—and administrative units—*gram, mousa, thana*, the villagers think of the *desh* surrounding Gameranga as divided in two fields of matrimonial operations. *Bhiler pichone* (behind the marsh) in a northwesterly direction, towards the subdivisional town and *boro nodir pichone* (behind the river), which is the territory of Jessore and Khulna district, constitute the two possible areas for those who are considering to bring in an outside wife or to give away a daughter beyond the village. In this context, the land beyond the swamp is seen as culturally alien or more distant, while Khulna-Jessore villages (i.e. an area beyond one's district) are seen as more similar and therefore preferable for the recruitment of wives or placement of daughters. What is interesting in this culture–geographical orientation, is that the cultural identity of a *desh* here is informed by a stereotypical view of "the ways of women" in respective directions. The less favourable *bhiler pichone* area consists of

[5] See chapter 12, n.5 and 10.
[6] 37 per cent of housewives in Uttor Para came from another village, i.e. an area denoted as *bidesh*—abroad. For a survey of wives' provenance in Matlab, see chapter 12, n. 10.

the villages with a large Hindu population which makes it largely ineligible, but one, Kathi-*gram*, has only Muslims who are reputedly wealthy. The saying goes in Gameranga that "daughters of Kathi are desirable for wealth but despised for their habits". On the other hand, the daughters from Jessore and Khulna, although administratively outsiders, are not objected to because they "make the same rice-pastry as we do here", "detest cooking with wheat flour and eating dry fish" and "show preference for canal water" (contrary to women in Ranchandropur—behind the *bhil*, who use tubewell water for drinking and cooking)[7]. The way of tying up the sari and the manner of speaking were other points mentioned disapprovingly of difference between the women in respective areas[8].

In Matlab, Aziz (1979:128) notes, that "the new daughters-in-law from different villages bring new ideas and specialities with them, and manners in the husband's houses" and from that concludes that "married [women] may act as an idea and information link between villages". This presumed potential for innovation and dissemination of alien ideas by outside women is exactly what the villagers in Gameranga aim to eliminate when they, in spite of economic prospects, object to women from "behind the marsh" as wives. The import of outside women, even though accompanied by cash or prestige-giving goods, always poses the basic dilemma of how to allow for the passage, yet maintain the internal order—*dhormo* imbued with agnatic ethos—unchanged. Bodily concern, as indicated above, is the main area of discord. Once, I saw a young mother using soap as she bathed her baby. It surprised me, as I knew of local resistance based on the belief that soap has a cooling effect (*thanda hoy*) and is therefore inappropriate for cleaning the body of a child or a sick person . As I was about to utter approval, another old woman behind the enclosure commented reproachfully, "He brought her from ..." and pointed to the direction of the *bhil*. It came out that the commentator's son had recently brought home a second wife with her unweaned child, the one who was now receiving, against local medical theory, a soap bath. When I returned a week later to see how the new co-wife was adapting to the local culture, I was told she had gone never to come back. The villagers believed and proved by a number of instances like this one, that a wife's adaptability to the new home is related to her provenance, not only in terms of her family's name and physical distance but cultural similarity as the case above illustrates; as if people assimilated their *desh* to their bodies.

However, locality (*sthan*), apart from the direction and degree of cultural diversity, is also considered in terms of distance. Bourdieu (1986:57) speaks

---

[7] For further details on water behaviour in Gameranga see Kotalová (1984).

[8] From another district in Bangladesh, Walraven (1985:44) reports similar distinction accorded to women's habits between the *para*s within a single village. People of the founding *para* (i.e. with proper ancestry) gave expression to their collective superior status and contempt by refusal to marry off their daughters to the *para* of Dhakaite newsettlers to the area. They grounded their objections on the difference in the way the Dhakaite women process paddy, "do not call a son-in-law by his name", "wear the sari differently", "talk differently" and "eat dry fish".

of the distance factor in matching spouses as "the choice between fission and fusion, the inside and the outside, security and adventure". The distance of two localities is thus assessed practically. People in Gameranga used to say that a daughter should not be given too far, neither too close to her natal home. Long distance makes visiting (*nayor din*) and sending news (of death for example) more difficult, and if a father wished to give a cow as dower, the transfer over numerous canals might prove unmanagable. Lastly, among those families who care for a daughter's post-marital well-being, it is felt that a daughter too far away is condemned to a life in exile. Closeness implied in *para* or *gram* endogamy means saving on wedding expenditure and more importantly, it has an impact on family relations beneficial for wives, as it gives an affective recourse to their agnates in case of ill-treatment ("brothers are near"). On the other hand, matches within *para* place a burden on the wife's family as she and her children (often with her husband's family's encouragement) keep making excessive demands on her natal home's resources. This is given expression in the worries by fathers, who feel they are being taken advantage of by affines because of physical proximity. On the one hand, daughters married endogamically are viewed as an instrument for strengthening the agnatic group; on the other, nearness may always turn a source of disputes instead of helpful alliance.

The most remarkable feature of the marriage-related concept of cultural geography is that it inverts the dominant definition of land (*desh*) and its people (*lok*). It should be recalled that the global self-definitions presented to outsiders by male and female informants, are male centered. Here, on the contrary, it is the domains of women which constitute the criteria by which a boundary is drawn around an area of optimal marriageability. This boundary is explained topographically in relation to the river and the marsh, and culturally in terms of consensus on three aspects of women's behaviour. These are: sartorial and linguistic style—the way women tie their saris and the dialect they speak, and culinary skills. A preference for dry fish and tubewell water in the villages beyond the boundary disqualifies their womenfolk from eligibility as wives. This is the way muted structures come into serious consideration.

Matching the spouses

The structural characteristics generically defining the value of the family by provenance, pedigree and wealth, discussed and specified as primary criteria on previous pages, are clearly not the only factors to affect the choice[9]. Personal qualities in the context of ritual display and viewing of what counts as

[9] One aspect of a bride's physical qualities—virginity—has been considered earlier as an index of *gushti*'s symbolic capital convertible at the time of marriage. Devaluation of women at second marriages has thus been explained as being based on the value placed on the intact female body.

proper gender attributes as well as convertible assets will be the focus of this section. At the event I am going to describe below—*bou dekha*—further physical traits come into consideration.

More systematic and detailed personal inquiries regarding a family's standing and the reputation of the prospective spouse are carried out via a matchmaker (*rajbar*) or a relative. As mentioned earlier, weekly markets are convenient occasions for soliciting marriage consultations. At that stage of a marriage project, the temperament and physical attraction of the spouses may be considered, though as a secondary factor. Again, there is a gender asymmetry in emphasis. Unfocused spending, heavy smoking, notorious stealing, a proclivity for violence, lack of mastery of simple *bajar* arithmetics, a highpitched voice or physical defect clearly count as a liability in a future husband-householder. The personality and appearance of the groom are discussed among the bride's sisters and unmarried peers following the suitor's visit to the bride-viewing or wedding ritual, but these attributes seldom enter the agenda of negotiations. In contrast, the bride's physical attributes—those related to unbroken hymen (i.e. modesty—*lojja*) and those which enhance her sexual attraction—vocal and bodily beauty—are ritually displayed and constitute an explicit, albeit secondary, topic in negotiations. The lack of physical accomplishments in a woman—broken hymen, dark skin, hair length, manner of talking and of walking—lessens her desirability and may have to be compensated for financially.

Viewing the bride

When a family with a bride is located and identified by geographical and collective status criteria, the event of selection turns into a ritual at which the families tend to display anything they have to show off. The tangible and movable endowments of respective *gushti*s that bear status messages are displayed—object by object, body part by body part. The process of attaining a mutual recognition of equality starts with that.

The proceedings are opened with the viewing of the bride—*bou dekha*. The groom, accompanied by his father or guardian and a company of male friends, comes to visit the family of the bride if she is from another village. The visiting party is well-groomed and dressed in their best clothes, often equipped with a transistor radio and digital wrist-watch, both of which may be borrowed for this occasion from a better-off neighbour or anthropologist. My sandals, camera and umbrella were frequently required for the trip, sometimes even my company. Invariably, I was instructed not to speak Bengali, but instead to drop a few English words after entering the hosts' compound, as if to enhance the lure of outsideness already associated with my physiognomy and skin colour. Introducing an exotic element into various stages of marriage rituals is not only tolerated but welcomed as auspicious[10].

---

[10] In West Bengal weddings are habitually attended by *hijri* singers and musicians.

Although impression management is a mutual effort of families involved in marriage, the bride's display is more elaborate, dramatic and costly. The family of one of my key informants received two different candidates to view their only daughter during the course of my fieldwork and I shall concentrate here on her. Baharon is light skinned (*ranga*), plump (*mota*), knows how to write her name and occasionally, in the company of an old matron and those female peers who shared her fate, attends religious meetings for women, held periodically in another village. Baharon was still unmarried four years after the commencement of the menses. She prayed desperately for a husband to come. So did all Gameranga girls in her situation[11].

Baharon is a landless farmer's daughter; her parents own nothing besides the hut in which they dwell and she is their only child. A long history of TB prevents her father from regular daily labour, her mother is severely anaemic and Baharon herself earns her meals by helping with domestic chores in the slightly better-off households of her neighbours. With this background, Baharon is representative of an ever increasing batch of young virgins in Gameranga, who remain unmarried long after the onset of menstruation. Morever, due to the absence of a regular breadwinner in the family, she is forced to work for others, including a non-Muslim anthropologist, a circumstance that has aggravated her vulnerability in the villagers' view and further damaged the image of a young sheltered virgin. The rest of her unmarried peers have been spared such disgrace. Baharon described fragmentarily two of the viewing events and one of her employers supplied further details. I have woven together these pieces of information.

The party of the groom arrived late in the evening from a village in a neighbouring district. They were treated with a sumptuous meal which put her father in debt. It consisted of the standard items of "guest" food like betel nuts, sweetmeats, milk, eggs, a fatty fish (*chol mach* and *koy mach*) and a chicken dish (*kurma polao*). The whole feast cost her father three hundred Taka.

The night's negotiation was followed by another meal in the morning. At that stage, after the meal, Baharon entered the scene. She was displayed in her neighbour's best sari and sandals, her face heavily made up and veiled. She was sitting with her legs under her to one side, her head inclined, eyes averted, her entire body wrapped in the sari. In that poise of retiring shyness she answered the questions asked by the viewers. She employed a deferential tone of voice, which made her words hardly comprehensible. The interrogation centered on her religiosity: regularity of praying and fasting (*namaj pora, roja thaka*)—the two pillars of Islam, particularly associated with female performance of the faith—her ability to read the Koran (*Koran Sharrif porcho?*), degree of literacy and years of schooling (*lekha pora jana, ki class?*). During the interview the interrogators acted casually and employed the familiar mode of address—*tumi*—used

---

[11] The accumulation of girls who remain unmarried such a long time after adolescence is a new phenomenon which causes a great deal of anxiety, not only to their parents; worried comments are voiced by the elders of the community. The girls themselves tend to attract unfavourable attention from unscrupulous bachelors.

for social inferiors. The oral examination was followed by a physical check-up. One of the visiting bystanders revealed her face by pulling away the end of her sari (*achol*)[12].

His companions commented loudly and appreciatively on the fairness and roundness of her face. To make sure that their impression was not distorted by a layer of white powder, the viewers lifted the sari even further from her arms to compare them with the shade of her face. Each exposure of additional body surface was loudly commented on with a total disregard of Baharon's feelings[13]. The last feature to be viewed was the length, gloss and colour of her hair: she was asked to untie her bun and display its length. At the end of the inspection, Baharon was asked to walk a few metres and when she resumed her sitting position, she was rewarded with twenty Taka which was thrown in her lap. The visitors voiced their opinion to her father and left.

On both occasions, Baharon was disqualified as a future wife. When asked next day about the outcome of the viewing, she attributed the negative outcome of it to her father's decision and named one or two of the candidate's drawbacks. When the circumstances were recounted to me by her neighbours, however, it was evident that the decision was not her father's but the suitor's and that her poverty was the main factor. One informant, a relative of the family, blamed Baharon's father who had on previous years received a couple of offers but refused them in the hope of placing his only child in better households than those of the then offering candidates. "She has now passed her prime and in a couple of years nobody will take her"[14]. Were the outcome of this first formal visit positive, the next step would be the negotiation of *muharana*, or of any other form of financial component in marriage.

In considering *bou dekha* in relation to the man and woman who will hopefully become spouses, several points may be noted on gender encompassment. Regarding it as a performance situated within the realm of appearances and make-believe (Morgan 1984), further insights can be gained about the process through which self-knowledge is acquired in ritual performance.

At both levels, with respect to ethnography of gender as well as epistemology, the performance *bou dekha* provides an ongoing structure for future experience of conjugal life, a kind of rehearsal of the wedding itself. Apart from the different material assets displayed by the bride and groom (traditional items of cloth like sari versus modern amenities attached to the groom), this structure is revealed through the style of communication whereby the groom acts as an initiator, looking at and questioning while the bride herself is unable

---

[12] As Selwyn informs us (1979), among the Hindus in Modhya Pradesh—this essential part of the female garment (*oli* in Hindi) serves as a denomination of the whole viewing ceremony.

[13] She said she had felt terribly shy but her male relative (one well versed in Islamic ethics) to whom I reported the matter, claimed approvingly that the custom of exposing a daughter's hair and face on this occasion is sanctioned by Islam. Later, I came across an explicit record of this: "It is permissible to cast a glance at the face and the palms of a woman whom one intends to marry" (Muslim 1973:717).

[14] As Bourdieu (1986:68) points out, "… a father can play with time so as to prolong the conjunctural advantage he derives from his position as receiver of offers, but only up to a certain point, or he will see his products devalued because they are thought to be unsaleable …" .

to look at or ask her viewer[15]. It is further marked by the features of duplicity, not only with respect to the pretended ownership of items to be displayed (and to enhance gender asymmetry) but as a kind of paradox intrinsic to perform-ances, one involved in the difference between "acting" and "active" (Gorfain 1986).

Here, Blair's (1981) insightful remarks on the ways a professional actress[16] consolidates her private and public self provide me with a way of thinking of Baharon's experience. Like an actress on the stage the bride-to-be displays herself in a way which in daily life is reserved for the most private context. The contention is that she is structurally (and ritually) located in a private rela-tionship to her viewers, men she hardly knows and by extension—society at large. As an object of exchange between men in the project of which she has so far lacked any control, a woman on *bou dekha* is valued by her viewers as an object to be given to a man; henceforward "her choice is between giving herself and acting that she gives herself" (ibid.). She portrays to her best the dramatis personae—bride (*bou*) she promises and hopes to become. To ac-complish this she changes her dress, posture, voice, borrows items she is short of and becomes in this way the not-Baharon and simultaneously Baharon, who is within her (cf. Schwartzman 1978)[17].

[15] Indeed, the details of his appearance are usually given to her after the rite is over, by onlooking peers.

[16] I resort to this comparison because of the features which this ritual shares with theatrical dis-play in films (particularly those of a Bengali production). *Bou dekha*, like all performances is "conspicuously artificial and theatrical yet designed to suggest the inevitability and absolute truth of their messages" (Myerhoff 1979:86 quoted by Morgan 1984).

[17] Berger (1977 whom Blaire 1981, quotes), generalises this shift within woman in terms of the incorporateness of the male's perspective on themselves, when he contends that while "men act ... women appear" and elaborates: "Men look at women. Women watch themselves being looked at ... which determines also the relation of women to themselves". Berger's view is particularly cogent in view of the agnatic orientation of all cultural spheres in Gameranga. Indeed, the verbal judgements women drop on each other's behaviour and exterior in other contexts, the way of commenting on husbands' sexual prowess or sons' sexual anatomy, the disgust for their own bodies they express at menstruation and parturition, brings forward sufficient evidence to the con-tention that "the surveyor of woman in herself is male: the surveyed female" (Berger ibid.).

However, remembering that all forms of representations are constructs that do not necessarily conflate with the process of thought and with experience, I would modify Berger's generalising stance and take the split within a woman on which the above assumption rests as related to the wider question of turning "herself into an object" (i.e. assuming a male view of society) in certain situations and contexts rather than as being indicative of an immanent essence of womanhood.

CHAPTER 16

Formalisation of marital union

The legalisation of marital union in Gameranga is marked by the co-existence of contradictory discourses both with respect to ritual forms of conclusion and with regard to the form of economic commitments. Each discourse is further imbued with dualities such as the ideal/practical, normative/strategic meaning. I shall start each section by introducing the local concepts that denote the ritual and economic discourse and elaborate on their moral connotations. Then I shall point to the different meaning a marriage has for a man and a woman.

Contract versus sacrament

Regarding the point of final settlement of a marriage, there is an official requirement according to which the signing of a contract suffices for a woman to become a man's wife (and vice versa). This is contraposed to the highly valued discourse of the wedding (*bie*) which emphasises the uniqueness of the first marriage and its ritual elaboration. I will show how, although not favoured by fundamentalist officials, the rituals have a particular meaning for women.

According to an observer of the customs and habits of Muslims in India at the beginning of the 19th century, marriages based solely on contract (referred to as *nikah* in the scriptures) were considered by the "ignorant"[1] people among the Muslims, as "secondary or half-marriages" and therefore "unlawful and disreputable ... equivalent to keeping a mistress" (Shurreef 1973:85). In Deccan plateau, where the ethnography was recorded, a word *shadee* was used synonymously with proper marriages, those embellished by rituals ("being merely the 'rejoicings' on the occasion"). It seems then, that a Hindu-inspired ceremony following the contract has among Muslims long been the folk requirement for a contract-based marriage (*nikah*) which will be considered a finalized, "full-marriage" (*bie*).

Today, villagers in Gameranga hold a similar view. According to current practice, the contract signature signals the consummation of the marriage, but the feast—*bie*—to follow is a pre-requisite for formal virilocal settlement. The time span between the two events depends on the ability of the exchang-

---

[1] The author's disparaging term for believers who practised unorthodox Islam in the subcontinent.

ing families to fulfill their economic obligations, including the transfer of movable property stipulated in the contract (*kabin*)[2].

Kabin constitutes the legal component of a wedding. According to Islam, the civil contract (*kabin*) is sufficient to legalize the conjugal relationship. Above all it stipulates the amount of money (*muharana*) the groom is due to pay the bride. No ceremony is prescribed to solemnize a matrimony, but the bride's agreement witnessed by two males is required. A religious official—a man from *madrasa* or a man known to be versed in Islamic matters—is called to pronounce the blessing. No oral or written reference is made to the permanency of the bond so concluded. In Muslim conjugal practice it suffices that a disappointed husband pronounces "I divorce you" (*talak debo*) three times, for the contract to be dissolved. *Kabin* is thus unambiguously associated with and is aimed at the possibility the failure of marriage.

Some older matrons with aspirations to literacy might have explain the meaning of the word by presenting the document which had legalized the marriages of their daughters, even quoted the various conditions stipulated there, but could not produce similar evidence with respect to their own marriages, as these were solemnized solely by a *moulana*'s blessing (*bie porano*) and wedding ceremony. Even today, those women who are aware of the *kabin* lack any knowledge of its exact content and the place where the document is kept (Blanchet 1986).

In discourse about marriage, particularly among women, the prevailing talk is of *bie*, which is the generic term covering a state of being married, marital union, the ritual that follows the signing of the contract, even coitus of humans and animals. As Blanchet (1986) also noted in Jamalpur, women in Gameranga, who had been married several times, specify their first husband as *bier shami*. It is to make a qualitative distinction between the first and all subsequent marriages or, viewed from a moral standpoint between the sacramental and contractual nature of marriages in general. As Blanchet (ibid.) writes, "A *biyer shami* referred to the first, and some say the only, husband of a woman. *Biye* occurs only once in a woman's life. Subsequent marital unions which are referred to as *nikah* are considered to be qualitatively different ... they are degraded and bring no prestige ... After knowing a number of [husbands], it is sometimes implied that a woman's nature becomes 'spoiled' and she may easily slip into prostitution" and adds, "Islamic law may legitimate such marital unions through *nikah* but this act is not sufficient to restore the moral purity"[3].

---

[2] Previously the period elapsing between the contract and the transfer of the bride would not exceed one year. In some cases today, this interlude may be filled by the visits of the couple to each other's homes. Nowadays, the contracted bride may continue residing with her natal family for two to four years, waiting for her husband to accumulate the wealth necessary to fulfill his *mahr* obligation, which in turn is a requirement for the wedding feast—*bie*—to materialize. In the meantime, the couple may have several children who reside with their mother in her father's home.

[3] In Gameranga I never heard the word *nikah* to be used by informants for marriages. This may be due to the fact that I failed to interview Islamic experts on this topic. As pointed out above, *kabin* was used to denote the legalistic aspect of marriage.

As shown, the distinction made by Muslims in Bangladesh nowadays has its historical parallel in Muslim communities in 19th century Deccan. Crucial to the distinction between the two ways of concluding marriage is the idea of uniqueness, permanency, (i. e. insolubility) intrinsic to the sacramental nature attached to the first marriage. Its permanency is further corroborated by the fatalist assumption with respect to the choice of the first partner: although the search is administered by male family members, ultimately, this very first choice is guided by the providence of God. All subsequent marriages are by contrast, mundane affairs concluded out of practical necessity (Blanchet ibid.).

The fatalistic–sacramental nature women ascribe to the first bond, that which imbues it with spiritual permanency, explains why women attach great virtue to being married only once. Even though re-marriage of widows is not proscribed among Muslims, it is considered meritorious if they remain unmarried, i.e. faithful to the divine arrangement of the first marriage. This is sustained by the similar Hindic tenet that a "marriage based on life-long fidelity is considered the highest *dhormo* of a wife and husband" (Khare 1982). The praxis of concremation of Hindu widows (*suttee*) on the death of their husband, widespread in Bengal until early 19th century (Stein 1978) and occasionally practised in India even these days (Hussain 1988, News 1987, Rao 1988, Vikasini 1988), is one extreme expression of this tenet[4].

In Gameranga practice today, this *dhorm*ic emphasis on life-long fidelity, although less radically expressed, is maintained exclusively by women. Widows past forty do not enter new marriages, (particularly those with grown-up sons) and state it with great pride, although at the same time they constitute the most vulnerable group among women, being either sexually used (often for remuneration) or offering sexual services to their patrons[5]. A village widow quoted by Blanchet (1986) concluded her account of the miseries in her married life by an exclamation, "I was blessed. My husband made my life miserable, but I have known only one husband". Saying this, a woman makes a clear comment on the score of her merits to be counted on the Day of Judgement. Similarly a woman in Gameranga who had survived her three husbands displayed an old silk sari for me as evidence of the piety she felt for her first husband—its donor. When I asked her to relate her marital history: "He

---

[4] Another notion underlying the practice of widow-burning is that at marriage, the wife is recognized as that half of the marital union which is transformable. While the groom continues to live after marriage where he was born, the bride is transfered and transformed through the wedding ritual. At the husband's funeral, burning herself to death is a further transformation of her body as well as a spacial transfer. Seen from this perspective, *sutee* may be viewed as an effort to reconstitute the union by diminishing the gap that the husband's death caused to the one-bodiedness of the marital bond.

[5] Widowed men of any age may re-marry, although it should be stressed that attaching a young woman to a man past his sexual age (50—60 in Gameranga) causes an embarrassment to all *gushti* (see chapter 11) and it should also be remembered that no prestige accrues to accumulation of wives either by chain marriages or concubinage. Re-marriages are now frequent among bereaved younger women.

was the best" she claimed, though "we had no land at that time and often went hungry".

The difference between these two components of marriage (legal and sacramental) is not only in degree of desirability or prestigiousness but the way each is emphasised and experienced differently by women and men.

As pointed out earlier, women can reach places and discourses where public search and queries are carried out only indirectly, if ever, and they are definitely excluded from the financial negotiations and ultimate decision. As I also stressed, mothers' concerns with their children's marital future differ from their husbands', their emphasis is on particularities and practicalities, not on symbolic collective gains of *gushti*'s *ijjat*. This does not mean, however, that brides, their mothers, sisters and peers are utterly unconcerned with moral or symbolic gains. It is precisely here through the wedding (*bie*) ceremony that women activate and articulate the meaning marriage has beyond legal and economic transactions orchestrated by men (and expressed as *kabin* or *muharana*). It is by ritual, not by legal means, that the sacramental value of *bie* is experienced and communicated to others.

On being questioned about the marriage formalities, timing and sequences, female informants spontaneously refer by words or gestures to the slaying of the cow (*goru kata*), smearing the body with turmeric paste (*holud gae*) or to carrying the palanquin with the wedded couple (*tulana* or *palki uthie dia*). Some refer to singing (*gan gae*) or the loudspeaker (*mayk*). Each of these are metaphoric references to rites that subsume *bie* and underpin the moral and emotional load of the first marital bond (and conjugal union in general). Such rituals are dispensed with on subsequent marriages.

In the village calendar, weddings are the most vital entertainments undertaken during the most abundant month of November. The length and intricacy of wedding feasts differ considerably, depending on status and economic resources. Only very few families in Gameranga can afford to kill a cow, rent a palanquin or a loudspeaker. In contrast to the rich and middle landowners, common people contract marriages in a simple manner, limiting the ritual to the killing of a goat or chicken and anointment with turmeric (*holud gae*). The transport of the bride, if required, is habitually effected by boat. Wedding rites are even more simplified in the case of cousin marriages. However, *holud gae* and a meat-dish are seen as indispensable prerequisites of the first marriage in order for it to qualify as *bie*. Elaboration and sumptuousness may often be lacking on the ground, either because of growing poverty which first cuts the budget for rituals, or because of the growing pressure of Islamic fundamentalists on local religious leaders (who in their fervour to convert "Muslims" into "good Muslims" tend to ban anything that is perceived as an element foreign to and threatening Islam)[6]. However, this official concern is reversed in the at-

---

[6] Reflecting on ritual impoverishment in connection with births among Muslim peasants in Jamalpur, Blanchet (1984: 11) notes "Islam is said to provide all that man needs ... not surprisingly, ... those beliefs and rituals of Bengali (tribal) origin which were easily intertwined with

tention these topics receive in women's conversations. The ritual events are vital to women's experience of marriedness. And so, on the night before the wedding, singing and dancing—the more lascivious of performances—are performed apart, for an audience of women and children. On many occasions in Gameranga, a female wedding singer or a dancer was threatened with denial of burial by one of the *madrasa*'s censors. Women themselves hinted to me that I should not disclose what I had seen and heard to my landlord or any man with whom I might talk, though many a young man favoured weddings because of these very events.

Nowadays, there is a growing category of villagers whose conjugal unions are effected without either a *kabin* or a feast; they are beggars, itinerant sellers, people whose kin and locale (*bari*) identity is shaky, but also notorious womanizers, who add and expel women from their households at will. Yet even women subjected to such circumstances cherish memories of their first marriages, and those who never experienced a true *bie* wax lyrical when describing the wedding of a sister or cousin. Even a female epileptic beggar I came to to know insisted on *holud gae* and *palki* as indispensable parts of marriage though she herself had been married a few times without any ritual at all. During my fieldwork, one of her marriages was contracted at a weekly market (*hat*) with a seller of betel. She was proposed to while buying a packet of betel and accepted[7]. Her neighbour–cum–relative, who happened to be present, was called to witness the oral agreement and when all the betel was sold she followed her groom to his village. When the news spread in Gameranga the same evening, people seemed amused but not disapproving. Some even used the word *bie* for this kind of casual arrangement but stressed that it was not a true marriage. A "true" marriage is authenticated by ritual. In this case, of course, such a marriage was now impossible, both because of the woman's epilepsy (classed as madness in local diagnostics) and the previous marriages which she had arranged more or less on her own. What was attained at the market was the social approval of sexual cohabitation rather than a sacral bond.

Hindu elements came to be regarded as "Hindu", making it doubly impossible for Muslims to claim them as theirs also, ... this move resulted in the cultural impoverishment of Muslims who were thus compelled to discard so many of their former practices". However, "public rituals" Blanchet adds, "have disappeared faster than the beliefs themselves".

[7] Markets are the male precinct par excellence; the only women I have seen there ocasionally were a beggar, a prostitute and a *churi-wallah*. My own appearances at *hat*s around Gameranga during fieldwork caused a great deal of entertainment and introduced a new topic into village discourse.

Marriage payments

The economic calculations behind each marriage are extremely complex not only because various systems are in operation but because each has a range of variations which the agents use strategically. As is the case with weddings, there also exist an overlapping system and double discourse within its contractual component—the forms of marrige payments. These differ in the direction the wealth flows with respect to wife-givers and wife-takers, by nature of the gifts that constitute each form and also by the way each system is historically and morally situated.

In relation to the moral system, the groom's financial commitment is associated with the old, "proper" order of the community. It also finds validation in Islamic scriptures[8]. Hence, it is placed within the moral space of the village, the past and the Book. Nowadays this co-exists with a form of prestation directed from the bride's side to the groom's. This latter form reverses the former system morally, as it comes from outside and lacks any authoritative justification other than necessity to secure husbands of a certain sort. To delineate the shift from one system to another, as well as the concomitant changes in spouse searching and selection, I shall rely on Lindenbaum's (1975, 1981) study where the introduction of a new marital discourse is placed historically in the context of a changing political situation in the subcontinent. The focus here will be on the strategies of exchanging families (polarised as wife-takers and wife-givers), rather than on the performances of bride and groom who represent them. Consideration of possible implications of the shift in the marriage market for women will conclude this chapter.

As I mentioned earlier, the amount of money to be paid by the groom to the bride (*muharana*) is the central issue in the marriage contract. The social identity of the person who produces the payment and that of the recipient are the criteria by which *muharana* is distinguished from other types of marriage prestations which are now in operation. Technically the total amount is specified under two headings as "prompt dower" which stipulates a lifetime support to the wife ("by installments or any time afterwards when she claims it"), and "deferred dower", which is the sum of money a husband agrees to pay as a divorce penalty "should the marriage be dissolved by divorce or death" (Carroll 1979). In Gameranga *muharana* is usually settled in terms of the portion of money to be spent on the gifts "*dai taka*" (given money), the amount of money to be given to the bride 'later on'—"*baki taka*" (outstanding money), and the sum to be pledged to the wife in case of divorce—"*talak taka*" (i.e. divorce insurance). Each amount is fixed in cash or its equivalent in kind with reference to the criteria of eligibility mentioned in the previous section. Though sexual cohabitation is sanctioned by the signature of *kabin*, a groom

---

[8] *Nika* marriages based on mere contract as corroborated by the scriptures carry an association of incompleteness and are generally held in disrespect.

who fails to fulfill his *muharana* obligations, is not entitled to bring his wife to live in his home[9]. This, together with the fact that many grooms today cannot afford the provisions of *muharana* in due time, explains why a growing number of contracted brides continue to reside with their natal families for a long time after marriage contract (*kabin*) has been signed and even after they give birth to a child or two. Waiting for their husbands to accumulate the wealth necessary to settle *muharana*, the costs of her maintenance—provision of food, clothing, toiletries and possible medical expenses—lie with her father or brothers who are also responsible for the additional costs of rearing her children, who in the future will belong to her husband's *gushti*.

In a separate chapter dealing with embodiment of *dhormo* I have shown that families in Gameranga express their anxiety about their daughters' upbringing in terms of control of sexuality and marriage-related costs. The latter worry may appear suprising against the background of *muharana*, which is intended to secure the transfer of valuables to women at marriage and to grant compensation in divorce. A further discussion of variations within the *muharana* system and the appearance of a novel payment system beyond *muharana* may clarify the economic context in which Bangladeshi parents perceive the marriages of daughters and not of sons (as the wording of the Muslim Family Law Ordinance may suggest)[10] as an extreme economic burden.

Implementation of muharana *and of the groom price*

There is an infinite range of variations in the way provisions of *muharana* are implemented in practice. Most often they are manipulated—by restriction, circumvention or total suspension—so that the legal promulgations aimed at securing women's position lose much of their effect. Even these strategies—the groom's attempts to be released from the payment of full *muharana*—have their precedents and ethnographic equivalent beyond Gameranga. The same observer of the Deccan Muslims mentioned above reports (around 1832):

"Men of property usually pay the whole, or sometimes a third of the dowry [here used to connote *muharana*] at the time of the marriage, while the poor pay it by installment. It being the divine command to give it, they must, partly by jewels, partly by valuable dresses, ... satisfy the woman to a certain extent to get the bride to remit the reminder". (Shurreef 1973:89, my insertion and emphasis).

---

[9] The husband may do so after obtaining permission from the wife's guardians, but then the extent of power he or his mother can exercise over such a daughter-in-law is very limited. A *bou* in this situation is more free to pay prolonged visits to her *babar bari* and to refuse tedious jobs—a circumstance envied by other women married into the *bari*.

[10] For the Muslims of the subcontinent marriage payment was encoded in 1961 in the Muslim Family Law Ordinance and has since then been applicable in Pakistan and Bangladesh. The Family Law Ordinance is a modified application of the Hanafi school of law. It was promulgated as a reform with the intention "to give women their proper place in society according to the fundamentals of Islam" (Carroll 1979, quoting the Commission 1956).

From Bangladesh beyond Gameranga, Aziz (1979:213), as well as Blanchet (1986), provide much data on evasive strategies. The commonest practice is to reduce the agreed sum of *muharana* to a nominal sum to be paid by the groom before the marriage is consummated. The outstanding amount (*baki taka*) is then usually remitted[11].

Another widespread practice which circumscribes the norm is the groom's habit of borrowing the items stipulated in *kabin* for the occasion of the wedding ceremony and subsequently withdrawing them from the bride and returning them to the actual owner after the bride takes up her residence with his *gushti* (Aziz ibid.,61). The divorce insurance (*talak taka*), usually constituting the essential portion of *muharana*, is likewise without effect at the time of divorce. In all the divorce cases I encountered or heared of at the time of fieldwork, the divorce penalty (if ever stipulated) remained unpaid[12].

Another factor indirectly contributing to the wife-giver's multiplied costs for daughters' marriages is the increasing period of time which now elapses between the signature of the contract (this signalling the consummation of marriage) and the actual marriage feast (*borjatra*), which legalizes the bride's transfer for permanent settlement in groom's house. As I said, during that interstitial period the costs of the daughter's and her children's livelihood are born by her family.

So far I have named the principles of *muharana* and the cultural elaboration of numerous strategies aimed at the circumvention of the norm. In addition to these the *muharana*-system nowadays co-exists with the application of marriage transactions which are distant, if not contradictory, to the Islamic code. One particular transaction gaining dominance in contemporary marriages, (particularly that of the upwardly moving peasants who have succeeded in accumulating some economic surplus and who are actively seeking to establish political alliances through hypergamy), is the transfer of specific wealth objects by the wife-givers to the groom. These items are foreign-made modern amenities such as radios, wrist watches, bicycles and possibly a gold ring (as a remnant of an old-style marriage exchange) given for the exclusive use of the groom (Lindenbaum 1981). As a stream of wealth flowing in the opposite direction of the *muharana*, this transmission reminds us of dowry, which in Gameranga is characteristic of marriage settlements underlying a daughter's second marriage[13] and of Hindu marriages in general (Caplan 1984). However, given the nature of the gifts—"male" objects—and the fact that the

---

[11] Aziz (1979:213) quotes his informants as claiming that "without paying a token amount of *mahr* [=*muharana*] the consummation cannot take place". Blanchet (1986), on the contrary, brings forward proud claims of elder women who deferred the total amount because "a wife who makes no demand to her husband is praised in the true spirit of *bie*."

[12] Lindenbaum (1981) informs us that in two thirds of her sample of 255 married couples in her research area (Comilla district), divorce occurred without *talak taka* being transferred (see also Blanchet 1986).

[13] See the case of Hosnara in chapter 14.

groom is their presumed recipient, this mode of payment violates the principles of dowry as a "property given to the daughter to take with her into marriage" and "property in her own control" (Tambiah 1973). That the occurrence of groom price[14] is in conflict with the traditional marriage proceedings, where the groom's family had formal responsibility for the payment of *muharana* (in gold, cloth or cash) and ultimately for the heavier costs of the marriage, is evident from the way people in Gameranga comment on this emerging form of marriage payment. The groom price does not usually receive great publicity, or it is disguised as a gift "out of heart" (cf. Caplan ibid.). Those among the rich and middle peasants who had been first to demand it but who care at the same time for their image as good Muslims are not ready to attest the receipt of the groom price by their sons and brothers openly. "We are not that sort of people" claimed a woman from a well-off family when asked about the expected groom price for her brother who was getting married. According to this informant, the parents agreed to the *muharana* amount of twenty thousand Taka (which silenced my further inquiry). On closer examination at the time of wedding ceremony, it became clear that the bride's family marriage expenses outdid those of the groom's and that the wrist watch and the gold ring with a ruby stone worn by the groom after the ceremony were acquired as wedding gifts from the bride. Another informant from the new-rich family of a self-respecting teacher–cum–*daktar* refered to this kind of transaction as voluntary gifts to the groom given "out of pleasure" (*shontusto ... kushi hoy de*). She claimed however, that the groom's total prestation should outweight the costs of the bride's family. In case of the traditionally respectable, *ijjat*-conscious families, it seems that the acceptance of any prestation from the bride must be discreet and covert so that the dominant ideology of *muharana* and the groom as the main giver, remains unspoiled[15]. The new-rich claimants to prestigious positions, on the other hand, may boast about the opulent wealth they might have managed to acquire through the import of an appropriate bride, as they have not yet absorbed the adequate discursive skills.

The economically weak majority of parents in Gameranga however, maintain that such gifts to the groom are demanded (hence *dimand* as groom price is sometimes refered to) and they bemoan such a practice. Excessive demands are not only considered a deviation from tradition. The novel custom of securing a husband is attributed to a general social decline and is contemptible on moral grounds. "Today, people are self-interested, greedy for money" (*ajke manush lubi, takar lubi, jomer lubi ajke*), attested a mother of two nubile girls.

The invasion of Gameranga by groom price during the last decade ("after the liberation war" informants claimed) coincides with the appearance of

---

[14] A term used by Bossen 1988, Kolenda 1984, Lindenbaum 1981, Tambiah 1973.

[15] The mode of transfer of tangible marriage gifts in Gameranga points to this: traditional objects—saris and gold—given to the bride are ostentatiously displayed for audience evaluation at the wedding ceremony, while modernities that flow in the opposite direction are given to the groom after the ceremony is over.

other "novelties" reversing the trends of the marriage market. Of these, the most remarkable is a change in the locus of intitiative in mate seeking. As some anthropologists have noticed and as female informants (of grand-mother category) also remember, traditionally the initial move to arrange a marriage was made by the father of the groom: "A decade ago ..." writes Aziz in 1979 "... it was more difficult for a man to find a wife than the reverse. But now a woman's family commonly takes the initiative in looking for a bridegroom", (ibid., 57) a move that places the wife-givers in a situation of strategic disadvantage (as initiators) and dependence on wife-takers (as receivers of offers).

According to older informants—women past forty—(i.e. the grandmother generation of women) their marriages were contracted according to the Islamic tradition, i.e. a *muharana* variant. Accordingly, the only marriage prestation (payment) they can recall came from the groom's family, who was thereby the main giver in the exchange. The wealth, mainly in the form of golden jewellery and saris, went from the wife-takers to the wife-givers. As a counter-balance, the bride's father might finance the wedding feast but the groom was always the main donor. My informants had no doubts as to the causes of the current shift in the flow of wealth and of attention. It was that in those days, "women had more value". "Nowadays, there are too many women" (*ajke meye beshi hoy*), grooms are hard to find and it costs a lot to get one. It is often added that "today women do not observe as strict purdah" (*ajke purdae thake na*), which further re-affirms the local truism that "women have no value". It is this moral-demographic disparity (decline in morals and surplus of women) that village matrons offer as an explanation for the emergence of a novel alternative, an unorthodox form of marriage payment that disadvantages wife-givers.

However, contrary to popular perception of a demographic disparity that apparently favours men, the statistical records (made available to me by a Circular Office employee in the subdivisional town in 1983), show that in Gameranga the males outnumber females by 47 (total population of 7 000)[16].

Quite a different understanding of the demographic imbalance is achieved, when it is considered in the light of historical precedents. In the Bangladesh case, Lindenbaum (1981) does so persuasively by pointing to the multiple links that tie the rural household with external economic-political forces. To pursue her argument, a shift is due from the local to the objectivist knowledge of the structures in the wider world beyond Gameranga. In Lindenbaum's interpretation the appearance of "groom shortage" and groom price resulting in the shift in power relationship between wife-givers and wife-takers, is placed within a wider epistemological, historical and geographical frame.

---

[16] Nationwide, men constitute 51,56 per cent of the total population of 87 119 965, women 48,43 percent (Demographic yearbook 1990:122). The population census carried out in 1982 registered 12 929 families ("*khana shonka*") in *thana* (lowest government administrative unit) where Gameranga pertains. According to the District Municipal Office these included 40 499 males and 36 510 females.

There is a general consensus among South Asianists that emphasis on dowry (of which groom price is a corrupt version), co-varies with social mobility, higher social position, urban employment and involvement in commerce (Aziz 1979:212, Tambiah 1973, Lindenbaum 1981). According to Lindenbaum (ibid.), the first opportunity for meeting these pre-requisites in this predominantly rural part of the British empire arose when the British administration in West Bengal offered government employment to Hindu males in the end of 19th century. This in India introduced money accumulation into the prestige system that had been based until then exclusively on land ownership. Thus education and employment possibilities gave rise to a new category of grooms—ones with salaried income. Henceforward, the rural householder's economic success depends on an ability to diversify a household's activities among landholding and private or government connected commerce. High demand for salaried grooms thus re-directed the focus from desirable brides to qualified grooms and opulent dowries were meant "as an inducement to the family of a qualified groom to make an alliance" (Lindenbaum 1975).

Lindenbaum goes on explaining: The departure of the British, followed by the formation of the Muslim state of East Pakistan in 1947, accompanied by continuous pauperization, dwindling land holdings and an ever increasing category of landless Muslim peasants, provided a political and economic framework for an aggravation of the male exodus from the villages. As Lindenbaum (ibid.) writes the educated minority could find an opportunity in the administrative and military services of the newly created state while the rest were absorbed by diverse odd jobs in the urban service and commercial sector.

Hence the "shortage"[17] of males in rural areas and the appearance of a new type of groom—one with an income potential (Lindenbaum ibid.).

A further factor contributing to the change was the economic re-orientation of East Pakistan towards the international market after 1947. East Pakistan's (now Bangladesh's) ever increasing dependence on foreign aid gave rise to a new sort of business class (whose surival depends on the continuing development efforts of foreign donors), and introduced to the local market a wide range of foreign-made consumer goods (Lindenbaum 1981). In this scenario, the groom is no longer an undifferentiated category. The modern groom, one with regular cash income and dual residence, corresponds to a new ideal which fathers strive to obtain for their daughters in marriage and it is "the suitable groom" my informants refer to when they complain about a shortage[18].

---

[17] A "shortage" in two senses: as a result of the exodus to urban centres and as a result of a culturally created image of scarcity around an item or a category.

[18] Scarcity surrounding the properly qualified groom is indeed serious. While urban newspapers advertise for business and bank-managers and engineers, a bus-driver, chawkidar, domestic servant or a messenger in the civil service makes up the bulk of lucrative occupations in Gameranga. Women married to this scarce category of men are refered to as *chakrir bou*, i.e. an employee's wife. Typically, a woman wearing wrist watch, spectacles and a hand bag is identified as *chakrir bou*.

Lindenbaum (1981) further points to the different implication the political-economic changes had for women and men. The diversified economic activities split the attachment of the new groom between the employment market and the home and lead to his commuting life-style. His income potential thus "surpasses previously valued attributes of the bride". Brides in contrast, remain, in spite of emerging educational opportunities, a relatively homogeneous, static and "secluded group, embedded in old values" (ibid.). Here I wish to narrow the scope and show how the form and origin of nuptial gifts highlights this contrast. While grooms demand externally designed objects (watch, radio, bicycle) that facilitate outward orientation and achievement (defined by speed and lineal consideration of time) through the acquisition of knowledge, speed, adjustment to outward forces, the valuables for the bride (stipulated in *kabin*) include the locally defined items of home manufacture. Garment (saris), jewellery, toiletries, (and possibly some kitchen utensils) reflect the concern of the users for change and modification of the bodily exterior, that facilitates orientation towards the locale of immediate residents, e.g. assertion vis à vis other affinal women. The sari, as I will show in the following chapter is the garment par excellence for communicating a woman's post-marital status of encompassment and submission to the male donor and of outward self-effacement or anonymity in the conjugal community. While the male objects permit the owner, manipulation of the environment by action on the basis of digital timing, radio information, and with the help of a vehicle, the gifts flowing to the female user re-affirm and encourage the manipulative skills of appearing, e.g. by assuming poses.

Summary and consideration of consequences for women

At this point, I shall swing away from the global–historical context back to the ground of Gameranga, where the changes, registered by Lindenbaum in the precincts of Dhaka in the sixties, started to affect marital transactions much later[19]. After reiterating the two systems of prestations I shall consider the actual constitution of the category "groom". Then I shall look at how the shifts in the marriage market "outside" are rationalised and dealt with locally. Lastly, I shall reflect on possible consequences of these changes for women.

Firstly, it should be stressed that the groom price co-exists with *muharana*[20] and that the initiative to search for a spouse may still be taken by the groom's

---

[19] This is also in accordance with Lindenbaum's observation that groom price first beagan to regulate urban rich and middle-class marriages in the late colonial period and has now spread into rural areas, affecting even the poorer categories of Muslims.

[20] This is true both within a family's or a person's marital history. A given marriage may subsume marriage payments that bear characteristics of *muharana*, dowry as well as groom price (see Aziz 1979:68).

family, depending on the family's wealth, sensitivity to prestige and its previous experience with marriage exchanges. The weakness of a 14-months' observation is that the system of marriage prestations is an on-going process which may cover several years and that it is a process from which women—my principal informants—are excluded. Yet, even in the absence of systematically collected data on the actual amount of marriage wealth or a family's history of marriages, the frequent comments by informants on these matters are suggestive of at least a double referential system of prestations. These two vary not only in the amount of wealth exchanged and the nature of the items but more importantly, by the direction in which the wealth flows and by the person who receives it. I shall thus summarize:

Muharana is a type of wealth in the form of cash, saris or gold, that flows from the groom to the bride who is the sole recipient. This payment is consonant with Islamic ideology as well as with the contemporary legal code; it receives publicity and moral approval. Informants hold *muharana* as one of the host of symbols carrying opposition to the "things Hindu", (whose marriages are marked by opulent dowries). Theoretically, the agreement to pay *muharana* is incumbent on all Muslims as an essential condition of the legitimacy of marriage, sexual rights and agnatic claims to the offspring—regulations which in praxis meet with widespread circumventions.

Groom price entails gifts by the bride's family to the groom for his personal use. The fact that the groom is the sole recipient corrupts the idea of dowry suggested by the direction of giving. This type of price is premissed on the culturally constructed scarcity of suitable grooms and subject to the fluctuations of commercial and political forces which are beyond the control of *shomaj*. It lacks support in the Islamic code and is euphemized as, "free gift" by those who apply it or "dimand" by those who lack the means. Groom price is concomittant with aspirations of social ascendancy implied in hypergamic alliance marriages (Caplan 1984).

Villagers admit there is a confusion as to the application of a clearly defined mode of payment; the boundaries are blurred; it is clear that if *muharana* system rendered wife-takers as evasive strategists the introduction of groom price will certainly generate a proliferation of similar strategies among the bride givers. In Uttor Para, where the majority of peasants are near-to-landless the actual range of marriage wealth given in either directions is rather limited. However, from the comments and conversations mentioned it is clear that the groom is now at the centre and that he is making demands and therefore a heavier burden of costs is expected from the bride-givers. On the other hand, for poor men and widowers it is as difficult to obtain a wife as it is for poor, or divorced women to get a husband. These grooms may feel superior while releasing a poor family from the inability to marry off their daughter but they do not usually make "*dimands*"; on the contrary, as obvious initiators of proposals they may contest for a bride's favour with a smaller gift. This category of grooms, although abundant, apparently does not count in folk hypergamic assessments of local demography and therefore there is a "shortage of men". This link between being in a position of the initiator and bearing responsibility for the heavier burden of marriage costs is not given attention by informants. Instead, the disparity in marriage obligations is rendered in a clearly gender polarized way, as a matter of numeric scarcity in men and moral scarcity in women.

Taking these shifts in marriage ideology as an effect of regulative forces that come from outside, a further point can be made regarding local conceptualisation and practice to incorporate otherness.

By explaining the appearance of novelties in different terms than sociologists, does not mean, that the villagers view their community as detached from the wider universe. It is only to claim that their interpretation is placed within a different frame of rationalisation. As has been shown, villagers conceptualise the nature of groom price and concomittant shifts in spouse seeking in terms of a framework of moral space, whereby persons, objects and ideas imported from outside are imbued with great ambiguity. In Gameranga, a family's perception of the present pattern of changes (the shift in emphasis on groom's qualities) is revealed in the comments on a daughters' up-bringing; which is primarily experienced as a pressing problem with marriage related costs and hence an anxiety about proper timing[21]; in marriage discourse, the effect of the external forces and historical transformation on marriage transactions is posed as the problem to the *shomaj* honour: a growing bulk of women staying umarried in their natal homes is given as evidence of this.

The unmarried daughters themselves may be fatalists with respect to the choice of *bier-shami*; they may be kept in purda and viewed structurally as passive objects of marriage exchange. Yet, even if lacking any say in the choice of their partner, they do have desires, and their desires are directed towards grooms that wear the insignia of modernity. Their parents, even those at bottom of community hierarchy, as much they may grumble about the morals of nowadays, their sacrifices made in order to accumulate marriage wealth, all cherish a hypergamic marriage ideal.

The fact that parents have to accumulate enough cash to meet wedding expenses means that many girls now remain unmarried long after puberty, thus giving worries to the family and bringing disgrace to the whole *gushti*. At the same time families in Gameranga are noting that a moderate education ("Some but not too much of schooling". "Too much education spoils a woman's behaviour" or "… affects negatively her sense of modesty") is now becoming an integral part of symbolic female assets at marriage negotiations; they see that young women with some education, even salaried jobs[22], possess quite a bargaining power even if they rate low on economic or aesthetic crite-

---

[21] See chapter 17.

[22] Interviews organized by a non-governmental organisation (just before the end of my fieldwork) for ten posts as family planning motivators in the area of Gameranga, attracted surprisingly a con-

ria. For a daughter herself, education is, contrary to the groom price (which her parents try hard, but fail to produce) a "property in her own control to take with her into marriage" to paraphrase Tambiah's (1973:62) definition of dowry. However, unlike dowry (pure or corrupt), it cannot be transferred to the husband's sister, as is often the case and unlike beauty education has a more permanent and dynamic potential for a married woman in the case of divorce or widowhood.

One consequence for women may also be that difficulty in finding a groom may extend the recruiting area and open new markets because fathers are now compelled to search for grooms further afield, beyond the culturally defined geographical boundary or kinship unit[23].

I would conclude by claiming that although in most families the range of marriage wealth (passing in either direction) is limited and groom price grudged (not least for its alien nature), it has entered the prestige system of even the poorest. As a possible medium for establishing hypergamic marriages it has now extended consciousness and vocabulary as a referent of social as well as moral standing: a stratifying factor, a possibility to calculate with, in negotiating one's position in the hierarchy. Particularly those on the verge of economic decline are alert to the possibilities involved[24].

siderable number of female Muslim candidates from a vast area. Most of them were divorced and widowed young women but even a few unmarried girls appeared and got the job (all candidates accomplished elementary education a few of them went through secondary school). Baharon, whose viewing is described on previous pages afterwards expressed regret for having neglected school when she was young ("today I could have had a job (*chakri*) and bought as many saris as I wish") which was the time when even rural schools started to be filled with girls.

[23] See chapter 15 "Spatial distance between affinal *gushti*s and provenance of wife".

[24] As may be the case of an educated–landless son who can amass some land and wealth by marrying a new-rich family's daughter.

PART SIX

Production and Reproduction of Womanhood in Marriages

CHAPTER 17

Why do all women marry?— Metafertility and unavoidability of marriage for women

As is evident from previous chapters, marriage equates building up credit whereby a lot of *gushti*'s prestige and material resources are at stake. However, inevitability of marriage in Bangladesh is grounded on yet another set of beliefs.

Universally in Bangladesh, it is felt that "a woman must be given (*bie dawa*) in marriage at least once" (Blanchet 1986); and moreover, she should be married "in time". Timing and timeliness of a daughter's marriage is an important aspect of male honour and family prestige, and her age since puberty affects her evaluation at the time of marriage negotiations. Keeping a post-menarchal daughter or sister at home for too long dishonours her guardians, lessens her own value and draws unfavourable attention to the whole family.

In this chapter I wish to explore the particular emphasis on daughter marriages within a wider symbolic system—the ideas of metafertility and well-being prevalent in Bangladesh. According to this ethos auspiciousness inheres in processes, substances and objects which are paralleled with the physical body[1]. This intertwining of the physical and conceptual realms in local cosmology provides a basis for legitimating cultural constructs as natural. Besides semantics of metafertility I wish to demonstrate how these constructs are used for evaluations of biological facts, and vice versa, how the "naturallness" attributed to non-biological processes renders them as inevitable and therefore legitimate.

General view and status of singleness

In this section I examine first the view of solitude (social apartness) and secondly the perception of the unmarried state of mature adults, showing how the bachelorhood of men is thought of and dealt with differently from the single-

---

[1] For instance the evaluation of the sexual biology of men and women reiterates the processes of food production (see notes 24, 25 below); conversely biological and physical attributes are ascribed to non-biological processes and elaborated into cultural concepts in many spheres of social reality (see note 26 below).

ness of women and how in both cases it is linked to beliefs about their nature, particularly their sexual, physical and mental capacities.

In Bangladesh a person is always viewed as enmeshed in a complex network of family (*poribar, ghor, bari*) and community (*shomaj*)[2]; hence connectedness with others possesses an intrinsic value, while any form of detachment from social bonds, be it an aspect either of personal temperament, a life style or a profession that demands concentration on texts rather than people, even an occasional withdrawal from the company of others[3] suggests denial of belongingness, the ultimate stage of which is social death. Significantly, in Gameranga, women would distract me from the deliberate solitude of reading or note-writing, expressing worries that I would turn mad; others would send their children before dark, suggesting they shared the bed with me. My refusals would invite doubts as to whether I was not frightened to sleep alone. This concern was quite apart from informants' preoccupations with the absence of conjugal pleasures in my attic. Encouragements to disclose "all my secrets" pertained to the same concern to rescue me from the few moments of isolation (which were so precious to me). A failure to reciprocate (in cash, food, tokens of attention, in disclosing news, gossip, secret) or to do so without leaving sufficient imbalance to prompt the receiver "to assume the role of the giver once again" (Khare 1976:103) is another expression of "withdrawal" in the context of social transactions (*shesha*). For further examples of strategies aimed at the sustenance of social continuity, negation of separation, see following pages in this chapter.

Singleness in the conjugal sense relates to another set of negative notions. The villagers in Gameranga recognize that the sexual drive is part of physical maturity in both men and women and that sexual abstinence has serious mental and physical consequences, particularly in men. Thus an infuriated man may be asked by his friends whether his head has got hot because he had not "stayed with a woman" for a time. Insanity or dermatological disorders are the consequences for women. The fundamental tenet is that sexuality should be expressed heterosexually, within marriage and with a procreative end. Mar-

---

[2] This is in accordance with belief systems which have currency in Asia, as stressed by Orientalists: "This is the belief in the unity of all being. Our separate selves, acording to Buddhism, Hinduism, and their offshoots, are not ultimately real. Philosophical Hinduism and Mahayana Buddhism reject dualism. For them ultimately there is no difference between myself and yourself, and this river and that mountain. We are all one and the conflict between us is therefore illusory." (Bellah 1979. See also Davis 1983:3, Khare 1976:118, 232–233, Leaf 1979:324, Maloney 1981: 248 for similar, but differently applied and formulated view and Ramanuyan 1989 who suggests the term "coherence" instead of "unity" in the Indian world-view).

[3] Such as a family's temporal non-participation in *shomaj* activities, or spatial isolation when a family decides to build a house on the outskirts of the community. It should be pointed out that in spite of strong disapproval of social withdrawal and in spite of over-crowdedness in public places, there are cultural forms of covert, inward withdrawal widely practised by people. Screening of the face or eyes behind the veil in order to achieve aloneness and privacy in the midst of a crowd is only one technique and is quite conspicuously employed by women.

riage is universally desired for both women and men in Bangladesh[4]. Inaptitude for conjugal life because of physical or mental infirmity thus presents a dilemma to solve in a culture which vigorously denies social status to an unmarried man or a woman (Bourdieu 1986:209).

The failure of a man to get married (*bie kora*) is equated with general impotency: "a man without a penis" (*kono jinish nei?*) or a man, whose " 'thing' does not do the job" (*kaj kore na*); not only physiologically but socially and mentally. By extension, this would also refer to a man who happens to be sexually impotent but is still capable of performing manual jobs. One was a leprous boatman in a neighbouring village, who does not see any sense in getting married—"For what? I lack the power" (*kono shokti nei*)—because true sexual impotency is recognized as physical (and even mental) incapacity. In fact he earned some money as a water bearer and a boat paddler. On the other hand, physical disability does not preclude sexual power. A man with a grave physical impairment prevented from doing productive manual work is not viewed as unmarriageable.

In a *gusthi* in Gameranga, there were two brothers severely deformed by polio. The elder one could not stand on his legs or sit. At the time of Islamic feasts, relatives transferred his body to Khulna town and placed him on the street amid other beggars. There, due to his pitiful condition, he could earn some money which affirmed him as a provider. In his *bari* in Gameranga he had a pretty wife—an orphaned "daughter" of the *gusthi*, who had just given him a son when I visited the place. People took it as evidence that even his younger brother (who could support himself standing, but not walking) was potent (*shokti hoy*) and they were looking for a suitable bride for him. Perpetuation of the line was a great concern for the elders, as that particular *gushti* had "too many daughters".

Unduly prolonged bachelorhood indicates avoidance of the full status of adulthood and thus suggests a deficiency in one's character (cf. Hirschon 1978). If he remains unmarried after thirty, a man is considered past the marriageable age and this attribute becomes a prominent mark of his personal identity. The few bachelors I knew of in the area around Gameranga were systematically excluded from their respective *shomaj*. During the rounds of family census I noticed that the first and only information people would volunteer about such men was "*bou nei, bie nei*", (no wife, no marriage).

For women, however, there is no way of remaining or imagining themselves unmarried. Even girls with grave physical defects are to be married at least once. They are given to widowers as second wives or to extremely poor men (even reputed wife-abusers) and it is anticipated that their marriages will not last long.

An epileptic woman and another who was deaf, both of whom I used to know, were given several times to various husbands and the only experience they recalled of their

---

[4] According to the national census over 99 percent of the women and 98 percent of men are married (quoted in Blanchet 1986). In the Matlab area Aziz (1979:160) recorded among the 40—45 years old category nil per cent of never married women in 1968 and 0,1 percent in 1974.

marriages was severe beating. They were beggars when I met them, and both expressed indignation over my "not belonging to a man".

Although various categories of women without husbands—widows, divorced, abandoned or women who remained unclaimed by their husbands after the conclusion of the marriage contract—abound in Gameranga, there is virtually no woman who would not have been formally married at least once in her life.

An interesting exception was Komiron, a servant in a neighbouring household, for whom her female peers and also her patron foresaw spinsterhood. Her employer attempted to dissuade me from giving Komiron a new blouse, explaining "She is a *bo-lot*[5]—sixteen years old and has not yet been menstruating, something is wrong". Komiron worked hard, yet her mother, a servant in the same household, had no hopes of marrying Komiron, unless, as she exclaimed (for she continued to hope), "if only a drop of blood appeared, we should give her away".

It is felt that a daughter is a debt of honour and there is hardly a more shameful failure for a man than the inability to marry off his daughter/sister. The recognition of these concerns in Gameranga brings to mind a Punjabi commentator quoted by Das (1979):

"Daughters are comparable to something kept in trust for another, you have to care for them, love them, and you will be held responsible for them but you are destined to lose them … once a daughter is properly married and goes to her own house, it is like a debt that has been paid".

The poorest families with daughters often resort to concubinage or arrangement of a marriage union with an old widower. Though for a daughter's family, such a solution always indicates the inability to attract a more adequate groom, the grooms in question tend to view their willingness to take over guardianship of a poor man's daughter or a divorcee as a meritorious deed. Frequently, it is viewed as a gesture whereby the groom releases the bride's family from the risk of shame if the daughter remains unmarried.

Apart from wifehood, there is no acceptable alternative career for an unmarried woman among Bengali Muslims[6]. It is believed that in the married state alone can a woman develop her potential and find satisfaction. The inevitability of marriage for women is most compellingly manifested in the long established Bengali practice, both Hindu and Islamic, of mock marriages of prostitutes. The Census of India (1911:325) recorded:

"In Bengal a girl who is intended for a life of shame goes through a form of marriage before or as soon as she reaches puberty. She is married either to a man, or to a plant, or to a sword or a knife. The man is generally an imbecile, but sometimes a Baishanab is hired to act as a bridegroom, or a prostitute's son takes the part. In any case, he is a

---

[5] *Bolot*—mentally retarded.

[6] For a woman in Gameranga, accepting a salaried job or searching for employment outside her home always points to the absence of a provider. This was the case for the candidates for the posts of family planning motivator mentioned in the previous chapter. Employment is perceived as a temporary solution out of necessity. Two of them told me that should a suitable man offer marriage they would happily resume housewifery duties.

husband pro forma only and goes away after the marriage. A regular marriage ceremony is however performed by a low Brahman ... while a Mullah officiates among
Musulmans. The ceremony is also performed if the girl is married to a plant [e.g. jas-
mine or rose] or a plantain tree, ... a sword or knife is invariably selected by Muha-
madan prostitutes, while a plant is preferred by Hindus. The symbolism is carried so
far that the sword is kept locked up in a box, in the belief that if [the knife] is lost the
girl becomes a widow ..."[7].

A recent study on brothels in Dhaka shows that mock marriages with banana
trees, and even with the sun or the moon, as rituals celebrating the introduction of girls to the profession, are still widely practised among prostitutes today (Khan:1988). The ritual performance of the wedding in their case thus
celebrates the life career which is the negation of marriage par excellence;
perhaps, as a substitute submission to the cultural imperative, an attempt to
yield a culturally proper woman[8].

To summarize: singleness in Bangladesh is universally perceived as a most
unnatural state. What is solitary negates sociability and is thus dangerously
detached from the premise of life. Separateness from *shomaj* is a suspect, imperfect state, because a person's full identity and intellectual creative potential
can only be attained in association with others, which in Bengal means assuming a proper social category and resolving the essential paradox of the human
situation: keeping the boundaries while establishing relationships across them
(Rhodes 1989). With respect to human fecundity only the marriage union can
free a mature person from unproductive separateness. In a culture which
places the supreme premium on creation and procreation, every social group
is viewed as a generative unit and the union of bride and groom is its minimal
form. The state of separateness is equated with sterility, dryness, emptiness,
hunger[9] and hence perceived as an impediment to prosperity, life itself[10].

The praxis of singleness, although extremely rare, has however different
consequences for women, who, if deliberately unmarried—like the prostitutes—abolish their actual civil state by a performance of symbolic marriage
with objects or an extremely brief union with any man available. Although

---

[7] My emphasis in the quote. Attribution "shame" to the career of prostitution reflects clearly an
anglocentric view, since in Bengali lore prostitutes have always assumed an auspicious position
(Marglin 1981).

[8] According to Manu, an unmarried woman represents one of the most vulnerable—*dhormo-*
harming—spots within the social system (Khare 1982).

[9] The act of giving food to beggars is to link this category of people to the human community as
much as to prove one's piety.

[10] An interesting inversion of this axiom (which I will not be able to explain here) is the sexually
anomalous category of *hijri*—transvestites—who enjoy an auspicious status in Bangladesh as
well as India, a virtue that make them particularly welcome guests at weddings in West Bengal
and even institutionalized receivers of government relief schemes (a *hijri* receives a free lungi or a
sari once a year in some states of India). From various informants I heard that whenever a group
of *hijri* invades a market in Faridpur or Jessore district, each of them is allowed to collect vegetables or a handful of rice free of charge; their "raids" are usually accompanied with obscene songs
and gestures. Cf. also Arens, van Beurden's (1977:48) experience in Kushtia and Rolt's (1991) in
Chittagong.

marriage is also an "inevitability" and imperative for a man and there is an intense pressure on bachelors approaching thirty to take a wife, the age limitation for men is more flexible and they are not as devalued as their sisters by advanced age or loss of chastity.

Most of my informants who reached menopause at the time of interview had been married before or immediately after menarche and lamented the current condition in which daughters nowadays stay at home unmarried a long time after they start to menstruate[11]. Some old matrons talked of "sinfulness" to specify the focus of their resentment and claimed that it is sinful to menstruate "while still living in the parental home". Others inverted this claim by saying "it is sinful to be still in one's father's home after menarche"[12]. It seems that claimed sinfulness here has a twofold implication. On the one hand it hints at the risk of exposure that a family undergoes should their mature daughter take control over her own sexuality; an eventuality which may produce undeniable, objectively manifested evidence—a baby. However, the informants' emphasis on sinfulness could also be interpreted as an aptitude to relate the marriage imperative to existing incest regulations as is the case among the Hindus[13]. Incest proscriptions constitute the only marriage rule among Bengali Muslims. Accordingly, sisters and daughters are proscribed as marriage partners and hence failure to exchange them as soon as they are consumable, invites an association with incest (i.e. keeping them for oneself).

Without intending to introduce the aspect of syncreticism (the problem of intrusion of foreign cosmological elements) into Islamic perceptions[14] (of which my informants were unaware in any case), it should be stressed in the context of this specific argument that the Brahmanic ideal of pre-pubescent marriage set out in the Vedic texts, still lingers in the way gender morality is constructed in Gameranga. These texts are explicit about the duty to marry off a daughter before the menarche (Bennett 1983:240,243, Hatti n.d., Khare 1982). It should also be remembered, that the marriages of older women had been in many other ways congruent with Hindic forms of marriage, as articulated in Brahmanic scriptures. Still today rituals and tenets stemming from these sources constitute the desired, and the only prestigious form of marriage (*bie* as contrary to contractual *nika* endorsed by Islam); this in spite of profound changes in other aspects of the marriage market.

---

[11] The increased age of the bride at marriage as concomittant with other shifts in South-Asian marriage market has been observed and commented upon by villagers as well as sociologists (Bennett 1983:235, Hatti 1983, Caplan 1984, Lindenbaum 1975, 1981).

[12] From a Hindu community in India Thompson (1983) reports that menstruating unmarried women cannot worship either with girls or married women because they are inauspicious until married.

[13] Fruzzetti (1975:112); see also Bennett's (1983:242) interesting discussion of the topic in her study of high caste women in Nepal.

[14] I abstain from systematic exploration of syncretic elements in local world-view, even from using the adjective, as my informants always referred to Islam whenever they invoked *dhorm*ic authority (see further chapter 6 and 16 n.6).

The difficulty with the incest consideration is that it does not apply to single sons and that, although a sister's/daughter's divorce or widowhood is considered a misfortune, it is a family's duty to take her back home. Thus a single marriage experience de-dramatizes significantly a daughter's attachment to the parental home. The crucial question here seems to be the insistence on timeliness of womens' marriages. This is expressed either as an emphasis on the normative sequence (i.e. a marriage before the onset of menarche) as remembered and experienced by older informants or as an effort to squeeze the interval between menarche and marriage, which I see as the modern transformation of the old axiom.

So far I have considered the general view of singleness, the avoidance of the risk that a daughter's uncontrolled sexuality after menarche may bear demonstrable evidence (therefore an urgent relegation of guardianship), the sinfulness of incest and textual authorization of non-Islamic origin as possible incentives that compel the parents of 99 per cent of Bangladeshi women to arrange marriages for their daughters. The problem remains, however, how to understand that female and not male bachelors are to be married to fictitious spouses and why women's marriages—fictive or actual—are to be timed more cautiously and narrowly than men's. Instead of rushing to a facile conclusion that any one of the above factors accounts for or explains marriage ideology, I shall present a set of cultural notions which point to yet another source of the different perception and praxis of female marriages.

My suggestion is that the universality and particular timing of women's marriages, apart from the factors already mentioned, are embedded in a wider context of ideas specific to Bengal about metafertility (see Greenough 1983). More specifically, that they are linked to the Bengali view of the female body and female blood (i.e. physical and biological attributes of women). I shall therefore delve further into my data to examine beliefs regarding these physiological attributes as these relate to the set of cultural perceptions surrounding two opposed states: that of the "full" (*bhora, purno*) and that of the "empty" (*khali, emni*).

Central to my argument is another anthropologist's assertion, that "a woman's status and her [need of timely marriage] can be seen to derive their rationale from the intermeshing of ideas regarding her physical nature [biology] and those concerned with her symbolic attributes" (Hirschon 1978)[15]. In the context of Bengali gender construction, the perception of a woman's body—as the embodiment of Lokhi, its metaphorical extensions in objects and substances, its states of fullness and emptiness, provide a dimension of the symbolic ordering of the world. The asymmetrical relationship between a husband and his wife is expressed and re-affirmed through this symbolic order.

---

[15] I am not concerned with the question of causality in biology-culture, rather my emphasis is on the mutuality of effects of the physical and the conceptual world in the constitution of the local meaning, thus following the suggestion of S. Ardener (1981), Hastrup (1978) and Jackson (1983b).

Cosmology of prosperity and scarcity

As suggested by the root *dhr* (to generate), by the existing moral order (*dhormo*) and the *ijjat*-emphasis on the numeric strength of the *gushti* (and *jat*), the outlook on life among Bengali Muslims revolves around the contrast between attributes beneficial to fecundity, life sustenance and those which impede it. Morever, in Bengal, fertility is not conceived of as mere survival; in addition to life sustenance, an important emphasis is placed on auspicious increase and strategies of multiplication (Lokhi and *borkot*). This orientation extends far beyond its obvious link with economic and biological reproduction. Persons, events, sequences of time, in fact all human activities are classified as auspicious or inauspicious, not only according to their propensity to maintain or destroy life but as to whether they are capable of enhancing, multiplying, inflating what is good. The idea of a good life in Bengal as in other parts of South Asia (Greenough 1983, Fruzzetti 1975:165, Bennett 1983:247, Wadley 1980) is epitomized in the image of the godess Lakshmi, which has been imported from the cosmological universe and traditions of Hindu Northern India and re-named by Muslim peasants as Lokhi. Lokhi represents and is intrinsic to prosperity, abundance, surplus i.e. all that adds to mere survival. This is what can never be attained without the aid of superior beings—social or metaphysical[16].

Scarcity in a household, or just any form of vulnerability to sterility is expressed as absence of Lokhi—Olokhi, which is ultimately connected with the perishing of life, patriline, and even mankind.

Lokhi is invoked conceptually as an image of moral order and physically as material abundance and is therefore revealed in the most diverse domains of culture. Lokhi represents an ideal state as well as an inherent quality of objects, substances and bodies with a potential to increase. In his excellent study of peasants' moral economy in Bengal, Greenough (1983) rightly points to the emphasis South Asian peasants place on deeds, rather than cosmic principles or supernatural forces. About Lokhi he writes "her boons tend to be pragmatic rather than transcendental … she is turned to by peasant devotees all over Bengal for their substantial, mundane needs rather than for spiritual benefits" (ibid.).

Greenough recognizes three interrelated features of favours believed to derive from Lokhi. First, there is indulgence, expressed by acts of parentlike feeding, second there is abundance of wealth, expressed by the "distribution of stocks of rice" to dependents and third, there is beauty expressed by the "vigorous and richly adorned adult body".

All of these features correspond to the kind of preoccupations raised in vari-

---

[16] In the first category, the villagers place government, foreigners, patrons, parents, whose duty it is to care for the needy.

ous contexts by the villagers among whom I lived. Morever, as I have already mentioned in a previous chapter, Lokhi is an ideal woman—a wife and a mother. Feeding and bodily metaphors thus constitute the link between a deity and her terrestrial correspondence.

Ordinarily in the Bengali moral economy, preservation envisages increase while decrease indicates extinction. In the domestic sphere in Gameranga the contrast between these—preservation:increase :: extinction:decrease—is expressed as an opposition between the state of fullness (*bhora* or *purna*) and the state of emptiness or voidness (*khali, emni, kitchu na*). This particular adjectivisation of Lokhi appears in practices of food and body management. "Filling" and "emptying" are the core practical operations involved in household production and reproduction—the tillage of land, food processing, cooking and the "work" of human procreation. These practices constitute the generative principle of *dhormo*, commonsensical knowledge, meaning and consensus of meaning (Bourdieu 1986:97). In the context of nurture, fullness promises vital energy and increase, is auspicious and therefore desirable; emptiness, on the contrary, is connected with misfortune parallelled with the suffering of an empty stomach (both words translated by a single gloss *khuda*) and of sterility (*khali*)[17].

Fullness and emptiness present two antithetical modes of orientation, which may be modified or reversed into their opposites in the full context of daily praxis. Moreover, the dichotomy is coupled with distinctions in other domains. Fullness for example connotes a positive commitment to the community. It is related to a wider set of positive notions regarding social and economic success as well as moral merits: openness to communication with others (a matter highly susceptible to contextuality), accumulation of social bonds and material goods, fullness of the house with people, backyard with cattle, granary with food, pockets with money, union of what should not be separated (*shil pata*—utensils for pounding spices); while emptiness suggests the absence of all sources of vital energy—food, foetus, maternal milk, oil in hair, water in the pitcher, sexual partner, affinal bonds etc. Ultimately, it is the equivalent of social as well as physical death. Many features of etiquette and social interaction could be recognized as means to safeguard against extinction of continuity, physical as well as social. Reluctance to finish a job once started, leaving leftovers on the plate as a guest, as a narrator never to bring a story to its end, saying on departure "I am coming" (*ami ashi*) instead of "I am leaving" (*ami jai*), are a few examples of strategic generation of positive (=fertile) disparities. It is believed that only the uncompleted, the imperfect, leaves a reminder as the transition point to continuity—"a seed towards the repetition of the same act" (Khare 1976:101).

---

[17] In an unpublished research proposal Dr. Claquin et. al (1982) suggest further research based on experience from his medical practice in Dhaka that his female patients tend to confuse digestive organs with reproductive. Thus it seems that voidness of food is viewed as a sign equal to reproductive sterility. A *bou* entering marriage empty-handed, unprovided with dowry is also *khali*.

I shall elaborate these notions with regard to an important and fixed area of a wife's life—her childbearing capacity and cooking. In a household's sexual, material and moral reproduction, both the housewife and the householder are concerned with the increase of the realm of prosperity, yet their functions and concerns differ and so their generative powers are expressed differently.

In an agricultural society like Bangladesh, while the householder's primary concern is management of crops (tillage of the fields and sowing and harvesting at the proper time), it is his wife's task to convert thecrops into edibles and to distribute them among family members. In spatial terms, it is a householder's duty to provide for the material, moral and spiritual needs of the family from the environment beyond the home—the field, the *bichar*, wrestling ground, market, the mosque; the locus of housewife's pursuits—feeding, protecting the weak and curing the sick—is the hearth. A woman's prominent role as a feeder, my informants claimed, is premised on her unique bodily disposition to feed and increase the foetus with uterine blood during pregnancy and later to secure the infant's growth with breastmilk. She is also a healer and a manager of domestic purity, a role premised on her assertedly unique predisposition to deal with bodily excretions e.g. infant incontinence. In either role a wife depends on her husband for attaining the auspicious condition of fullness—of her body and of storage vessels—as he is the legitimate lover, tiller of the fields and provider of alimentary supplies from the outside. Man has the role of initiator and also takes care of the ultimate product: money, the circumcision ceremony, marriage negotiations for mature children. However, it is by a woman's association with the supernatural realm that an increase of what has been provided by the householder, can be attained. The nature of a married woman's contacts with the supernatural vary from that of men. Because the mosque is regarded as a male precinct from which mature women are strictly excluded, the point from which housewives communicate with Allah is quite circumscribed. On the other hand, the array of supernatural powers the wives invoke and elaborate on is much wider.

From the perspective of *dhormo*, to create, distribute, cook and increase food is considered a moral act (Cantlie 1981, Khare 1976:117) and observance of gender division in carrying out these tasks is perceived as a moral duty. Accordingly, a woman's *dhormo* is premised on the perception of herself as a feeder. As already noted, Bengali Muslim culture does not provide women with a career alternative to housewifery cum motherhood[18], and therefore the perception of a woman's "nature" is embedded in the singular semantic field of nurture, feeding and in the social space of cooking. As also mentioned above, even prostitutes in Bangladesh model their careers on the image

---

[18] This is contrary to Bengali Catholics among whom a high merit attaches to families whose daughters pursue the career of a nun. Also among Banchhadas, tribal communities in Madhya Pradesh, considerable respect accrues to women who pursue the career of prostitute (*khelawaneese*—pleasure givers). Long tradition demands that at least one woman in a family must take to prostitution (Ganguly 1982).

of Lokhi as they cling tenaciously to the very rites that define the *dhormo* of wifehood (Khan, ibid).

Fertility of objects and substances: jars, earth and water

The ideal of metafertility is reinforced in a wide range of pan-Indian metaphors, of which some have currency in Gameranga. Thus, in the context of household management, the domain of female anatomy and of biology are linked with kitchen objects in a symbolic resemblance between the auspiciousness of the filled female body and of vessels (*kholosh, hari*). In their feeding capacity housewife and vessel are perceived as equal and synonymous symbols of increase. When a daughter turns bride and is about to leave her father's house for her husband's, a new *kholosh* filled with rice has to be supplied, as it is believed that otherwise a daughter-turned-bride takes the household's Lokhi with her. Being made of clay, *hari* and *kholosh* partake in the earthy substance I deal with in the section that follows.

In the realm of domestic increase, fullness is sponsored by Lokhi, but Lokhi's presence or absence in the female body, cattle, cooking objects and substances (food, water, cowdung) depends largely on the wife's culinary and bodily management, including negotiations with superior powers. When a mother's lactative capacity decreases or ceases altogether too early, because "the milk got spoiled" (*duth noshto hoye geche*) it is due to the intervention of malevolent spirits provoked by her erroneous behaviour.

In a wider context of metaphysical increase a further analogy is made between female reproductive sexuality and earth, both of which are subject to a householder's care (Fruzzetti 1975:165–202, Khare 1982, Marglin 1981, Selwyn 1979) as well as Allah's benevolence. The beliefs widespread in the subcontinent regarding ploughing illustrate the nature of that care. As acts of creation, marriage (never divorced from sexuality) and ploughing are both conceived as male acts of opening and filling. In Bengal, it is a maxim that earth—and also a woman—is to be "ploughed for sowing and reaping" (Fruzzetti 1975:27) and not merely for indulgence. Doing it with other intentions, would be considered a wasteful effort. According to my informants, the only morally sanctioned coital position is that of "*shami upor*", i.e. one that replicates the earth tiller's over his field as he is ploughing and sowing. All other techniques, if heard about from men who have some experience with urban prostitutes, are condemned as sexual aberrations, detrimental to the husband's health and the quality of offspring.

Accordingly, sexual intercourse, in polite discourse is referred to as *kaj*—work[19], the female sex organ as "the place" (*oi jaigata*) and the penis as "the

---

[19] "Bad work" (*kharap kaj*) denotes illicit sex.

thing" (*ei jinish*). When I asked housewives to indicate where exactly their land was located, they would just point in the approximate direction using the same descriptive "*oi jaigata.*"

This singular mode of household production and reproduction—a husband's mounting position over "the place"—provides a justification of distribution and exercise of household authority as reiterated in dialogues about wife-beating. Female informants objected emphatically to my suggestion "why do not you hit back when you receive a blow?", claiming that "a husband is always *upor* ("above", "on top of")". A husband's right to physical abuse is indisputable because of the embeddedness of the whole question of authority and moral order in a set of metaphoric associations between proper human anatomy and the non-biological tenets of a broader cosmological order. The physiology of coitus and the manner of ploughing, provide a suitable validation of domestic authority. Thus the act of procreation, itself imagined as land cultivation, provides domestic authority and the whole gender ideology with a status of naturalness.

It is reported by various ethnographers (Cantlie 1989), that tillage is suspended in various communities in India for a few days when land is rendered infertile and impure because it menstruates. In neighbouring Orissa a festival is held to mark this event (Marglin 1981). Bengali villagers familiar with the urban life-style frown upon the habit of the rich (in whose urban homes they may have served), of planting their gardens with decorative trees or grass-lawns and consider it a useless waste of resources. The same cosmology underlies the condemnation of male masturbation (*hata mara*) or overindulgence in sex, as both are considered thoroughly wasteful (of semen—the supreme source of vital energy) and therefore aberrant behaviour[20].

Both decorative planting and sex "just for pleasure" (*aramer jonno*) are considered as a work of culture that compromises the fecundity of nature (Bourdieu 1986:126–127,137). Likewise, village women often express contempt over the alleged trend among town people or other *jat*s, to marry "just for pleasure" or "for easiness" (*bie kore aramer jonno* or *khelar* jonno). My answers to endless inquiries about my *jat*'s notions of conjugal well-being, although strictly self-censored, confirmed the worst of their premonitions. Not only marriages out of "love", but late first marriages or abstention from marriage altogether is judged with disapproval, because "waste land—like a woman without a husband" (*Jeye jomi choran jai na, ar je meyer shami nay*) lacks any meaning[21].

In so far as the householder's primary task is to convert every available piece of land into a productive field (Thoorp 1982) by ploughing, sowing and

---

[20] Recall here the serious scolding a mother gives exclusively to a child who plays with rice grains (see "Rice—superfood" in chapter 10).

[21] This adage brought to my attention the parallel made between tillage of land and of a woman in Gameranga. It was served to me as an explanation of exhaustive inquiries regarding my marital credentials and childlessness.

reaping, so it is a father's duty to give away his daughter, and it should be done in time. For it is only through a timely marriage exchange that her body's generative potential may achieve full benefit and waste be avoided. The cultural preoccupation with the timeliness of a daughter's marriage is reflected in the close monitoring (*choke, choke rakha*) to which a daughter's maturation is subjected. At that time, her body is figuratively assessed as belonging to the semantic category of ripening plants, rather than soil[22].

Preoccupation with timeliness does not end at marriage however. It is auspicious if the first child be a son, but more important, that it is born soon after the wedding night (*bashor rat*), though not so early as to suggest pre-marital conception. More than a year's lapse without sign of pregnancy invokes the worst of suspicions—barrenness. Failure to conceive is always attributed to the woman. Because women are considered an intrinsic source of auspicious increase in all spheres of reality, they assume responsibility for all generative failure (Reynolds 1983) —still births, births of daughters only, etc. Male sterility, on the other hand, tends to be represented by impotence only; people assume that, were a man sterile, it would show as sexual inadequacy on the wedding night[23]. Although a quality of paddy seeds (always in the wife's custody) is recognized as important for the outcome of the harvest, "if a crop is not forthcoming, it is because of the condition of the land and its moisture, rather that because of the seed" (Maloney 1981:120). Male infertility is never publicly acknowledged. Because sexual performance bears on a man's *ijjat* it is important to cast the blame for any sort of procreative inadequacy on woman.

Theoretically, singleness for a Muslim woman is the worst of status alternatives (not widowhood as among Hindus), but because, as I said, in Gameranga, it is unimaginable, barrenness assumes its status instead. Marriage that does not yield birth renders the sexual activity it implies inauspicious, without meaning, because it leaves a wife's belly and breast empty. While it is marriage that confers on a woman adult status, pregnancy grants her the full body promising increase, and a surviving son affirms her aspirations to domestic power and gives a security against the calamity of widowhood.

Emptiness of the house and of women

The multiple symbolism of metafertility discussed so far is well conveyed by the poetic imagery of Hindustani folk songs (Dar 1982:167):

"See how fleshy and well-nourished is the oilman's sprightly daughter; Large and round and smooth like oilman's jars or pitchers of the potter".

---

[22] See "Late adolescence", chapter 8.

[23] One of my female informants continued to assume responsibility for the couple's failure to conceive even after the medical test administered by a foreign doctor clearly pointed to her husband's sterility of which both she and the husband were aware. Her husband, however abstained from bringing home second wife, a solution he had been pressed to by his brothers.

or

"The potter's gawky wife is swollen like an undried cowdung cake; By being spanked and tumbled both their rounded form are known to take".

The first captures the indisputable attributes of female beauty, the latter is explicit about the ways of turning an unattractive wife into an appealing woman. In both cases female beauty is defined in terms of aesthetics that develops from operations of domestic work, objects and substances. Apart from the close association between fertility of the female body and a field, and the ripening process of a young girl and a paddy plant which render women, earth, earthen vessels and paddy grains a source of life generation and increase, the villagers hold a view of the ideal female body as plump, filled and juicy—"as fat as a live palm tree yielding plenty of sap, so does a fat woman give birth to many sons"[24].

From the semantic field of the culinary domain stems also the metaphor expressing the view of the optimal condition of a woman's sexual readiness and desirability. A friend reported to one of my male informants the satisfactory result of the sexual conquest he had attempted the previous night as —"like eating rice pastry soaked in hot date palm sap"[25].

Wetness as a pre-condition of auspicious increase is suggested in the poetic records above of the oilman's daughter's beauty as well as the potter's wife's metamorphosis[26]. While wetness is the core indicator of a disposition to open, fill and procreate, dryness (*shukhno hoy*) is a sign of sterility, attributed to unhealthy women (Kotalová 1986) widows, divorced and others, whose husbands are not providing sufficiently or are not alive. According to young men, this process of drying out of women starts at 25 and reaches its height with cessation of menses at menopause. However, dryness may inflict a mature woman at any life-stage in a variety of forms, always connoting an impediment of procreation and beauty and always, during her fertile years, a temporary condition open to doubt and amenable to remedy. By extension wetness is also a mere indicator, a promise of increase which may remain unrealised in the process of sowing, growing or harvesting[27]. In a household where I used to buy cow's milk, the young housewife had a history of still births. I was disap-

---

[24] "*Narkel gach taja mota, bou mota, onek chele hoy*"—a *gachi* (palm tapper) in Gameranga.

[25] "*Bhija pithar motto*"—the pastry my informant referred to is moulded in the shape of vagina.

[26] Note the consensus of female as well as male villagers regarding the beneficial effect of wife-battering. Here again, the text suggests a parallel between domestic authority secured by physical violence and sexual intercourse (i.e. dominance and biology). Another adage that specifies auspicious wetness as the rewarding effect of harsh treatment was revealed to me by a palm tapper (*gachi*) in Uttor Para, who claimed that "the more you beat it [the tree], the more juice will it give", thus rendering a botanic species he mounts at a particular season (in order to make an incision in it and so to yield its juice) as the same source of metafertility as is the female body and tilled earth in their potential of auspicious generative increase.

[27] Note however, that excessive wetness or "open body" of a woman after delivery is succeptible to harm. The body has to recover through a diet consisting of drying substances and literally to be dried; a woman after delivery achieves this dryness by positioning her body over a fire.

pointed when one day she announced that there was no milk to sell, and tried to find out why. It irritated her husband, who exclaimed in desperation, "Barren woman and this cow do not give any milk, what shall I do with these two?" (*Bhaja magi ar je goru dudh dai na tadia ki kori?*).

We can see that even unyielding pregnancy (one that results in still birth) is specified as a state of emptiness or is compared to anything that is drained. Married childless women are contemptuously called *bhaja* but in their presence the euphemism *khali* is used and their condition is likened to an empty granary (*khali maja*) or empty jar (*khali kholosh*). This parallel between the emptiness of a woman's body and food containers is, I believe, at the root of other metaphors of inauspiciousness in Gameranga. Within the household (the minimal unit of reproduction), the prosperity is secured through storage in food and water containers (*hari* and *kholosh*) which are formed rounded and curved as the body of an adult woman is supposed to be[28]. Jars containing rice are lined up in a granary while a *kholosh* is always placed in a shallow damp pit on the kitchen floor. Also this praxis is given attention in the imagery of metafertility in the poem above depicting the charms of an oilman's daughter. The parallel between the fertility potential of female body and *kholosh* is clear from sorcery practices. A young female patient who had been treated for a mental disorder (*pagol hoye geche*) in the village hospital near Gameranga, insisted that her co-wife had placed a *tabij* (amulet) with *mantra* (incantation) under the *kholosh* in her kitchen (*kheti hoyche tabij dia*) in order to instill sterility into her. She believed the magic had proved effective as the only son she had given birth to died after that, and soon she herself turned dry (*shukno*). This deprived her of her husband's sexual attention and so the possibility of conceiving. The nurses who attended her had no doubts about her exegesis and supplied further data on similar cases, each telling a tale from their homes of a woman's pregnancy or fertility being impeded by some magic action on a cow, a granary or a pitcher.

According to the evil eye paradigm (*kharap drishti*), the clues for understanding misfortune related to fertility are also taken from imaginary representations of the female body. The water pitcher should never be completely drained: its contents should be replenished when there are still some drops of residual water. Neither should jar (*hari*) containing processed rice ever be completely emptied, but refilled when there are still a few grains left. As mentioned above, mere maintenance of the assets is not sufficient in the Bengali notion of fertility. Because a housewife is the feeder of her husband, children and domestic animals, it is a part of her culinary skill and mythical power not only to avoid emptiness, but to ensure the increment (*borkot*) of resources in her custody[29]. A housewife's increase strategies include almsgiving, and fast-

---

[28] Prosperity is also signalled by a dowry a bride may bring with her to her conjugal home. Therefore, a woman entering marriage empty-handed is referred to as *khali*.

[29] "Muslims as a contrast to the austerity of daily life claim that God is able to increase the quantity of food available, by several times the normal bulk … this is a part of a widespread belief that

ing (*roja*)—practices intended not only to please God (in accordance with one of the Islamic tenets), but to yield increment (heap up wealth). What to me seemed cleerly a deprivation is based on the local premise that "subtraction yields addition", according to the Hindu notion of *dawa* (what has been given or abstained from would be got doubled, Khare 1982)[30]. Fasting (*roja*) practised in connection with Islamic feasts may be considered a strategy based on the same logic. In Gameranga, women fast more frequently and fastidiously than men.

Another opportunity for a wife to pursue multiplication of resources is her direct involvement with rice cooking. She does so by removing a fistful of rice (*mushti tuli*) from the portion she has previously rationed for cooking of a day's meal and throwing it back into the storage jar. To enhance the efficacy of the action she may invert the normal practice and use her left hand (cf. Lindenbaum 1968); in response to my wondering glance at the performance, a succinct comment was made—"*borkot hobe*" (it will bring increase)[31]. While almsgiving and fasting is claimed to be aimed at "pleasing God" (*Allahr shate bhalo hobe*), this gesture is explained pragmatically as a safeguard against contingencies, for example, "if suddenly an uninvited guest appears, what could I give him to eat?". The use of left—"dirty"—hand was probably aimed at averting the malevolent forces.

In order to be able to link the "fullness" of an ideal female body to the universality and timing of daughters' marriages and to show how women's "emptiness" affects male *ijjat*, and how the concept in itself presents an issue of existential order to a Bengali peasant, I shall briefly consider the lexical meaning of the attribute *khali*.

The adjective, which literally means empty, is used as well to designate voidness, anything "without purpose" or "false", like in expression *khali kotha*—meaningless statement, empty words or a lie. It may be recalled that, when attributed to a woman, emptiness denotes one who has been given for fecundity (the quality built into her father's *gushti's* credit) but who has failed to attain that purpose (to increase her husband's patriline). This renders her family, the givers, equal to liars. By the same line of reasoning, women in Gameranga commented on the filled, rounded breasts of foreign female visi-

---

behaviour in accordance with *dhormo* is rewarded by God showering believers with blessings, such as filling the *kholosh* with money or gold" (Murphy 1986). Many dreams re-told to me by women in Gameranga conveyed this imagery of a deity distributing boons (by filling their *kholosh* with exactly the same items as above example attests to)—evidence of a deeply rooted and widely spread cosmology.

[30] The summarized version of Mauss' (1969) theory of the gift which has it that one has to give in order to receive points to a similar logic. Recall also the previous claim with regard to creation of rank, that dispossession ensures the persistence of possession (see "Strategies of social distinction", chapter 13).

[31] *Borkot*—derived from the Arabic *baraka*—"to bless" or "to be blessed". In Urdu and Persian the word translates as "increase, abundance, prosperity, blessing, auspiciousness, inherent prosperity which produces success and abundance" (Murphy 1986).

tors[32] as *khali*, after it had been proved that no milk was forthcoming (Kota-lová 1986). A round filled breast, the promise of an adult woman's lactative capacity thus proved "forged" because unproductive. Gathering data on the nature of my womanhood, village women in whose homes I appeared as a visitor frequently attempted physical check-ups as they found the verbal comments I could supply on the way I was, astonishing. The memory of these experiences brings to my mind Fortes'(1983) claim with respect to personal–cultural identity:

"… the main point about [gender] identity is that it is not enough to experience it, it has to be shown all the time. If it is not shown, it is not real, and it must be shown in objective ways".

In Gameranga, chain pregnancies are taken for granted. A newly arrived woman whose body does not show any observable sign of fecundity such as advanced pregnancy or an attached suckling infant in her lap is habitually asked whether her child has just died or whether there is just one in her belly (*pete bacha hoy na*? or gesticulated to by pointing to the lower abdomen). To show that one is a woman should be done in an objectively visible form (Fortes 1983). The only conceivable explanation of a woman's apparent emptiness is some kind of misfortune, never a deliberate choice, because in an agricultural society like Bangladesh an adult woman and a man are assessed and differentiated as much in terms of belongingness as by her or his reproductive and productive skill. Whenever I returned to Gameranga after a few days visit to the district town women who had known me were eager to know whether I had been "together with my husband" and in that case whether there are some signs of pregnancy (*bacha hobe*).

At the end of my fieldwork, as the family planners started their campaigns and introduced an appropriate jargon into the area, some female informants who adopted the new vocabulary, tried anew and wondered whether I was *bondho*, which now is the local term applied for the deplorable act of tubectomy on a woman's body. On the contrary, the credibility of family planners themselves was put to the test when they were flooded by questions whether, if they can "close" a woman, they can also arrange for barren women to be "opened".

Emptiness—fullness: extinction–increase of *gushti*

So far I have dealt with the cosmology of metafertility in terms of the attributes attached to the various physical and metaphysical containers that are believed to possess an intrinsic quality of auspicious increase. After having

---

[32] An American graduate student of anthropology and two Swedish colleagues from my previous job in Dhaka who paid a brief visit to me in Gameranga.

considered these and the various strategies women employ in order to approximate the realities of daily life to the cultural ideal of abundance, by transforming the content of these containers, I shall turn my attention to the substance which marks a woman's maturity and which is the source of biological increase par exellence.

From a previous chapter it should be recalled that blood shared ancestrally and fraternally defines belongingness in the context of the agnatic ethos and the fiction of filial and fraternal solidarity is based on this concept of male blood. In the domestic discourse of physiology and dietics (never divorced from each other), it is claimed that semen, mother's milk, in fact all bodily substances, are all transformations of one essence—blood. In turn, the quality of the blood is determined by food. Thus, to summarize the chain of local moral-dietary logic: proper eating of proper food produces proper offspring. While in daily conversation faeces are taken as an instant evidence of the quality of food a person has digested, body vigour, sexual performance, the foetus, mother's milk, are more long-term manifestations of the particular cooking and moral skill in each household. Both male and female blood are believed to contribute to the generation of the foetus, but female blood is distinctive in that it is perceived as a source of its increase, i.e. undeniable evidence of a woman's unique ability to feed (the foetus with blood and lactate the infant). This particular feature of female sexuality—regular occurrence of bleeding at a certain life-stage—is linked with the notion of beauty and health. According to local standards female bodies are viewed as beautiful when "filled", fat, juicy, white[33] and "opened" and as inauspicious when "empty", "dry" and "closed."

Another distinctive feature of female blood is that it marks a woman's status at a given time, status over a period of time and changes of status (Fortes 1983). Although ritual attention is given neither to its appearance and disappearence at a particular life stage, nor to hymenal bleeding on wedding night it divides a woman's life into non-sexual and sexual stages; the latter being further punctuated by empty versus auspicious periods, depending on what happens with the blood.

There are three sorts of female blood related to sexuality: menarche, which signalizes maturity, hymenal blood of defloration and regular bleedings subsequent to menarche. Menarche differs from subsequent bleedings in that its occurrence can be estimated but not exactly predicted. When it appears, news may be spread announcing the daughter's marriageability but no celebration comparable to South Indian, Sri Lankese (Winslow 1980) or Orissa (Marglin 1981) culture ensues from it. A girl is not available for consummation before that. In the case of a pre-adolescent marriage, it is the pre-menarchal wife's mother-in-law's responsibility to see to it that defloration is not effected prior

---

[33] Although an important criterion of female beauty, I do not elaborate on skin colour in the context of this argument as it does not directly relate to the semantic field of auspicious increase.

to the first menstruation. Although great merit has traditionally accrued to early marriages and most of my menopausal informants had been married "in time", the practice of child marriages has nearly disappeared nowadays (to the great discontent of the old).

Then there is the hymenal blood of defloration which marks the consumption of legitimately transferred women on the wedding night (*bashor rat*). Contrary to the menarache, hymenal bleeding occurs only once in a woman's life and is subject to cultural determination in that its time and circumstances are induced and predicted by human agency (Callaway 1978). Unlike menstruation, hymenal bleeding is not elaborated or clearly marked as an independent category. Instead, defloration and its consequences are connoted by wider, overlapping concepts. For example, the link between wedding and defloration is suggested by the word *bie* which refers to the wedding ceremony, married state (*bie hoy* or *bie bosha* for women and *bie kora* for men) and also coitus of both humans and breeding animals[34]. In village parlance sexual intercourse is a statement of marriage, these two are not separated.[35] Separating these two by practising pre-marital sex or by being raped renders a woman spoiled (*noshto hoye geche*), a condition that points as much to her body and character as to the marriage plans of her guardians. Within the broader cosmological scheme it provides undeniable evidence of the spoiled chronology of biological and cultural events—a failure to synchronize the natural pace of a woman's biology with cultural demands. Infants of such untimely unions are illegitimate and therefore abandoned in the jungle. On the other hand, a time separation as a result of a groom's failure to consummate a marriage on the wedding night (i.e. delaying his moral duty) is a serious drawback which, if reported to the bride's family, is sufficient reason for divorce. Hymenal bleeding, as evidence of defloration is not particularly dramatized in Gameranga, just implicit in the term *bashor rat*—wedding night—the locus of which is a flower-decorated bed provided with an embroidered canopy. It should ideally occur and concur with the bride's transfer.

Menstruation, like anything linked to sexuality in South Asia has an ambiguous status and is an object of great concern. Writing about Sri Lanka, Winslow (1980) presents tellingly the dilemma of a mature woman as an issue of chronology:

"When a young woman menstruates the implications tend to be negative; she is not married and should be, or she is not pregnant and should be".

The nonappearance of menses after menarche is a disastrous prospect for a nubile daughter, yet a promise for a married woman that her body is auspiciously

---

[34] Villagers refer to insemination appointments for their cattle as *bie kora*.
[35] Bachelors refer to their pre-marital sexual explorations by derisive *annondo kora* (enjoyment); illicit sex is referred to as *kharap kaj* (bad work).

filled. Whatever a woman's marital status is, her menstrual blood is an auspicious sign, but polluting (*chutho*) matter[36].

Following the suggestion of Marglin (1981), we can think of the ambiguity Bengali Muslims attach to women and their reproductive biology in terms of "auspicious impurity"[37]. The first sense is conveyed in a mother's comment on her daughter's first menses: "Your son is born" (recorded by Blanchet 1984:38)[38] and a belief widespread in Bangladesh, that a woman has to get rid of the "bad [i.e.menstrual] blood" (Maloney 1981:188, 201); the second sense is expressed in a wide range of restrictions a menstruating woman is to follow to reduce the danger that emanates from her and which she attracts during the period (to insulate her mystical danger to men, fields and animals). Insulation of menstruating women is authorized by Islamic as well as Vedic textual sources; my informants were well aware that a menstruating woman is not supposed to cook or serve food to her husband, to be approached sexually, and that menses invalidates fasting as well as prayer. The Holy Book should be out of the reach of women in that condition[39].

While women in most households could not follow the injunction with respect to cooking ("who will do it?"), the rest of the rules were strictly followed[40]. I myself have been told not to go out during my period, "people will speak badly of you," as I could pay a servant to arrange the practical neccessities on these few days each month. Whatever the practical possibilities, a wife always tries to provide a deputy to cook and cater for her husband, and the menses are always surrounded by secrecy.

Some observers of Bangladesh culture claim that menstrual bleeding is perceived as an anti-thesis of fecundity, which is based on the local perception that "no conception can happen as pressure of menstrual blood prevents semen from entering the uterus" (Maloney 1981:188). We may recall the previous reference to Indian ethnography, that land should not be cut when it menstruates because this condition renders the field infertile. This would affirm the pervasively negative attitude villagers hold towards any pursuit directed at anything that does not yield an increase. Scholars dealing with the problem in Hindu communities validate similar assertion that the menses are ontologi-

---

[36] In a physical sense, a menstruating woman is "unclean" (*oporishkar*). It is the word used by a doctor questioning the patient before attempting to carry out a gynaecological check. In a metaphysical sense, menses renders women *chutho*, i.e. contagious, dangerous to men in particular.

[37] For attention given to the same congruence between impurity–auspiciousness see Das (1976) and Khare (1976b:184).

[38] Note here again, how verbal and physical treatment of the young female body is persistently oriented towards the prospect of marriage (Cf. chapter 8).

[39] When a villager sold me a copy of Al Hadith he had volunteered to buy for me in a Dhaka bookshop, he asked emphatically, "And please do not touch the book during your periods" at the same time as he overcharged me for the copy. It seems he could dispense with the Islamic injunction proscribing usury but not with one which proscribes use by a menstruating woman.

[40] As a consequence of that I had to manage without tubewell water during the three days each month when my female helper had her menses, as the only tubewell was situated on *madrasa*'s precincts.

cally connected with death (Reynolds 1983, Bennett 1983:215–216) with reference to a Hindu myth of Brahmanicide[41].

The difficulty with this interpretation is that, in Gameranga, women are considered polluted in various degrees on occasions which are the signs and the acts of fecundity par excellence—menses, sexual intercouse[42], and 40 days following childbirth. This means that the most auspicious event for the *gushti*, that "a son has been born" renders his mother untouchable. I will not be able to resolve this complex problem here, but instead of adopting the tempting, but facile equation—menses equals death, I wish to place it within a wider cosmological spectrum.

If plumpness is not a prominent feature of female physiology among women in Gameranga[43], so neither is menstruation a common condition among those who have a husband. Many an older informant, (those who had been married in due time), attested boastfully that they had not experienced menstruation as a way of saying that their timely marriage was followed by a chain of pregnancies. "Just a couple of times before it definitely disappeared" said a mother of three sons, whose other siblings, altogether twenty, died as infants. She was exceptionally productive and unfortunate; however, as demographic studies of Bangladesh show, the completed fertililty average per woman is around seven pregnancies (Maloney 1981:186). This, added to a prolonged post-natal lactation[44], makes even today a woman who had not been (like her mother or grandmother) married as a child, experience menses only occasionally and some time before menopause. No matter what the exact frequency is, all women in Gameranga held the view that repeated pregnancies alternated with two—three years of lactation, rendered them auspiciously filled, fullbodied, complete adult humans. In Bangladesh a person's social position is always expressed in terms of collective belonging—to a *jat*, *dhormo* or family. But personhood cannot be legitimized unless "put into social space", either in the form of labour, skill or of the products of the body (Fortes 1983). For the majority of housewives, who fail to attain the auspicious condi-

[41] "... a condition that results because women, rivers, and trees graciously assumed part of India's sin of killing the half-Brahman Vrtra who held back the waters necessary for life" (Reynolds 1983). Given the host of explanations and practices my Muslim informants based on the cosmologies of "foreign" origin, it is plausible that even the message of this myth may linger in the equation they make between menstruation and negation of life.

[42] The sexual act itself requires a thorough ablution (*phoroj goshol*) for both partners. Although pregnancy itself is not polluting, it is seen as a shameful condition. To my inquiries as to the expected date of delivery, the pregnant woman would cover her head with *achol* and another who overheard my question could comment "She has just eaten too much rice today" or "How could she be pregnant, her husband is too old by now?".

[43] Most of my informants were chronically undernourished.

[44] The actual average birth interval in Bangladesh is estimated to 34 months (Maloney 1981:186 referring to Chen et.al 1974). Throughout much of this interval most women do not ovulate (ibid. 183, 247). Lactational amenorrhea was found in different studies to range from 17 to 20 months. Another factor contributing to the absence of ovulation may be poor nutrition which is widespread particularly among women (ibid. 133).

tion in household management (abundance in the granaries), the fiction of embodying Lokhi can be maintained and objectively manifested by the virtue of their biological potential for increase.

Unlike menarche, subsequent bleedings are predictable, markers of the periodicity of an "incomplete" woman's life. They are subject to the control of human agency—if transformed into filling substances a wife's life is instead marked by auspicious alternations between pregnancies and breastfeedings. In Gameranga a woman's behaviour is always judged in relation to this menstrual periodicity: menarche or menopause. Widows for example are categorized according to whether they still menstruate or not.

Reprise

From previous evidence it is apparent that the ideal of metafertility is vouched for by the whole symbolic system. Like elsewhere in Bengal (Greenough 1983) villagers in Gameranga do not speak of their worries and contentments with crops, cows, children, granaries in terms of metafertility or scarcity. Instead they speak of Olokhi or emptiness and see to it that humans, animals and objects that embody the capacity of auspicious increase be continuously filled.

A woman's capacity to increase is signalled biologically by menarche; her womb and breast are conceived as containers, henceforth to be filled with substances generated out of uterine blood; each menstrual bleeding following the first announcement of maturity, is the most conspicuous sign of a woman's body being emptied, an evidence that she failed to come to fruition. Because her being opened and filled can only be effected by a legitimately acquired man, a daughter after the initial signal has to be given away. Only marriage holds the promise of a mature woman's body being filled. In terms of *gushti*'s *ijjat*, keeping menstruating daughters at home is facing the risk that pre-marital sexuality can result in socially demonstrable evidence. In terms of *dhormo* a father, who fails to marry off his daughter as soon as she is due to be filled, witholds from her the disposition to reproduce, to bring all her inherent potential into the fullness of realisation. Framed in a wider cosmological context, such a father fails to synchronize his daughter's biology with the transfer to an affinal household and thus obstructs the proper coming together of biolgy, time and space, in the natural and appropriate pace of human reproduction. Emptiness, of what should be filled within the cosmological order of metafertility has an intrinsic quality of falseness. Emptiness of vessels like "empty women" (unexchanged or barren or sterilized) are Olokhi and therefore feared and avoided, because in the end emptiness, physical or metaphysical, means cessation of becoming as well as of being (Khare 1976:118).

It seems that ideas of emptiness, unproductivity and inauspiciousness have equated to supply one major rationale for the unavoidability and strict timing of a daughter's marriage. In contrast, ideas of fullness, fertility and auspiciousness meet in the ideal image of woman and the ideal pace (i.e. proper chronology) of human reproduction. Within the conceptual framework of female beauty and biology, menarche echoes birth and because all the biologically inevitable stages of the reproduction—defloration and conception—are of the same symbolic order, menarche, wedding, conception and birth should ideally concur. To combine them into one also means to minimize the risk of a daughter's body becoming spoiled. This fiction is performed at wedding ceremonies, where ritual images of sexual intercourse and birth are enacted as conflated events. *Holud gae*, sprinkling with mud and water, activating of *dekhi*, compulsory invitation of children, replacement of an old *kholosh* in the bride's home by a new one, filled with rice—are the key sequences alluding to the ideal chronology of a woman's career.

Thereafter, to maximize the purity and presence of Lokhi an adult female body should never be emptied. The womb and the breast of a wife ought to be filled alternately with bodily substances promising and showing off what she is, because as Fortes (1983) observed of another people, in Gameranga also "a woman is a woman only if she actually produces children, or at least, shows that she is capable of this; and this is not only a social or cultural definition but a very personal assumption. A woman cannot feel or know, let alone show herself to be a woman, if she lacks these signs". Impeding or delaying a daughter from realizing her physical–cum–moral completeness, is to affront *dhormo* and one's *ijjat*.

CHAPTER 18

Wifehood ritualized:
wedding and incorporation of bride

Problems of interpretation

In the following chapter I shall discuss the symbolism and the rites surrounding the final phase of a marriage exchange. Before that, I wish to consider the methodological dilemma ensuing from to the tension between text and experience.

A marriage in Bangladesh reproduces social structure on many different levels. As a result its ritual version—the wedding (*bie*), instead of comprising a single event, extends into a series of ritual performances. This multiplicity leads to the methodological problem of seeing a wedding as a coherent event.

During my more than four-years' stay in Bangladesh I participated as a guest in Muslim, Hindu and Christian weddings in Dhaka and other districts, but as a wedding can extend over a period of three years, and as even in weddings completed in four days fragments of rituals may go on simultaneously in the bride's and groom's house, I was never able to witness a single wedding in its totality. Apart from this lack of omnipresent vision, it was also difficult to associate the stereotypic, shorthand statements provided by informants with the actual performances. In Gameranga vernacular, the marriage ceremony is presented as encapsulated in discrete performances, each being a fixed, bounded unit with beginning and end: *holud gae*, *goru katbe*, *khawae dawa*, etc. However, informants were ill at ease when pressed for consistent chronology or to account for the way performances are linked to each other. In addition, what was in local vernacular presented as a lavish, spectacular feast was often in practice reduced to absolutely essential gestures. Linked to this is the question of how the wedding discourse conforms with the actual performance.

Dealing with *bie*, I shall focus on the final phase of the marital project that spans the bride's departure from the familiar world of her father's home and landing among "others" (*tule ana*, *mukh dekha*, *bou bhat* and *bashor rat*). I have chosen these particular rites for exegesis for several reasons. First, because they are so vital in marriage discourse and because the repetitions (in previous stages) of various themes cumulate here into an agnatic definition of married womanhood. Second, because the theme that stands out as central here is the transformation of outside women into "goddess-like bringers of household prosperity and continuity" (Moore 1986:269). The complementary strategies that operate in the daily management of otherness, the control that outsideness requires as well as that portion of laxness that is inveitable for generating an auspicious increase, are ritually enacted in this final phase of the wedding.

In spite of the fragmentary nature of observation, the incongruities between narrative and actual event and the ways each event is recorded in field-notes (cf. Leach 1982:199), and in spite of shifts in emphasis of particular details in each wedding, there are components that re-appear in every wedding both in informants' accounts and in other ethnographic sources. From the repetitive character of certain themes thus emerges a pattern similar to the pattern of messages on which I myself was able to predict and act while living in Game- ranga. Indeterminate, shadowy and provisional as this pattern may seem, it may well be that its blurred contours and openendedness constitute the very core of the Bengali Muslim construction of reality.

In addition, the meaning of some of the narrative and scenic fragments— "things" and acts—become apparent when they appear in other contexts, rit- ual or quotidian (though they do not necessarily communicate identical mes- sages). Finally, there exists a continuity in South Asian wedding scenes re- corded in written ethnographic records as well as accounts by colleague an- thropologists. Thus, in accordance with Leach's instructive notes on the di- lemmas intrinsic to the interpretation of a Sinhalese wedding, I shall extract these repetitions and try to put them together into units, which seem to form a meaningful chain of symbolism but which at the same time "may turn up in quite different ritual (and practical) contexts" (Leach 1982:199) and therefore gain a different meaning (Winslow 1980).

In doing so, I shall present the events by reference to their larger cultural contexts as well as to the anthropological theory of initiation. This means that in the course of description I shall separate symbolic objects (sari), acts (cook- ing) and phenomena (darkness) which in the course of ritual are tightly inter- woven and constitute the semantic field of *bie* (Kapferer 1984). I shall also elaborate on the paradoxes intrinsic to the performative genre adopted in the *mukh dekha* stage of the *bie* ceremony. I take these paradoxes as instrumental in clarifying the meaning in situation in which a bride finds herself at the verge of wifehood, i.e. a position between two worlds.

In order to facilitate orientation to the sequential sructure of the whole *bie*, I present here a summary, drawn from two accounts of middle class semi-urban Muslim weddings[1].

---

[1] There is a great variety in *bie* performances, with respect to region, status, family ambition, birth-order of the person to be married and obviously with respect to the male/female perspective. The summary version I present is far richer than those I observed in Gameranga, but poorer than the one recorded among Deccan Muslims at the beginning of the last century (Shurreef 1973) or among North Indian Muslims at about the same period (Ali 1978:252).

1. *Bou dekha*—("Viewing of the bride") Ceremonial viewing of a girl for marriage is described in chapter 15. Usually several *bou dekha* takes place before a girl is chosen for marriage. If the outcome of the viewing is positive, the parents of the prospective spouses enter into marriage negotiations.

2. *Pan chini*—("Betel and sugar, sweets"). The boys' parents go to see the parents of the girl, chosen on *bou dekha*. The conditions of *kabin* are negotiated, a date for the wedding and number of the guests is fixed. To re-affirm their interest, if there is a need to delay *bie*, the parties may exchange a ring or other smaller gifts as a sign of a serious commitment.

3. *Holud gae*—("Application of turmeric"). The day before the wedding feast in the bride's home, the bodies of the groom and bride are smeared with a mixture of smashed raw turmeric with water (or mustard oil) in their respective homes. It remains on the body until the next day when the groom and the bride are ritually bathed before puting on their wedding clothes. A barber is called to shave and cut the hair of the groom.

Turmeric occupies a prominent place in Bengali dietary, medical and cleansing traditions (Inden, Nicholas 1977:41, Ellickson 1972:116, Fruzzetti 1975:249). Its root is smashed and mixed with water before being used as a condiment and yellow dye in food preparation. It may also be smeared on the body to cure skin infections, and young women occasionally rub turmeric on their bodies before their midday bath to cool themselves and to remove pollution accumulated during the day. In India turmeric is universally and unanimously associated with auspiciousness. Its use in sacrificial rituals among Hindus or in the anointing of humans, animals, idols or clothes before being given as gifts is designed to effect beneficial changes (Beck 1969). Its sacredness is upheld by the semi-liquid state in which it is preserved and applied. Writing about the ritual use of anointment liquids in Indian rituals, Eichinger Ferro-Luzzi (1981) draws attention to the physical attributes of humidity and its effect on everyday experience "... (humidity) carried smells, sounds to a greater distance, enlivens colours and makes engravings on flat surfaces more easily distinguishable ... and thus reveals additional hidden features". These properties make it possible to classify turmeric paste as one of those substances that cause divine powers "hidden in the idol(s)" to emanate. Although idols are not admitted in official Islam, the apparel and manner of travelling of the bridal couple suggest royal identification. The chromatic aspect of the turmeric, its yellowness, is picked up in the border of the bride's wedding sari and golden jewellery. Thus in the notion of *holud* in the context of *bie* is contained the synonymity of the turmeric, gold, sari (its blood-like redness bounded by yellow border), exposure of the skin to prolonged moisture of turmeric paste with auspicious increase, biological as well as alimental. Urban Muslims may substitute turmeric with henna (*mehendi*). Smearing, massaging and sprinkling of the body with various liquid and semi-liquid substances like oil, milk, mud or smashed leaves of various plants is a widespread practice in rural Bangladesh. In daily body care it is attributed with a soothing effect because of the cooling and purificatory properties of the substances. In the ritual context of *holud gae*, smearing of the body and splashing it with water is designed to produce the optimal condition of metafertility, particularly in view of the coming *bashor rat*.

4. *Borjatra*—("groom's journey") is the procession that follows the groom to the home of the bride, where the major feast (*goru khawai*) takes place. *Borjatra* is the core ceremony without which a *bie* confers little status. It requires

the invitation of *shomaj matubors*. The groom's party—relatives and friends—which constitutes the procession is equipped with a trunk containing the wedding gifts to the bride—saris, jewellery, cosmetics, hair-care paraphernalia and a mirror, all of which are viewed as indispensible to present and render a bride as Lokhi. The groom, dressed in white costume, wears a crown and a golden ring and he travells so his feet do not touch the ground—in a rickshaw or *nouka* from which his friends carry him to the entrance of the bride's home. During the journey, the groom keeps silent and covers his mouth with a handkerchief. The gateway, specially constructed of banana trunks for the occasion, is decorated with flowers and red/white ribbons. The groom's party has to buy free passage through the entrance which is blocked with a red ribbon. After the amount of *gater taka* is negotiated, the ribbon is cut and the groom is offered a spoon of sugar. Once the groom's people reach the yard, male and female guests separate—women gather around the bride hidden in a house and men around the groom outside. The bride is sitting modestly, with her head bent towards the ground, eyes closed, under a canopy, still in her ordinary sari (or *salwar kamiz*). An older relative holds up her face to the view of the spectactors. All the guests are served *mishti* before all are invited to the backyard to have a meal in which meat (beef, frequently substituted by goatmeat or chicken) is an indispensable item. Meanwhile, the content of the trunk brought by the groom's party is laid out for scrutiny by the bride's relatives who usually drop depreciatory comments. Afterwards, the bride is meticulously dressed and made up by the groom's sister (*bhabi*) and her own friends and sisters. This is the opportunity for singing wedding songs. After the guests who are not closely related to the families leave, the two witness of the wedding (*ukil*) representing the bride and groom respectively, enter the bride's quarter to solicit the bride's agreement to the marriage. They approach her through a curtain asking "XY, the son of ... agreed to *muharana* amount of taka ..., do you consent to this marriage?" After the bride repeats her consent three times, the witnesses announce it publically to all guests present and the *moulana* reads the prayer (*kolema*)—*bie porano*. After that, *kabin* is signed by each party. These two acts are the minimal requirements to legitimize the sexual union—they constitute the essence of *nika*. Afterwards the groom ceremonially greets (*salaam*) his parents-in-law and is prepared to face the bride. There is variation in when and how exactly the bride and the groom first meet. According to some informants, their glances are first exchanged in the mirror, after the prayer; others claim this happens during *tule ana* inside the carriage (*palki*, rickshaw or *nouka*). In no case do they face each other directly. One way of exchanging the first glance is by way of reflection in a mirror which is placed in front of them. The groom's sister may ask her brother "What have you seen in the mirror?", to which he answers "The half-moon". Sweet rice porridge (*paesh*) is then served to the couple, which they eat from one plate.

5. *Tule ana* or *Palki uthie dia* ("Lifting of palanquin"). On the following day

or after a couple of days, the *bou* is transferred to the house of the *jamai*, usually accompanied by a related widow or her brother. The details of the journey and the events during the course of the ceremonial reception of the bride that culminates in defloration —*bashor rat*—are the main concern of this chapter.

6. *Bou bhat* ("Bride's rice").
The bride's family comes to the groom's home and together with the in-laws eats *bou bhat* (rice cooked by the bride). The bride returns afterwards to her father's home for two-and-a-half days (*bou firano*) before she returns for permanent settlement in her *shashur bari* (in-laws).

Initiation into female adulthood—spatial, social, bodily and moral transformation

As mentioned, *bie* is not a single rite, but a number of ceremonies spread over a period of time. Each of these comprises ritual acts that address various themes and emphasise different aspects of the transformation in social status: affinity, control of outsiders, the married state, wifehood, female beauty and health, fertility, female space, domestic prosperity, cultural didactics.

Before going into details of the ceremony I should mention that the aspect of social structure that runs through the whole of *bie*—establishment of affinity—but receives different treatment in various stages, is here specifically concerned with one person—the bride. The transformation of a girl into a woman, a virgin into a wife, is here presented in terms of the bride's relation to the household's authority, space, body and food.

It has been suggested that wives in patrilineal households are welcome but feared (Jacobson-Widding 1984). This dilemma inheres in the patrilineal ethos and residence pattern according to which the group's prosperity and survival depend on the food-processing skills and the fertility of strangers—"the daughters of others" (*porer meyera*). In a culture lacking preferential or prescriptive marriage rules, locality and spatial propinquity[2] become critical factors in marriage choices. The insistence on outsideness, (conceived in spatial terms), is apparent from the zig-zag form of "travelling" employed in the bride's transfer in cases when the spouses' natal homes are too close. Unlike the *shoja* manner of walking (pursuing as direct and short a path as possible) in case of long-distance marriages and non-ritual situations, the procession of cousin spouses takes a circuitous route so as to create the desired distance ritually. At weddings, the metaphor of a woman's distance—outsideness—is thus activated and given literal value (Jackson 1983b). Space and time to be traversed become the symbolic precursor of a real and permanent existential problem of a woman's married life (Turner 1982:25).

[2] See "Spatial distance between affinal *gushti*s and provenance of wife", chapter 15.

Events

A married woman's passage between her father's and her husband's home constitutes a metaphor of affinity and adult womanhood. It presents, apart from a concrete logistic problem to her guardians, a problem for her of socio-psychological adjustment. This becomes of central concern in her experience of *bie*, and of married life.

To cope with the attachment of new wives in everyday life, each household in Gameranga deals with its own specific forms of control[3]. The standard controls and anxieties with regard to the new wife's incorporation into the collectivity of the patrilineal group are enacted in a welcoming ceremony which follows the bride's arrival.

This consists of the following performances:
- respectful greeting by the bride to her mother-in-law
- changing of the sari
- welcoming drink offered to the bride
- bride's ritual seclusion.

The sexual union with her husband and her cooking of rice (*bou bhat*) for the members of his household constitute the concluding events.

The first act of the rite is preceded by a territorial passage from the bride's parental home; the final act, *bou bhat*, is followed by her return to father's home (*bou firano*) "to think it over" after which the marital project is considered finalized and a woman who has passed through these rites is considered as properly married (*bie bosha* or *bie hoy*).

The ceremonial reception (including seclusion) lasts about two and a half days during which the bride, concealed behind veils, is the focus of attention. The transformation occurs through a series of rites performed with and on her body[4]. On this occasion the corporal acts are aimed at reducing the uncertainties ensuing from confrontation with an outsider and the dangers which emanate from the liminal situation itself, i.e. the dangers from and to the bride. It is believed in Gameranga that anything in the process of preparation, becoming, transition into a more complete cultural or moral state, may it be grains, foods, infants, virgins, may turn out badly and is therefore in need of protection from malevolent forces.

Precautionary measures are relaxed after a couple of days, as the bride is introduced to the cooking sphere to display her culinary skill (*bou bhat*).

Either withdrawn or on show, the bride is the center of ritual attention. The reason is two-fold: first, the groom continues to live where he has been born and circumcised; his familiarity with the surroundings where he will spend his marital life does not require the same elaborate transformation as in the case

[3] These vary, depending upon the developmental cycle of the family, the personal idiosyncracies of its members (particularly the mother-in-law), the amount of wealth the bride brings with her to the conjugal household, and distance from her natal family.
[4] Cf. chapter 8.

of his wife. Second is the differential ritual attention paid to a boy's and girl's personal life-cycle. In the absence of ritual concern with menarche among Bengali Muslims, and in view of the ideal timing according to which menarche and betrothal "coincide", a daughter's *bie* subsumes both succession to adulthood as well as to wifehood. Because families in Gameranga do not organize a woman's maturation into separate puberty and nuptial rites (consistent with the fact that menarche, *bie* and birth are conceptualized as one event), a *bie* conflates transition from juniority to seniority with socio-sexual conjunction; the undue lapse of time that most families today experience, is perceived as *dhorm*ic failure[5]. It is also for this reason that without a *bie* a daughter can never become a complete woman, in contrast to the son whose manhood has been marked and celebrated by circumcision at an early age.

Structurally and stylistically *bie* shares attributes with rites of passage as outlined by van Gennep and explicated by Turner (1969, 1982). The whole ritual contains the familiar stages of separation, transition (liminality) and integration, thus replicating the same themes from preceding stages of the wedding ceremony over and over again. Turner (1982:44) focused much of his analysis on the period of transition. He saw liminality as anti-structure—a reversal of daily reality, and subsequently as a ritual analogue of the subjunctive mood, used in classical languages to express supposition, desire, hypotheses, possibility, when "For a while almost anything goes: taboos are lifted, fantasies are enacted" (Turner 1984)[6].

In Bengali *bie* the bride passes through at least two phases which bear a certain resemblance to liminality. During her cosmological journey (*tule ana*) and seclusion after landing of the palanquin the bride occupies "privileged space where people are allowed to think about how they think, about the terms in which they conduct their thinking, or to feel about how they feel in daily life". As Turner (ibid.) points out "Here the rules are themselves the referent of the knowing; the knowledge propositions themselves are the object of knowledge". Liminality is thus achieved in the sense of spatial and temporary seclusion from the ordinary, a condition that makes an optimal occasion for reflexivity[7]. However, apart from this epistemological, metacommunicative sense, the bride's posture and behaviour in no sense suggest reversal or confu-

---

[5] This contrasts with the life-cycle of their brothers whose initiation into manhood—the circumcision ceremony (*musulmani*) precedes their *bie* by many years. It also differs from the life-cycle of women among those religious groups in South Asia who celebrate menarche (see Winslow 1980). Physical maturity among Hindus, Christians and Buddhists in Sri Lanka is not so unambiguously equated with married status, though structurally and stylistically the rites of first menstruation studied by Winslow (ibid.) share some common features with wedding rites.

[6] Both attributes, anti-structure and subjunctivity, are used as generic indices denoting a wide variety of performative genres of culture (Turner 1984).

[7] Recall the opportunity implied in a wife's journeying between husband's and father's residence discussed in chapter 12.

sion of roles or irregularities of any sort. Neither does *bie* provide space for acting out individual, idiosyncratic features of the initiant's personality[8]. Rather than suspension or challenge to the daily structures, the liminal period appears as an unequivocal, exaggerated abstraction of an idealised image of social reality. What is merging, fuzzy and complementary in ordinary life is presented as bounded, distinct and juxtaposed in *bie*. Contrary to the intermediate timing of the liminal phase identified by Turner, in Bengali *bie* a sort of reversal of the ordinary is attained during the final incorporation phase of "bride's rice", but it lacks the other indices of liminality. In one sense, Kolenda's (1984) characterization of Hindu weddings as "... 'hyperstructural', presenting a sharpened, highlighted social structure in which each actor carries out highly stereotypic acts dictated by a rigid scenario ...", applies equally to *bie* in Gameranga. Moreover, the bride's reception entails elements by which Goffman (1975:24–25) characterizes the admission procedure employed by total institutions[9], such as "stripping", "dispossession", "barrier setting between the inmate and the wider world", all marking the first curtailment of self. Yet it is important to keep in mind that the structure omnipresent as it may appear, is in no sense as totalizing as to remain unchallenged; there are features in its presentation which tend to produce paradoxes about its own powers (Gorfain 1986).

In the domestic context of rural Bangladesh and in terms of personhood, the rite addresses first of all the elevation of a Bengali Muslim woman into the status of adulthood. It is enacted as a public display of the domesticated virgin, seated first in a milieu, attire and bodily posture which corresponds to the public stereotypic image of an ideal wife. The bride has to prove that she is capable of self-control, separation and submission. Her affines on the other hand demonstrate their acceptance of the new bride. The control which is externally exerted at the onset of the rite is internaized as self-control on its consummation.

Cosmological journey (tule ana) *and landing*

A bride's physical separation from the father's home is the climax of the wedding, as well as the most radical shift in her life career. It is refered to as *tule*

---

[8] Those features that may be thought of as providing a link between social role and personal experience, are elements of style embedded in the scenic frame (silence and sartorial equipment) and therefore difficult to describe in the same terms as are the messages that define the situation structurally (Karp 1987). Cf. the metacommunicative aspect of *bichar* discussed in chapter 9.

[9] From the bride's point of view, her affinal family shares some but not all the characteristics of the total institutions explored by Goffman (1975). The most important of these are their encompassing character symbolized by the "barrier to social intercourse with the outside", often inbuilt in the physical plan, surveillance under the same single authority, physical punishment to enforce discipline and co-operation (Goffman 1975). Another is the restriction on the bride from voicing her need for autonomously managing bodily elimination. This less because of the lack of appropriate edifice or because of the bride's lack of orientation in the new locale, but rather because it is an act of self-assertion, a sign that some autonomy still remains, that she has some freedom.

ana which literally means "bringing by lifting (or rising)", an expression that points both to the mode of transportation as well as to the moral up-lift of the person so treated. The same expression also indicates the groom's ability to bring home his betrothed. It is used as a synonym for a properly concluded marriage and the very operation marks the final removal of the bride from her land, people and and the security of the familiar past.

After bidding farewell to her mother and friends, the bride is lifted, installed in the palanquin and carried away towards her new home. She is draped in one of her best saris, provided by her father[10]. The invisibility of the travelling bride is further secured by the walls of the palanquin, which is a wooden cage (a miniature replica of a house), and by the curtains drawn over its small windows. The physical transfer of the bride from her father's home (*babar bari*) is thus embellished with symbolic devices which distinguish it from an ordinary trip. The palanquin, like other seclusion devices for women—a house, a rickshaw, sun glasses, or a sari—allows observation from within, without revealing the whole face and/or the body of the occupant. The bride is mute and so is the groom, who sits besides her, or if the palanquin is too small, or its bearers too feeble, walks alongside. The groom's silence is sealed with a handkerchief which he presses to his mouth.

The manner of transportation—being carried "above Earth", seclusion and imposed silence—are as much the attributes of "sacred liminality" (Turner 1969:89) as of an "out of time" experience which in Turner's terms constitutes "a time beyond the time which measures secular processes and routines" (Turner 1982:24). At the outset of this cosmological journey the bride (with the groom) is extracted from her profane existence (time and space) by being lifted above and isolated from what surrounds her. "Held between heaven and earth" (van Gennep 1977:186) and carried between the two homes to descend to the ground of her husband when the trip is accomplished, she assumes sacred status. When the party is noticed on reaching the groom's *para*, it is announced by the children screaming "new wife, new wife!" which specifies the status category she is going to assume during the integration period of her new career. In this sense, bodily elevation correlates with social and moral elevation into wifehood.

Greeting—salaam

After landing the bride disembarks from the palanquin, and is led forward to greet her mother-in-law (*shashuri*). She bows deeply to touch the mother-in-law's feet with her right hand and then, with the same hand, touches her own forehead, thus stating—the lowest part of your body is equal to the highest and therefore pre-eminent part of my body[11]. The *shashuri* responds by touch-

---

[10] This was the case in the rite I directly observed. If *tule ana* follows soon after *bie porano*, the bride is clad in the sari which the groom supplied on the previous ceremony.

[11] In India, this ceremonial greeting at weddings is called *parcaran*—touching of feet (Lewis 1958:185). Among Bengali Hindus the same respectful greeting is rendered as *pronam*.

ing the bride's head with her right hand, acknowledging the statement and releasing the bride from the posture of extreme subjugation.

As Firth (1975:299) points out, forms of greeting are symbolic devices of
incorporation and continuance of persons in a social scheme. In Bangladesh,
many of these forms are non-verbal actions involving a gesture or body posture as substitutes for speech. This form of greeting—lowering one's head to
the point of the receptor's feet[12]—exploits the body parts as metaphors of the
differential rank of greeted and greeter. In non-marital contexts it is employed
by adult daughters and sons to greet their parents before and after a significant
separation, by ordinary believers to welcome pilgrims after their arrival from
Mecca, or by a pubescent girl on receipt of her first sari. This bodily posture is
also assumed as a sign of apology when a low status person inadvertently hits
a person of higher rank with feet or umbrella. Also a petty thief, if of lower
status than the owner, is first physically punished and thereafter expected to
ask forgiveness of the owner by touching his feet. The person who makes the
initial move is always of lower status than the person greeted. For example
once during my fieldwork I refused to eat dinner and an old man was dispatched to see what was wrong with me. When he found me in tears, the old
female cook of the family where I was a guest immediately assumed responsibility for my discomfort and came to express her apologies for "the bad food
she was serving" by touching my feet in the same way as the bride greets her
mother-in-law, a son his father etc.

In the case of the bride the greeting removes some of the uncertainty and
threat from the encounter between two strangers (Firth 1975:324) and more,
between the future rivals for the affection of a man who is the son of one and
the husband to the other. It creates the link and framework for future communication between persons of the same sex who belong to two generations—an
old and a new wife and the "diachronic synthesis of the opposing affinal and
consaguineal categories of female kin" (Bennett 1983:254) in a single household. The vertical body movement downwards and the amount of physical energy expended by the bride not only conveys her status position, but specifies
the amount of respect she owes to the most powerful woman in her new
home—her husband's mother. Sinking her head to the ground she incorporates depreciation of the self to the level of the other woman's feet, thus acknowledging the lowly status she is assuming as a new wife even among the
low-status group of women.

Encompassment—change of sari

After the greeting the bride is taken off-stage to a mat laid on the ground for
her. There she changes the sari (*kapor*) she is wearing for the one given to her

---

[12] Normally, feet are associated primarily with contempt, rejection and pollution in Bangladesh.

as a wedding gift by the groom's father[13] at the solemnization of marriage. The new sari is distinguished from the original (and ordinary) one by a large embroidered border which marks the loose end of the garment—the *achol*. Of the few personal possessions a Bengali woman has, the sari has a special relation to the self. It is considered and used as an extension of a woman's body whereby she "exerts some control over the guise in which [she] apears before others" (Goffman 1975:28). Because the social identity of the giver (kin or affinally related male) is of crucial importance, one can say that this piece of clothing is also an extension of her social persona (Sharma 1978). Though pubescent girls increasingly try to wear a sister's or mother's sari (desired elevation into bridehood, i.e. adulthood), the garment is chiefly associated with weddings and therefore with the married state and adult womanhood. Sari is a key symbol of mature womanhood. It is always purchased by a male guardian, be it a brother, father or husband, never by a woman herself. Women all around Bangladesh would open the initial encounter with me by asking "Who has bought your sari?" which is a round-about way of soliciting information about the marital credentials of its wearer. A sari always presumes a provider whose social identity (father, brother, husband or a son) and economic status (conveyed by the sari's quality) discloses the nature of a woman's belongingness. To admit to purchasing one's own sari suggests the absence of any guardian, an independent, self-providing woman, one who has escaped the authority of parents, husband or husband's parents or a widow neglected by her son; each of these conditions is close to being a prostitute.

However, the girl's first sari (required by physical maturity when it does not coincide with *bie*) is always given to her by her mother or, in the case of a young female servant, by her employer's wife. The first sari is the only gift formally and ceremonially acknowledged[14] by touching the feet in gratitude in the gesture described above.

Because of the male monopoly on sari purchase and provision we can see the bride's change of saris on entering the husband's home as a transfer of guardianship. In his study of the costumes of India, Dar (1969:157) points out that the concept of modesty as well is transferred from the woman to the garment and notes that "at one time they would not permit the garments worn by their women to fall into the hands of strange men, and to this end did not have them laundered but had them burnt or washed at home". It is clear that for male members of a household the conceptualization of sari as an extension of the female body has not only economic consequences; the replacement of an "old" sari for one the bride receives from her husband brings into focus a *gushti*'s symbolic capital, that portion of *ijjat* that lingers in a mature woman's body.

---

[13] Sometimes, because of a long interval between the marriage contract and *tule ana* (i.e. the ceremony of incorporation I am describing here), it is deemed necessary for the first sari received from the groom on *bie porano* to be replaced. This not only because it is worn out but because symbolically the bride's encompassment has to be re-affirmed.

[14] Normally, in Bangladesh a gift is given and accepted in a matter of fact manner and disparaging remarks are made as to its value, quality and quantity.

The way a sari is worn and the technique of draping it on one's body—spiral encompassment in an upward direction—suggests a further metaphor, that of the total encompassment of the self by the donor and his control over the recipient, the groom's family over the bride. The manipulative potential of a sari's loose end permits for some self-expression, but is mainly used for covering the wearer's head. This habit invokes another theme which runs through a married woman's life and which the integration rite emphasises—that of anonymity.

The theme of control through encompassment, boundedness, is reiterated in a number of other articles and signs which form the stylistic ensemble of a bride's outfit. Thus a bride's hair is firmly tied into a bun, her neck, ears and forearms are "constrained" (Das 1976) by necklace, rings and bangles, all of which emphasise and encircle the peripheries of her body. The edges of the blouse's short sleeves cut firmly into her arms. Her sari, which figures prominently in this, is tucked into the waistband of her slip, tied firmly round her waist, and the rest encircles the body upwards. Its loose upper end is edged with a border which is particularly emphasised on wedding saris and richly embroidered with golden thread.

One dimension of meaning of the border becomes apparent if it is considered in relation to the whole piece of the cloth and compared with the occasions on which the sari border is de-emphasised. First: that end of the sari which is tucked into the tightly strung waist-string is hidden under the cloth's outer layers and has no border at all; the other end—*achol*—which remains visible and operational is always finished with a more or less conspicuous line. This contrast between interior and exterior aspect of objects, is reinforced linguistically: the loose end is distinguished by a name, *achol*, while the invisible, hidden end lacks any denomination. Second: the marking of the border is discrete, if not invisible, on saris used daily for activities within the fenced in-area of the household; the white saris worn by elder widows also lack any prominent border.

The full meaning of *achol* is disclosed when we consider its (daily as well as ritual) use. *Achol* serves many practical mundane purposes, such as wiping one's own or a child's face, nose, ears, tying-up coins, keys, hiding stolen objects, "beating" children. More important is its symbolic use as a tool of communication—"the management of personal front" (Goffman 1975:29). *Achol* can be positioned in many different ways thus allowing women to convey their mood, enhance their grace, conceal their face, cover the head or just the mouth, depending on the degree of embarrassment or perceived danger. It can also be arranged so as to denote respect or contempt, depending on social situation and space[15].

---

[15] As mentioned in a previous chapter married women going *nayor din* leave their affinal homes thoroughly "veiled" in *burkha* or under an umbrella, but uncover their face as soon as they sense their natal home is on the horizon.

In view of its expressive potential, the emphasis on the border introduced on wedding saris appears to point to the boundary associated with the married, i.e. adult state, a symbolic barrier imposed by those who will have supreme authority over the bride during the life-stage to come. Viewed socio-spatially, the praxis of concealment behind *achol* is linked to the view of woman's adult sexuality as well as to the kinship seniority in the affinal home. The affinal space is sub-divided into the fenced courtyard of her in-laws and the larger affinal community outside and each space requires a different degree of seclusion. Strict concealment is enjoined in encounters with males who are in superior positions to her husband. As Sharma (1978) pointed out, it is not by chance that all those to whom she may appeal to hear her claims of justice (i.e. men elder than her husband), are included in this category. The theme of control and self-control is further reiterated in the style of under-wear—the articles of clothing which are in immediate contact with the female body and without which a woman is not considered fully dressed—the bodice (*blaus* or *choli*) and the petticoat (*saya*). Bengalis are particularly concerned that their clothes cling tightly so that "the sweat of the body is immediately absorbed". However, in the semantic field of female apparel (or body anatomy), the concern with tightness has additional meanings. The waistband of the slip which cuts into a woman's waist emphasizes the symbolic boundary important in Bangladesh, that between the upper and lower parts of body. According to the Bengali view of anatomy, the human body is constituted in terms of a hierarchical opposition between its upper–lower and right–left parts. A child's understanding and maturation is sometimes assessed in terms of its grasping this spatial bodily orientation, i.e. the habituation of withdrawing the left hand and both feet from social communication. The ability to communicate generational hierarchy by appropriate body posture at greeting, described above, (which the bride and her mother-in-law assume on their first meeting), operates on this corporeal asymmetry, that accords preeminence, power, centrality and authority to the head and the right hand and inferiority, withdrawal, strangeness, intrusion to the feet and the left hand. Preoccupation with the head and neglect of the feet in the local medical paradigm belong to the same hierarchization of bodily space[16]. The extremities above and below the dividing horizontal line of the body receive similar asymmetrical attention in daily bodily management. Tying the waistcloth with a knot is exclusively a wom-

---

[16] Bengalis seem to share the extreme concern for the head with most people in South Asia. My observations and experience of this particular preoccupation in Gameranga are identical to those described by Obeyeskere (1976) among Sinhalese people. "The head must be protected from heat, and particularly from cold ... Mothers of all social classes and educational backgrounds worry if their children are exposed to even the most meagre drizzle. The concern is so great that adults may often be seen covering their heads in the rain with an ineffectual piece of cloth rather than leave it totally unprotected. To walk in the rain with the head unprotected is unthinkable; yet wet feet are of no cultural concern. ... a basic distinction is drawn between a head bath and a body bath ... the neglect of the head may cause ... diseases [or] may make people especially vulnerable to [them]".

an's practice; men adjust their lungi by means of an overlapping tuck. During the days of hard physical work women frequently re-tie the string with which the petticoat is fastened so as to tie the knot more firmly. Pregnancy in particular demands that the string be fitting tightly, so that the embryo does not move upwards. The concern for maintaining the waist boundary (based on the belief that neglect of the boundary may cause the embryo in a pregnant woman's body to move upwards) underpins the arguments on which female clients frequently ground their refusal of the IUD-preventive method: all heard of cases of a user whose coil "floated up from the reproductive area to her throat". It seems that the loose edge of the blouse or loose waist-string stands for a woman's "easy virtue" as became apparent from the comments which the western fondness for loose and airy dress evokes among village women. From this it is apparent that laxity of morals is denoted by the metaphor of loose string, that tightness denotes self-control of a virtuous woman, that the string and the knot are the symbolic custodians of woman's sexual honour and bodily well-being. Hence, the accomplishment of adulthood rests also in the distinction between the upper and lower parts of the body and the distinction between appropriate tightness and looseness of apparel. That the string is suggestive of the secret charms of the female body (which if uncontrolled may have disastrous effect for her guardians) is well depicted in poetic imagery, as documented by an Indian writer in the following lines:

"… a shimmering string encircling the snowy whiteness of a slender waist is comparable to the iridescent lights of the rainbow as an indicator of approaching pleasures" (Dar 1969:156).

Apart from the control and anonymity suggested in the conventional use of the clothing attached to the bride's body, the operation itself—putting off the "old" sari—may be seen as a marker of a definite separation from her previous lifestage. Removed from the familiar world of her father's house the bride puts off at the same time her former self, which lingers in the sari given by her father. By putting on the cloth given by her in-laws she invests herself with a new status, that of a wife (*bou*). This shift in garments, which for men indicates the shift of *ijjat*-loaded capital, denotes for women an existential shift in their life career; the design woven in the new cloth and its firm adjustment to the body specify its most outstanding feature—encompassment by the other and the self-control which binds her words, sexuality and mobility to only one man.

Conditioning—shorbet *drinking*

Now, in the new sari, the bride resumes her usual posture of subordination and anonymity—with her head inclined to one side, covered by the sari—and receives a welcoming drink offered by her mother-in-law. It is a glass of *shorbet*—sweetened juice of seasonal fruit.

Like betel (*pan shupari*), sweet drinks and sweets in general are standard items of welcome in Bangladesh. They are indispensable starters at weddings and a new-born child is welcomed with honey and sugar water which the mother smears into its mouth. Betel is always offered to visiting outsiders with plain water to drink, the sweets and *shorbet*s are reserved for special occasions.

In South Asian dietary symbolism, sweet foods, including some of the betel ingredients (*khejurer mitha*) are associated with purity, self-control, "freedom from anger, conceit and greed" (Kakar 1984:248). It should be noted that the contrast between sweetness and bitterness in olfatory semantics, is translated into the domain of human relationship as an opposition between acceptance and rejection. The same infant which has been welcomed by honey on his birth is weaned by application of a bitter substance to the mother's breast. This contrast further parallels a distinction between union and separation in social events: festive meals are always started with sweets and ended with bitter *pan-shupari*, thus marking how the union and the forthcoming separation are perceived. Thus sweet items are served on occasions when good and fruitful relations are sought, but also to avert hostility or to propitiate the suspected anger of a visiting outsider. In the field of language prosody, the sweet tone of voice (*mishti kotha*) is a feature of much social interaction in South Asia. As Kirkpatrick (1980:48) noted, "anyone wishing to influence another's will uses the tone of super sweetness". Also the singers of the love songs broadcast by Radio Bangladesh employ this voice modulation to express the feeling of erotic longing. Sweetness is a quality of voice very desirable for young ladies. The degree of sweetness of a girl's voice is one of the aesthetic criteria that guide suitors' evaluation of a future wife.

The sweet drink offered to the newly-arrived bride is used to overcome the tension of the first encounter and to spare the groom's family, particularly the mother-in-law, the bride's resentment at the inconvenience suffered as a consequence of her separation from the familiar world of her home. It is also an expression of the hope and desire for affinal co-operation among those who are "intimate strangers" (Khare 1976b:214). Ultimately, it is hoped, the sweetness will give the new bride a sense of warm satisfaction and restore of self-esteem, and thus upholds such desired qualities in a young wife, as self-control and an agreeable voice.

Bride's seclusion and "viewing the face" (mukh dekha)

Now that the bride is encompassed, appeased and neutralized she is to be removed from the outer area of the courtyard and led inside one of the huts. During at least two and a half days she remains sitting there motionless and silent, with downcast eyes, her head and face covered with the bordered end of her new sari. Replicating the posture of "bride-viewing" (*bou dekha*) she has passed through prior to the wedding, she is not supposed to make any requests, nor complain of physical discomfort. One of my informants was five months pregnant when she was brought to her husband's home as a new wife. After four days of maintaining a stationary position, which was customary in her husband's village, her feet swelled to such a size that she could not stand and walk when she was due to return to her father's home, she said.

The new bride accepts food when offered, which on this occasion is guest-food. Small girls in the family, ideally the groom's sisters, are expected to arrange for her bodily elimination, by first asking, and if needed, leading her behind the hut where she can attend to her needs. Neighbouring women and children drop in to see the new wife. They lift up the *achol* from her face, comment loudly on her looks and soon the news about her face and hair are spread in the neighbourhood. The viewers may throw one or two Taka in the bride's lap.

After two and a half days, *mukh dekha* dissolves into *bou bhat* ("bride's rice") whereby the bride is released from the frozen liminal posture and assumes an active stance to celebrate her productive skill.

Outsideness, insideness, penetrability, the house

During the *mukh dekha*, the bride may be seated on the ground inside of the sleeping hut (*shua ghor*) or it may be a screened area within the big house (*boro ghor*) of the in-laws. Exceptionally it is a separate hut constructed for the young couple.

We may recall that the cosmological journey (*tule ana*) is effected in a *palki* which is a miniature replica of the house on the ground where the bride undergoes *mukh dekha*. Because a house will remain the main locus of reproduction for the rest of a wife's life, and because the house is the immediate structural microcosm in which principles of gender ideology are generated and communicated, I shall briefly examine its place in local cosmology.

In Gameranga the house (*ghor* in the sense of the architectural structure, *bari* in the sense of a home) is the centre of sustenance, the focal point on which the division of space into inside (*bitore*) and outside (*baire*) is modelled. The walls, made of interlaced jute matting, provide the physical border around the living space, occupied by a minimal social unit—the conjugal family. The lack of fenestration (windows if inbuilt are ventilation devices, closed as soon as dusk falls to prevent intrusion of *bhut*) insures constant darkness or semidarkness. This facilitates outward vision through the chinks in the matting but the walls are not sound-proof and the residents occasionally communicate with passers-by from within. Outside conversation inside the house can also be picked up. In view of this, conversations inside are usually whispered. Summing up, the walls that surround the inside of the house prevent observation from the outside, facilitate it from the inside but are permeable to sound. As with the lifting of the veiling contrivances used by women, non-family members very seldom enter the inside of the house. In general terms the two areas of the house—its dark inside and light outside—invoke the interior–exterior aspect of space, behaviour and experience. By extension they also provide the ground for the rules according to which the sexual division of concerns, labour and the roles are organized.

The inside of the house, where the bride now acts out her *lojja*, is divided into the sleeping area and the granary, both pertaining to the natural activities of life and food preservation (production, reproduction and increase), that is to say, the female sphere of concern and activities. It is a place where lives are made and sustained and multiplied through food containers, sleeping, sexual intercourse, birth and death. It is also a region of concealment, secrets and darkness—indices of female knowledge and creativity—and the backstage of external social life—public presentation of self.

Contrasted with the house's interior is the outside—the front, back and rear area immediately surrounding the house; paths and canals opening the homestead's interior to markets, towns and foreign lands (*bidesh*).

The area immediately outside the village—the field (*danga* or *bhil*), the jungle (*jongol* or *baghan*), market (*bajar* or *hat*) and the mosque (*mojdjid*) constitute the mainstay of the economic, political and Islamic realms reserved for men. The landmarks linking these points—the canals, rivers and paths—take them out to cultivate fields, negotiate exchanges (of food, women and news), or to journeys towards outsiders. Outside is where money is made, rank negotiated and anti-*dhormic* acts relegated. Inside is where women are kept and where *ijjat* and sins are generated.

An area of the outside that lacks an explicit gender association is the "jungle" or garden[17]. The jungle is dense, and inhabited by wild animals. One can enter it for calls of nature or for occasional male activities like tree-cutting, but generally it is perceived as a non-social area. I have been warned on several occasions not to walk there unaccompanied, particularly at inauspicious times of the day. It is a place where the dead are buried, latrines set up, and where malevolent spirits lurk at night.

The total space may be said to be divided into the inside associated with married women[18] (who, in structural sense, come from outside), the outside associated with men and the genderless interstitial area of jungle with wild fauna, flora and dead humans. However, the superordination of outside over inside or exterior over interior is not as consistent as the corresponding relationship between male–female or right–left tends to be. When considered from within and from a female perspective, the interior of the house and the yard area is understood as a cultural space contrasted with the non-social wilderness of the jungle as well as with the outsideness of the fields where raw grains are harvested by men. By both men and women the interior of the vil-

---

[17] *Jongol* refers to dwindling patches of jungle interspersing the fields (*danga*) in the vicinity of the hamlets; *baghan* is an overgrown area behind each house.

[18] Not in any legal sense, as women have no rights in their husband's house.

lage is favourably contrasted with the dangerous and amoral realm of towns. The eminence women accord to the interior is manifested by the assiduous measures they take to ward off the dwellers of the wild—ants, jackals, civet cats, chameleons, mongooses and malevolent spirits. Similarly the courtyards are meticulously cleaned of grass (the flora of the wild) and plastered with cow-dung (the spill of the culturally most eminent animal) before raw grains are processed there.

Darkness, silence and transparency

From the solidity of physical construction I shall shift to more transient aspects of *mukh dekha*, which are neither symbolic acts nor objects, but which in combination are capable of sustaining a frame which questions the situation defined by the ritual. I start by examinining darkness and silence in the sense imputed to it ritually, i.e. as a means of restriction (or fixity).

Darkness, seclusion and silence—the indices of anonymity, uncertainty, submission and ultimately of death—that mark the bride's journey are also highly characteristic of *mukh dekha* enacted on the ground. These are also the prominent attributes of liminality in Turner's theory of initiation (and death is its epitome par excellence). Here too, the process of becoming is indicated by the "seclusion from the normal", via a milieu "that represents both a grave and a womb" (Turner 1969:81,158). However, in the case of the Bengali Muslim bride, her behaviour and ultimate seclusion are enacted as exaggerations (amounting to caricature) and not ritual reversal of the ordinary[19]. Here the bride's stylized behaviour within the semi-dark interior of the hut reiterates and exaggerates the essential facts of what is expected from a woman in her role as a wife. What is celebrated and confirmed is the idealized image of social reality, the agnatic dogma of total control over imported women. Rather than providing scope for personal features of the initiant or for highlighting the variety of methods for coping with outside women, the rite provides a definition of and acknowledgement of a unitary, universalistic, undiversified, bounded category of a virgin on the verge of wifehood.

It may well be that chaos intrinsic to initial unknowing is a prevailing feature of a bride's experience during seclusion, but this is in no obvious way suggested in her manner of expression. The bride's inaudibility (or soft-spokenness, if an answer is due), her body posture—manner of sitting, eyes

---

[19] In ethnographic contexts studied by Turner (1969:94–165, 1974:231–270) these scenic artifices generate and affirm the mood of a ritual state during which the stringency of social structure and the categoric principles of daily behaviour—generational and gender hierarchy in particular—are played down if not overtly reversed. Also among the Kuranko described by Jackson, in order to become adults the initiates have to undergo a period of confusion during the seclusion phase of the rite, an interval where normal behaviour and boundaries round categories are suspended and space is left for individual expression, "as if chaos had to be entertained before order (i.e. adulthood) could be achieved" (Jackson 1983a).

cast downwards, tilt of head, care that the *achol* does not reveal the hair and face—constitute a visible manifestation of the central, specifically feminine virtue of modesty—*lojja*. *Lojja* denotes a wide range of restraints for which self-control is the common denominator. It subsumes shame, shyness, social sensitivity, modesty and reserve and also the acknowledgement of embarrassment. The exterior tangible locus of *lojja* for a Bengali woman is her head and face. Female *lojja* directs a woman's eyes, head, the whole female body downwards and inside. The male virtue, equivalent to *lojja* is honour, *ijjat*, and self-respect, *mannagonno*. A husband's *ijjat* depends largely on the behaviour of dependent women, his wife and daughters. The most important aspect of female *lojja* which acts on male *ijjat* is a woman's ability to control her words, movements and sexuality. It is partially achieved with the help of the paraphernalia—jewellery and sari—focused on at *bie*. *Lojja* and *ijjat* are complementary even in bodily expression; the sense of honour turns a man's face upwards and drives his body and interests outwards to the company of other men. *Lojja* is incorporated in the posture a bride assumes on ritual seclusion.

Against this wide cultural background *mukh dekha* can be seen as the climax of a journey whereby a stranger, the bride, reaches her destination—the husband's birth-place which is her future home. Her final absorption among strangers is preceded by the ritual display of her body which affirms the appropriate place of an adult woman in the physical and moral universe.

First, as I have shown, the seclusion of the journey and the interior staging of *mukh dekha* established an association between the female world and the secluded interior and darkness. This association is picked up in other non-ritual contexts such as transport arrangements on the streets of towns, where the rickshaws carrying female passangers can be identified by the umbrella-like hood pulled over the passenger while she enjoys an excellent view from the semi-dark interior of the carriage. In contrast, male passengers always sit upright—with the hood pushed down behind the seat—looking around, letting nothing that happens on the street escape them while remaining clearly visible to other passers-by. The idea of an appropriate use of space and time by women is made poignantly explicit in a father's advice to his daughter documented by an Indian Muslim writer:

"Hold yourself my dear! in the heaven of safety, turn your face to the wall, your back to the door. If at all you have to desire to peep through an aperture, let this aperture be the eye of your needle" (Amir Khusro in Sher-ul-Ajam, Lahore in Dar 1969:30)

Woman's invisibility and seclusion is further suggested in the layers of cloth that separate her from the total outside space of which the outsideness of her natal home is a part (its previous familiarity converted into outsideness). The walls and fences provide additional privacy from the public space of men within her affinal village. Added to the multiple enclosure is darkness and inaudibility which further enhance the bride's anonymity. Depersonalization of a wife also finds expression in the form of address and reference employed by her affines. A woman's personal name is dropped or "forgotten" as soon as she gets married. Instead, in her affinal home she is referred to as a *bou* or as a "so-and-so's wife or mother", depending on her life stage.

Knowledge through paradox—a commentary on and in mukh dekha

So far I have elaborated the definitional emphasis of the rite. Yet, as I suggested at one point, the performative nature of *mukh dekha* provides a paradoxical frame that raises the distinction between appearance and reality. I shall now shift from the indicative mood of the ritual to the interrogatory nature of the performance (Turner 1984).

The additional meanings that I shall attempt to explicate are exposed by the term denoting the bride's seclusion. The very notion of "viewing the face" itself admits that there may exist more than one face to a communicating body. It betrays the existence of a hidden truth waiting to be unfolded. The act of showing further suggests the presentation of what has been hidden, a screen that falls between an authentic reality and a mere 'version' of it (Gorfain 1986). It also indicates that internal experience and its outward presentation (e.g., *lojja*, which is on the face) are related in such a way that behind that screen, thoughts may be going on quite independent of the formal structure imputed to the performance. Such a perspective would make it possible to think of *mukh dekha* not only as a communicative event carrying the agnatic definition of married women but as a play that stimulates imaginative ideas of an alternative reality (Hodder 1982:171).

The second factor, pointing to the ludic[20] quality of this performance is also a realization that *bie*—the first and only marriage—in fact is not the first time a woman stages as a bride. Various events of *bie*, particularly *mukh dekha*, have earlier been invoked in make-believe games. Small girls in Gameranga often play "a *bie*" or a "kitchen" with rice straw toys representing a bride (the groom is present in absentia in make-believe games). Older girls also play make believe-weddings, themselves caricaturing the *lojja* of a new wife. In these rehearsals, the bride is always mocked as a helpless, clumsy intruder, so disoriented and overwhelmed by shyness that at one point she slips and falls on the ground. The children sing: "New wife, new wife, it was raining when she came; she slipped, fell down and ate the mud ..." (*Notun bou, notun bou, brishtite ashche, pore geche, kheda khaiche*). These playful dramatizations of the new wife capitalize on the consequences of literal, unreflective internalization of submission. This provokes ridicule.

---

[20] By this term I point to the process of playing described by Schwartzman (1978:232–247, inspired by Bateson 1956) as "a way of saying something about the roles and powers of players", or in other words, as a process of negotiation in which players both deny and express their social identities (see Bateson 1972).

Fajans (1983) defines (in a different cultural field) an equivalent emotion to *lojja* as "the movement between internal and external domain which acts to promote and demarcate the boundaries of the person". The mockery that surrounds the make-believe *bou* seems to capitalize on a newcomer's failure to distinguish between the internal and external (consensual) aspects of a person's actions; to overemphasize doctrinal truth at the expense of imagination is the propensity of apprentices in their initial stage of unknowing. The *lojja* of the bride in the above song is so thoroughly and unreflectively internalized and her "veil" so unimaginatively positioned over her eyes as to hinder the minimum of vision indispensable for the praxis of "going on" in an unknown ambient. Attempting to conform to the rules literally, the "bride" elicits laughter. My pretence, at times, of taking their roles seriously, (as I attempted to enter into their games) was vigorously objected to. The young co-actors felt compelled to correct my erroneous perception of the event and pointed out emphatically "she is not a *bou*, can't you see, it is Kulsum (or Hosnara, or Rohima …)?!". Or, as I approached their make-believe *"chula"* and pretended a guest's inquiry about various meals they were in the process of preparing, the "cooks" assured me: "it is not *dal*, just sand"[21]. However, unlike childhood rehearsals of adult roles, at which the small girls pretend not to be girls but wives or mothers, (yet are quick to discard the illusion and expose their actual identity as soon as a naive intruder takes the stage at face value), the role "bride" (*bou*) on actual *bie* is not reversible. If divorced, a married woman can never be a girl again. Were she Mahinia, Jahanara, or Kulsum a bride is translated into a social position of a *"bou"* and nobody in the *shashur bari* but herself ever remembers her personal name. And more, as Roy (1975) claims in her monograph, Bengali women seem to believe that they change their nature as they move from one life stage to another.

On the other hand, in spite of assuming the role of a model wife, the initite remains perceptibly herself (Jackson 1983a). This is apparent from the complaints many a bride voices in her father's home (on *bou firano*) after disengagement from the ritual persona, about the physical strain and discomfort she had experienced during *mukh dekha*. In one case which I mentioned earlier a bride thought she had become paralyzed for life as her legs swelled to such an extent that she could not return to her father's home in due time. Others recalled their worries regarding incontinence[22].

The third indicator that provides me with clues to see the *mukh dekha* as play with what is real, is the ostentatious and intense manner of asserting invisibility. While the bride (and married women in daily practice) exhibits herself as

---

[21] This latter point exemplifies what Schwartzman (1978:210–247) calls "saying play", i.e. "a process of negotiations in which players both deny and express their social identities", and where they are both "playing and saying" ("It is a play") and where also the actor is both a subject as well as an object—in mutual dialogue: "I am *bou*, I am not a *bou*" (Schwartzman ibid.,220, 232–47).

[22] Bodily processes seem so often to betray the representational models and impose a limit on the inflexible compliance intended by the novices.

blatantly cloistered and invisible, it may enhance rather than diminish her sex-
appeal and thus produce the reverse effect on the onlookers. Translated to the
everyday domestic scheme: for a male outsider visiting a household a new wife
is readily recognizable by the dense employment of signs intended to avert his
attention: veiling, silence, surreptitiousness or total absence of women from the
front scene. Postmaritally, in the sphere of conjugal politics, the usual way
women draw the attention of their husbands and sons to their grievances by refusing food. Even the public domain provides examples of extreme withdrawal
calculated to provoke attention. I have noticed instances of provocative reticence on public buses, where college girls or wage labouring women occupying the seats in a scrupulously marked ladies section, may provoke the attention of a male fellow-passenger by fainting or by a more subtle demonstrations
of bodily indisposition like sighs of exhaustion or provocative fanning[23].

Conspicuous concealment is not always successful in producing its intended effect, because to conceal inevitably draws attention to what is concealed. This is poetically elaborated in the following verses by a Bengali
poet—"her belly gave itself to be guessed through her garment and her beauty
broke forth like light from all her veils" (Das 1927).

Ultimately, the most salient and tangible pointer to the metacommunicative
dimension of *mukh dekha* is the bride's sartorial equipment. The permanence
and the rigid, structural, unitary definition of wifehood attained by stylistic
exaggeration[24] is made refractable via the veil (*achol*) that obscures the bride's
face. Intended to protect, control, depersonalize, the veil provides a woman
with the possibility of refracting the social expectations and the order of the ritual. In this way it serves simultaneously as a stylistic variation of the same refraction, just as the little girls attempted to convince a naive onlooker "It is just
a game". The veil's conspicuous decoration on a transparent texture adds to its
elusiveness, sharpens the paradox and leads to awareness of the simultaneity
of saying and playing (Shwartzman 1978:ibid.) embedded in the ritual.

---

[23] The first time I witnessed these demonstrations was during a bustrip from Chittagong to Ranga-
matti in 1981. When I drew the attention of my Bengali escort to what I interpreted as signs of se-
ductive strategy he commented "It is what purdah is for".

On another occasion in a train compartment a Bengali fellow-passenger, a man of 40, cast a
deprecatory glance at me when a shawl slipped from my shoulders. My uncovered arms incited
his interest sufficiently to bring into debate the question of the moral superiority of the Islamic
over the Christian life-style. As my discussant solicited support from two other passengers, any
defence of a liberal outlook seemed futile. To my surprise, however, one of them asserted the superiority of Islamic ways by claiming that "after all, *burkha* is more tricky as one never exactly
knows what is underneath; one can only guess". His cultural juxtaposition in terms of female sartorial style implied the opposition I am trying to elaborate here—between the transparent and
opaque manner of communication.

[24] As I have shown, the main actor—the bride—assumes an exaggerated posture and expression
(whereby she abstracts the essential features of the structural position she is about to occupy),
which the practicalities of daily life to come will prevent her from attaining. (Ideally women
should be kept from productive work and be kept sedentary, ordinarily even the *bhodro lok*er *bou*
is constantly on move preoccupied with supervision of food, children, servants and domestic animals.)

The mounting emphasis on anonymity and depersonalisation via costume, site, immobility, obscurity and muteness is functional and effective in one sense, since it impedes overt communication and vision, yet in another it admits such a potential in women—for inappropriate speech, movements and even their aspirations to activities in spheres occupied by men (Sharma 1978)[25].

In this way, the *achol* seems to claim as well as to disclaim the bride's social belonging that is promoted in the ritual. At the beginning of this chapter I have named some circumstances that parallel a new wife's (*notun bou*'s) position in the affinal household with that of the inmates in total institutions. Indeed, as I have shown in chapter 9, housewives in Gameranga are extremely subordinated and dependent, but they are not entirely powerless. To recognize this and to understand the nature of their powers one has to admit that such powers often reside in the symbols whose efficacy "is not simply a matter of something that is inherent in custom. It is created and re-created in what people do and often in the ephemeral embellishments through which they enhance their actions" (Karp 1987). The recourse to "the infinitely small", labile aspects of expression, (for which Bourdieu, 1983, praises Erving Goffman) is particularly important in cultures whose official ideology and controlling practices are committed to keeping certain sections of the population muted. Under such conditions, nuances of style and gesture may prove "powerful means of expression available to people whose communicative options are otherwise constrained ..." (Karp ibid.). Thus in her manner of enacting the ritual given to her a woman can make it something other than it is.

Wife's rice (bou bhat)

The gradual employment of tranquilizing gadgets and scenic artifices in the preceding sequences of the ceremony invokes an image of ultimate inertia, an important marker of liminal states outlined by van Gennep (1977:10,21–25) and explicated by Turner (1969). Likewise, in Gameranga a virgin has to die, or at least "be reduced or ground down to a uniform[26] condition to be fashioned anew and endowed with additional powers to enable [her] to cope with [her] new station in life" (Turner ibid., 95). Following *mukha dekha* the

---

[25] In this context we may recall Gorfain's allusion to Handelman's comment on Naven, where also "Person and role become absorbed in a pure symbol, which does not represent another figure but penetrates the immediate cultural construction to make a 'direct superimposition on social action ... and through this medium, social discontinuities are objectified and recontextualized' (Gorfain 1986, Handelman 1970:86–87).

[26] It may be of interest to note that virgin's "death" is modelled on the body management that attends the actual biological death; dead body has to be processed (washed and sprinkled) and decked like the body of a bride. (cf. Das 1976). The view of death as a precondition of birth, rather than a termination of life is only an extension of South Asian conceptualization of time as cyclical, non-lineal phenomenon. This optimistic attitude pervades even forms that mark less radical separations like journeys or terminations of visits: in Gameranga the person leaving greets "I am coming" (*Ami ashi*) and not "I am leaving" as is the case in cultures that maintain lineal view of time. (Educated urbanites may leave saying "See you again" (*Dekha hobe*).

bride assumes a new platform, a "relatively stable, well defined position" (Turner 1982:24) characteristic of the ultimate incorporation phase in van Gennep's/Turner's ritual scheme. I shall briefly sketch the concluding rite at which these "additional" powers of the initiant are articulated.

Bou bhat ("bride's rice") is the feast where the groom's family first eats rice (*bhat*) cooked by the bride (*bou*)[27]. It conflates with the *bashor rat* which is the night of defloration. After a few days of maintaining an immobile posture the bride is conducted to the cooking area or *ranna ghor* (cooking hut) by her mother-in-law. There she cooks rice in water poured from a brand new water pitcher (*kholosh*) on a hearth (*chula*) that has been newly plastered for the occasion. *Chula* is a portion of the floor space in the cooking area. As a prominent portion of female space it is secluded from the rest of the courtyard by a fence made of hanging mats (*pati*) or jute sticks. As a physical construction, *chula* consists of one large cavity (69 cm deep and wide) covered with plastered clay. A small opening is left for feeding the fire and two larger circular openings for cooking. These two have slightly elevated edges to support the earthenware pot (*matir hari*) in which rice is boiled and an iron or alluminium wok (*koroi*) for cooking side dishes like *shobji* or *torkari*[28]. Seen from above the openings form a triangle of which the central smaller cavity absorbs fuel generating energy that transforms the content of the pots placed on the lateral openings into edible substance[29].

Contained in the notion "*chula*" (hearth) is not only the synonymity of its shape and function with the procreative powers of female bodies, (or the synonymity of the process of cooking and eating as a metaphor for sharing other bodily substances, e.g. during sexual intercourse); linguistically, the term is frequently used to denote a "household". For instance, an inquiry regarding the exact relationship of two apparently related persons may be opened by "Do you eat (food cooked) from the same *chula*?"[30].

As I have elaborated extensively on the essences *bhat* and *kholosh* on previous pages[31], I shall here point to the various meanings given to the sharing of food and the process of cooking (*pak kora*, *ranna kora*) at and after the *bou bhat* event.

---

[27] There was a disagreement among my informants about the order of precedence: some claimed that the first sexual conjunction of the couple follows the night immediately after the bride is released from the frozen liminal posture; others stated, defloration is preceded by *bou bhat*. In all cases these two events are contained in one ceremony. In some parts of Bangladesh the defloration night is referred to as *phul shojja rat*—the night of flowered bed and in upper class urban families I have been told this locus of sexual inauguration is decorated with flowers. The term as well as the custom draws obviously on the parallel established between the female body and those botanical species whose seasons are marked by the appearance and disappearance of flowers— paddy, jasmin.

[28] A wide ranging term denoting a category of vegetarian dishes (see Rizvi 1979).

[29] All three circular openings of *chula* (the middle one receiving fuel, the lateral ones producing food) create a triangle reminiscent of the points of female anatomy involved vitally in life generation and sustenance.

[30] In order to assess as accurately as possible the number of family members during the family census I carried out in the middle of my fieldwork, my assistent opened this part of the interview by "How many people eat from this *chula*?"

[31] See "Extra-household commensality", chapter 10.

At the *bou bhat* feast, the bridal couple is served first and eats together—which is a commensal order that reverses the daily praxis following the *bie*. Ordinarily during food preparation, a daughter-in-law at her *notun bou*-stage of marriage occupies the lowest rank of a helper[32] in the cooking team[33] under the supervision of and subordinate to the mother-in-law. The serving of food to the bride's husband remains the mother-in-law's prerogative so long as the young couple resides in the same household[34]. The bride herself eats alone after everyone else has been served—a commensal order that persists during the rest of a married woman's life.

At *bou bhat* however, the bride enacts her structural position and a wife's typified obligation vis à vis her conjugal family. The rite is not as much concerned with control as with the cultural elaboration of those powers whereby a wife can influence the household's prosperity. A bride's cooking rice and the groom's family's acceptance of cooked food from their *bou* "is a feast of encompassed otherness" (Khare 1976:235). For the bride it marks a newly acquired belongingness: henceforward she will be refered to as "our wife"—*amra bou*[35].

In Bengal, sharing and giving food is the foremost expression of love (*ador*), filial as well as conjugal[36]. Prior or subsequent to the night on which her body is also used in the physical consummation at *bashor rat*, *bou bhat* expresses bodily as well as affective conjunction between a woman and a man who have so far been strangers to each other ("the daughter of others" and "a son of others"—*porer meye, porer chele*)[37].

---

[32] The division of labour among women responsible for daily cooking follows a hierarchical order according to which the lowest tasks—grinding spices, cleaning vegetables and fish, collecting water are a servant's or new wife's jobs while rice boiling, cooking *torkari*, meat or fish dish is the mother-in-law's responsibility.

[33] The number of women involved in household's cooking depends on the economic standing and the stage of a family's life cycle. There may always be a servant or at the time of the first son's marriage there may still be his unmarried sisters, all working under the supervision of *malik*'s wife.

[34] After the couple splits from groom's parents and establishes a separate *chula*, the serving of food (apart from sexual intercourse and beating) becomes the most critical ranking transaction between the couple (Khare 1976:78–79). Universally in South Asia, a wife's subordination is communicated in the unquestioned precedence of the husband in serving and "his authority is emphasized by his demands on the wife for a service that meets his exact requirements. Should the wife fail to comply with the commands issued by the husband, or should her cooking not be to his liking, he has the right to beat her" (David 1980). In Gameranga the particular failure of a wife that leads most frequently to conjugal discord and wife-beating is failed timing, i.e. when food is not prepared for instant consumption at the very time of the husband's demand. The same applies for sexual intercourse.

[35] In some parts of India the adjective *notun*—"new" is detached from *notun bou* after the bride's ritual cooking at *bou bhat*. In Gameranga, the status of newness ceases only after the wife gives birth to her first child.

[36] Khare (1976:254) asserts a similar view in his analysis of commensality among Brahmans in Lucknow when he states "To be a wife and to be able to cook for one's husband are traditionally reinforcing and emotionally convergent connections".

[37] The parallel between sexual intercourse and eating replicates in the language of extramarital

Apart from being a moral substance, food, as Lindenbaum (1976) has noted is an "incendiary" matter in Bengal, causing fires, anger, disputes and—as *bou bhat* asserts—incorporation of outsiders.

In the daily life of a Bengali family the sharing of food (cooked on *chula*) for which boiled rice is a synonym is a reinforcing action bringing a family together (Inden/Nicholas 1977:18,49) and it is a wife's foremost duty to prepare and serve it.

Being the main motive for a *gushti*'s import of outside women, culinary and procreative ability becomes the point of attention at the rite of incorporation that finalizes a *bie*. The bride's acting as a rice-giver is parallelled to Lokhi's power to secure universal prosperity through auspicious increase; the consumption of her food and body is acknowledgement of her as a new wife. The conditioning of her body with turmeric, water splashing and *shorbet*-drinking at previous stages of *bie* was aimed at activating the conditions of her optimal receptivity that would hopefully result in manifest increase of the *gushti*[38].

Structurally, the *bou bhat* rite reverses not only the hierarchical order of the daily cooking and serving routine but the trend of the preceding sequences of the *bie*. Throughout the welcoming ceremony the bride has been acted upon. Her gradual encompassement has been effected through the acts on and with her passive body. At *bou bhat* however, the cultural emphasis is shifted on the creative aspect of female powers. The contemplative "knowing" of the preceding rite is here shown off and instrumentalized as a skill useful to others. The movements with hands required for the lighting and maintenance of the fire in *chula*, and those movements of carrying and gripping embedded in food preparation—peeling layers of onions, pouring of water, attending to the pots, adjustments of the sari, visually depict the style of knowing and working specific to married women. The simultaneity of these bodily movements with the records of culinary skills established at the mother's *chula* and the subordination to *shashuri*'s (mother-in-law's) sets out the paradigm of an adult woman's knowledge, creativity and strategy.

The bride's otherness is here absorbed in life-giving acts. Conversion by the wives of the most prestigious grain—paddy—into the cultural super-food—rice and focusing their sexuality into successful pregnancies is a shift from controlled to absorbed otherness[39].

---

sexual conquest. An inquiry about a young man's sexual experience may be introduced by question "How many girls have you eaten"? (*Koyjon meyera khaycho*).

[38] See the chronology of the rites constituting a *bie* in the beginning of this chapter.

[39] To contribute with an "increase" is an expectation through which villagers paralleled both outside women—new wife and the anthropologist. The particular expectations directed towards the anthropologist have been derived from the local equation of the category "the Westerner" with unlimited affluence. Indeed, the villagers' claims based on this assumption never faded. However, the parallel between these two outsiders refracts when it comes to the point of their respective ambitions. The strategies of the genuine *notun bou* are aimed to make herself manifestly auspicious in the house whose prosperity she came to influence whereas my aim was simply to make myself acceptable in spite of my engagement in activities which villagers viewed as meaningless (i.e. collecting data for writing a book about them).

Summary

In order to position the career of Bangladeshi Muslim womanhood, I have placed the principles and processes through which a person becomes a woman into a wider cultural context. Hence a large part of the study deals with the dominant structure and discourse of belonging within which actors operate and within which flexibility and negotiation is possible. As evidenced among Muslims in Bangladesh, agnation and affinity constitute the cultural context of becoming a complete woman.

My intention has been to move between phenomenological and an objectivist approaches, i.e. the experience people themselves convey of their world and the outsider's knowledge of the structure of this world (Abu Lughod 1989). My style of writing is deliberately eclectic, processual and circular, to replicate the ways women in Gameranga place themselves in agnation and to mark my own position in academic anthropology. Beyond ethnography and epistemology the aim has also been to convey the process of thinking throughout this writing enterprise—to produce a text that also reflects on its becoming. The text is structured along a lineal axis that reveals a six-part division encompassing eighteen chapters. The lineal reading shows different levels of social relatedness—the units of belonging and the official imagery of agnation and affinity.

As an explicit precept in the local theory of species (*jats*), gender distinction provides a basic premise of moral order—*dhormo*. Its principles are acquired, upheld and reproduced through systematic didactics that incorporate metaphors from various domains of culture. Bodily metaphor is particularly instrumental in the process of learning to belong.

In Part Two I have shown how the patri-lineality of basic social units is construed through lexical, moral, biogenetic and botanical metaphors of belonging and is recreated in ritual activities—prayers, slaughter of animals, commensal feasts, funerals, feuds—from which women are excluded. The administration of moral order within a community is achieved through hearings which admit women but are embedded in forms of procedure that make assertion of claims by women difficult.

Dealing with the various representations of the agnatic ethos I have also shown how the symbolic logic of bamboo corresponding to the social logic of agnation provides an idiom in the play of and for power. The bamboo stick links maleness with positively sanctioned violence—the defence and assertion of people with whom one shares blood and the sense of honour; in domestic politics too discipline is enforced with bamboo rods. Albeit an agnatic construction, the ideology of pure blood (that denies adoption as a solution to sterility) and honour (as the idiom of esteem that affects and reflects a person's status and sense of self) are points of mutual gender concern. Women have a stake in honour in two senses: literally, through their reproductive capacity and feeding skills; and symbolically, through their sense of modesty.

Albeit oriented to the understanding of dominant categories I place significance on the transformational nature not only of women, but on the flux and shifts within the dominant agnatic discourse itself. My argument has been, that whether or not agnatic groups (*gushti*, *shomaj*) operate cohesively or possess all the characteristics of their emblems, they exist in their members' perception of a preferred self-image and image for others. Like other people, Muslims in Bangladesh construct and re-construct their birthgroups metaphorically, making them "a source and repository of meaning, and a referent of their [belonging]" (Cohen 1985:118).

The rhetoric of social perfection—unbreakable fraternal unity and lineal growth represented by the botanical species bamboo—is betrayed by the deformities and divisions involved in pregnancy and delivery. The agnatic discourse is thus contradicted by the equally important orientation of Bengali Muslims towards the creation of auspiciousness achieved by adding and multiplying anything that yields life. Birth, the most auspicious division, is carried by women. Thus the import of women—dividers of *gushti*—is indispensable for the auspicious increase of the patriline as well as for its affinal linking to the rest of the world.

The objects and actions most effectively yielding auspiciousness are those which compound such attributes as inflation, enlargement, swelling, protrusion, bulging or fullness. This is in sharp contrast to the aesthetics of vertical ordering of reality abstracted in bamboo. As a state of being a woman, auspiciousness is linked to the image of her body as a vessel to be filled, wet and open at a culturally specified time. As an attribute it is revealed in the praise she receives for keeping storage vessels in the same way. All these conditions enhance the maintenance of a metaphoric link with the deity Lokhi. In order to produce all her benefits and be auspicious, a daughter has to be exchanged in marriage. The locus of a woman's creativity thus becomes strictly limited to her affinal group.

Essential to the construction of womanhood in Bangladesh is the assumption of women as detachable in two senses: from their home of origin and from one husband to another (in the case of divorce). In relation to the agnatic structure women are thus generalised as daughters or wives and a woman's status of completeness is bound to a chain of transitions—of guardianship, space, knowledge and body. These transfers are administered through marriage arrangements and ritualised in wedding. Parts 5 and 6 deal with this.

In order to find an answer to the question raised in the Introduction regarding women's assimilation to the structure that mutes them I suggest a non-lineal reading of the book. This will follow the practice Bengali Muslim women adopt with regard to their social organisation.

The volume is framed by an analysis of two events through which two women are moulded into the agnatic image of complete womanhood. One is the anthropologist at the point of entry into the community; the other is the bride on her ritualised arrival at the conjugal home. Both are cases of a performance that changes the sense of self through confrontation with otherness, and the bodily adjustment that ensues from this confrontation. Taken together, the performances provide a highly condensed, dramatic metaphor of the agnatic view of womanhood on the one hand and heightens the dilemmas of double belonging (one inherent in the anthropological enterprise, the other in a state of marriedness). The ethnographic concern in each event is the use of symbolic devices aimed at rendering women invisible and mute yet at the same time tending to work towards the opposite .

This dialectic of belonging—non-belonging, exposure and hiding, has epistemological consequences and is crucial to the understanding of how different forms of discourse come to be produced and maintained in a Bangladeshi community. The emphasis in the opening event is on the shifting nature of norms applied to a female outsider over time. The final chapter points to the complementarity of self-denial and self-assertion. Both are enacted as complementary virtues of in-married women in two sequences of the wedding ceremony— *mukh dekha* and *bou bhat*.

Epistemologically, the episodes of the first event highlight the dialogical nature of interpretation where "the interlocutors are equally played out and from which their result changed in some way" (Vattimo 1988). Their mutual understanding is achieved from their "being situated within a horizon they do not have any control over but within which and by which they are placed" (ibid., see Kondo 1986). The last event is a description by a "neutral" observer, biased toward ordering principles according to rules.

Inserted within this external frame is chapter 12, the most salient part of the text. The ambiguous position of women vis à vis patriline is here enacted as an institutionalized post-marital journey to their natal group whereby the travelling wife is rendered as moving between two points of orientation—the different realities of her parental and her conjugal homes. These journeys are presented as a key metaphor of affinity, married womanhood and of anthropological knowledge.

In response to the general question of my inquiry, I contend that *nayor*—the journey—is a metaphor of woman's presence in agnation as well as a source of insight grounded in shifting points of view. In contrast to the appearance of self-containment suggested in the agnatic abstraction of bamboo, *nayor* is an event of crossing boundaries through which a plurality of meaning is attained and manipulated. Because, as I have shown *nayor* enables the participant to achieve a distance that implies the understanding of the world from an external point of view, it generates double awareness and hence the potential for a critical view. In *nayor* the concerns of a wife intersect with those shared with the fieldworking anthropologist in terms of the relation between internal and external understanding of situation. Therefore, *nayor* also constitutes a meta-phor of inter-subjectivity.

Lastly, I revert to my special concern and the most pertinent question of this inquiry—how do muted groups, women in particular, assimilate to the structure in a culture that denies them visibility?

As I have shown, there are forms of divisions immanent in the process of communication, besides those accommodated in the cultural elaboration of affinity. The meanings conveyed in structural terms become refracted by non-verbal means. Bengali Muslim women achieve dissent from authoritative discourse by resorting to the very means that are meant to silence them.

In structural terms a housewife demonstrates her awareness of the authoritative discourse, her proficiency as a decent wife and not least her eagerness to comply with the image of Lokhi. The veil is thus a metaphor of encompassed otherness. In terms of inter-subjective interpretation I render the veil as the very means that tends to celebrate subversion—"a transparent masque that admits a view of what it seems to hide" (Handelman 1979:80). Throughout this volume I have pointed to the use of *achol* as a means of highlighting the transience of meaning in different ritual contexts (*bichar, bou dekha, mukh dekha*). The didactics of double awareness generated in rituals extends to daily experience and provides a wife with the possibility to affirm and communicate the agnatic definition of self yet question it at the same time. The meanings transmitted through the sartorial camouflage available to Muslim women in Bangladesh may contradict, reverse or merely comment on *dhormo* which the authoritative discourse seeks to sustain. Equally, to its observer the veil suggests the possibility of viewing the informant behind it and the social reality they share—encompassed otherness—as factual:fictional, indicative: interrogatory, concensual:subversive and/or objective:subjective.

Bibliography

Abdullah, T.A. 1974(1966). *Village women as I saw them*. Dacca: Bangladesh Academy for Rural Development.

Abu-Lughod, L. 1986. *Veiled sentiments. Honor and poetry in a Bedouin society.* Berkeley: University of California Press.

Abu-Lughod, L. 1989. Zones of theory in the anthropology of the Arab world. *Annual Review of Anthropology* **18**, 267–306.

Ahmed, R. 1981. *The Bengali Muslims 1871–1906. A quest for identity.* Delhi: Oxford University Press.

Ali, (Mrs.) Meer Hassan, 1978(1832). *Observations on the Mussulmauns of India. Descriptive of their manners, customs, habits and religious opinion made during a twelve years residence in their immediate society.* Oxford: Oxford University Press.

Allen, M.R. 1976. Kumari or 'virgin' worship in Kathmandu valley. *Contributions to Indian Sociology* (n.s.) **10**, 293–316.

Appadurai, A. 1986. Is homo hierarchicus? Review article. *American Ethnologist* **13**, 795–761.

Ardener, E. 1977a. Belief and the problem of women. In *Perceiving women* (ed.) S. Ardener. London: Dent. New York: Wiley.

Ardener, E. 1977b. The 'problem' revisited. In *Perceiving women* (ed.) S.Ardener. London: Dent. New York: Wiley.

Ardener, E. 1982. Social anthropology, language and reality. In *Semantic anthropology*. ASA Monographs 22 (ed.) D. Parkin. London: Academic Press.

Ardener, S. 1978. Introduction: the nature of women in society. In *Defining females* (ed.) S. Ardener. London: Croom Helm.

Ariès, P. 1974. *Western attitudes toward death from Middle Ages to the present.* Baltimore: John Hopkins University Press.

Arens, J. & van Beurden, J. 1988(1977). *Jhagrapur. Poor peasants and women in a village in Bangladesh.* Amsterdam: Arens & van Beurden.

Aziz, K.M.A. 1979. *Kinship in Bangladesh*. Dacca: International Cenre for Diarrhoeal Disease Research, Bangladesh.

Aziz, K.M.A. & Maloney, C. 1985. *Life stages, gender and fertility in Bangladesh.* Dhaka: International Centre for Diarrhoeal Disease Research, Bangladesh.

Babcock, B.A. 1978. Introduction. In *The reversible world: symbolic inversion in art and society* (ed.) B.A. Babcock. London: Cornell University Press.

Babcock, B.A. 1984. Arrange me into disorder: Fragments and reflections on ritual clowning. In *Rite, drama, festival, spectacle. Rehearsals toward a theory of cultural performance* (ed.) J.J. McAloon. Philadelphia: Institute for the Study of Human Issues.

Bakhtin, M. 1986 (1965). *Rabelais och skrattets historia.* Grabo: Anthropos.

Bakhtin, M. 1991. *Det dialogiska ordet.* Grabo: Anthropos.

Bangladesh at a glance. 1980. Chittagong: Literature Division.

Bateson, G. 1956. The message "this is play". In *Group processes*. Transactions of the second conference. New York: Josiah Macey Jr. Foundation.

Beck, B.E.F. 1969. Colour and heat in South Indian ritual. *Man* **4**, 553–573.

Bellah, R.N. 1979. New religious consciousness and the crises of modernity. In *Interpretative social science* (eds.) P. Rabinow & W.M. Sullivan. Berkeley: University of California Press.

Bennett, L. 1983. *Dangerous wives and sacred sisters. Social and symbolic roles of high-caste women in Nepal*. New York: Columbia University Press.

Benveniste, E. 1986. *Problems in general linguistics*. (Miami Linguistics Series No. 8, 195–237). Coral Gables, Florida: University of Miami Press.

Berger, J. 1977 (1971). *Ways of seeing*. Harmondsworth: Pelican.

Bertocci, P.J. 1970. *Ellusive villages: social structure and community organisation in the rural East Pakistan*. Unpublished PhD thesis. East Lansing: Michigan State University.

Bertocci, P.J. 1972. Community structure and social rank in two villages in Bangladesh. *Contributions to Indian sociology* (n.s.) **6**, 28–52.

Bertocci, P.J. 1974. Rural communities in Bangladesh: Hajipur and Tinapara. In *South Asia: seven community profiles* (ed.) C. Maloney. New York: Holt, Rinehart and Winston.

Bertocci, P.J. 1977. *Notes on the political culture of Bangladesh*. Unpublished MS.

Bertocci, P.J. 1984. Bengalis. In *Muslim peoples. A world ethnographic survey* (ed.) R.V. Weekes. Westport, Connecticut: Greenwood Press.

Bettelheim, B. 1987 (1960). *The informed heart*. Hammondsworth: Penguin Books.

Blair, J. 1981. Private parts in public places: the case of actresses. In *Women and space* (ed.) S. Ardener. London: Croom Helm.

Blanchet, T. 1984. *Women, pollution and marginality. Meanings and rituals of birth in rural Bangladesh*. Dhaka: The University Press Limited.

Blanchet, T. 1986. *Marriage and divorce in Bengali Muslim society*. Unpublished MS. Dhaka.

Bloch, M. & Parry, J.P. 1982. Introduction. In *Death and the regeneration of life* (eds.) M. Bloch & J.P. Parry. Cambridge: Cambridge University Press.

Boon, J.A. 1987. *Other tribes, other scribes. Symbolic anthropology in the comparative study of cultures, histories, religions, and texts*. Cambridge: Cambridge University Press.

Bossen, L. 1988. Toward a theory of marriage: the economic anthropology of marriage payment. *Ethnology* **27**, 127–143.

Bourdieu, P. 1983. Erving Goffman, discoverer of the infinitely small. *Theory, Culture and Society* **2**, 112–113.

Bourdieu, P. (1977) 1986. *Outline of a theory of practice*. Cambridge: Cambridge University Press.

Bourdieu, P. 1987. *False dichotomies*. Lecture given on 20th May in Stockholm.

Broady, D. 1990. Sociologi och epistemologi. Om Pierre Bourdieus författarskap och den historiska epistemologin. Stockholm: HLS Förlag.

Bruner, E.M. 1986. Ethnography of narrative. In *The anthropology of experience* (ed.) V.W. Turner & E.M. Bruner. Urbana: University of Illinois Press.

Callaway, H. 1978. 'The most essentially female function of all': giving birth. In *Defining females* (ed.) S. Ardener. London: Croom Helm.

Campbell, J.G. 1976. *Saints and householders: a study of Hindu ritual and myth among the Kangra Rajputs*. Kathmandu: Bibliotheca Himalayica, Ratna Pustak Bhandar.

Cantlie, A. 1981. The moral significance of food among Assamese Hindus. In *Culture and morality. Essays in the honour of Christopher von Fürer-Haimendorf* (ed.) A.C. Mayer. Delhi: Oxford University Press.

Cantlie, A. 1984. *The Assamese*. London: Curzon Press.

Cantlie, A. 1988–89. *Personal communication*.

Carstairs, G.M. 1957. *The twice born: a study of a community of high-caste Hindus*. London: Hogarth Press.

Caplan, L. 1984. Bridegroom price in urban India: class, caste and 'dowry evil' among Christians in Madras. *Man* **19**, 216–233.

Carroll, L. 1979. The Muslim family laws ordinance, 1961: provisions and procedures. *Contributions to Indian Sociology* (n.s.) **13**, 117–142.

Carter, A.C. 1982. Hierarchy and the concept of the person in Western India. In *Concepts of person. Kinship, caste and marriage in India* (eds. A'. Östör, L. Fruzzetti & S. Barnett. London: Harvard University Press.

Caton, S.C. 1987. Contributions of Roman Jakobson. In *Annual Review of Anthropology* **16**, 223–260.

Census of India, 1911. Bengal, Bihar, Orissa and Sikkim. Part 1. 1913. By O'Malley, L.S.S. Calcutta.

Chaudhuri, N.C. 1965. *The continent of Circe*. Delhi: Jaico Publishing House.

Chen, L., Gersche, M.C., Chowdhury, A.I. & Mosley, W.H. 1974. *Maternal mortality in rural Bangladesh*. Dacca The Ford Foundation.

Claquin, P., Rahman, S. & Begum, F. 1982. *A study of body concepts and beliefs regarding the anatomy and physiology of sexual, reproductive and digestive organs among some rural Bangladeshi women*. Dacca: International Centre for Diarhoeal Disease Research.

Clark, K. & Holquist, M. 1984. *Mikhail Bakhtin*. Cambridge, Mass.: Harvard University Press.

Cohen, A.P. 1985. *The symbolic construction of community*. London: Tavistock Publications.

Cohn, B.S. 1971. *India: the social anthropology of a civilization*. Chicago: Chicago University Press.

Cragg, K. 1956. *The call of the minaret*. Oxford: Oxford University Press.

Crapanzano, V. 1987. Editorial. *Journal of Cultural Anthropology* **2**, 179–189.

Crapanzano, V. 1980. *Tuhami, portrait of a Moroccan*. Chicago: University of Chicago Press.

Csordas, T.J. 1989. Embodiment as a paradigm for anthropology. *Ethos* **18**, 5–47.

Dar, S.N. 1982 (1969). *Costumes of India and Pakistan. A historical and cultural study*. Bombay: D.B. Taraporevala Sons.

Das, Ch. 1927. Loves of Radha and Krishna. In *Eastern lore*. London.

Das, V. 1976. The uses of liminality: society and cosmos in Hinduism. *Contributions to Indian Sociology* (n.s.) **10**, 245–263.

Das, V. 1979. Reflections on the social constructions of adulthood. In *Identity and adulthood in India* (ed.) S. Kakar. Delhi: Oxford University Press.

Das, V. 1985. Paradigms of body symbolism: an analysis of selected themes in Hindu culture. In *Indian religion* (eds.) R. Burghart & A. Cantlie. London: Curzon Press.

David, K. 1980. Hidden powers: culture, socio-economic accounts of Jaffna women. In *The powers of Tamil women* (ed.) S.S. Wadley. Syracuse: Maxwell School of Citizenship and Public Affairs.

Davis, M. 1983. *Rank and rivalry: the politics of inequality in rural West Bengal*. Cambridge: Cambridge University Press.

Demographic yearbook. 1990 (1988). New York: United Nations.

Douglas, M. 1970 (1966). *Purity and danger. An analysis of concepts of pollution and taboo*. Harmondsworth: Pelican Books.

Dufferin, (Lord). 1888. *Conditions of the people of India. Bengal, Assam, Punjab, Central Provinces, North & West Provinces, Oudh, Bombay*. (Appendix A to No. 2). London: India Office Library and Records.

Dumont, L. 1966. Marriage in India: the present state of the question, part 3. *Contributions to Indian Sociology* (n.s.) **9**, 90–114.

Dumont, L. 1980. *Homo hierarchicus. The caste system and its implications*. Chicago: University of Chicago.

Eichinger Ferro-Luzzi, G. 1981. *Abhiseka*, the Indian rite that defies definition. *Anthropos* **76**, 707–742.

Ellickson, J. 1972. *A believer among believers; a village in Bangladesh*. Ph.D. thesis. East Lansing: Michigan State University.

Ewing, K.P. 1988. Glossary of selected terms. In *Shariat and ambiguity in South Asian Islam* (ed.) K.P. Ewing. Berkeley: University of California.

Fajans, J. 1983. Shame, social action and the person among the Baining. *Ethos* **11**, 166–180.

Fernandez, J.W. 1980. Reflections on looking into mirrors. *Semiotica* **30**, 27–39.

Fernandez, J.W. 1985. Exploded worlds–text as a metaphor for ethnography (and vice versa). *Dialectical Anthropology* **10**, 15–26.

Firth, R.W. 1975. *Symbols: public and private*. Ithaca: Cornell University Press.

Fortes, M. 1983. Problems of identity and person. In *Identity: personal and sociocultural* (ed.) A. Jacobson-Widding. Uppsala: Almqvist & Wiksell.

Foster, S.N. 1986. Reading Pierre Bourdieu. *Cultural Anthropology* **1**, 103–109.

Fruzzetti, L. 1975. *Conch-shells bangles, iron bangles: an analyses of women, marriage and ritual in Bengali society*. Ph D thesis. University of Minnesota.

Fruzzetti, L. & Östör, A'. 1976a. Seed and earth: cultural analysis of kinship in a Bengali town. *Contributions to Indian Sociology* (n.s.) **10**, 97–132.

Fruzzetti, L. & Östör, A'. 1976b. Is there structure to north Indian kinship terminology? *Contributions to Indian Sociology* (n.s.) **10**, 63–261.

Fruzzetti, L. & Östör A'. 1982. Bad blood in Bengal: category and affect in the study of kinship, caste and marriage. In *Concepts of person. Kinship, caste and marriage in India*. (eds.) A'. Östör, L. Fruzzetti & S. Barnett. London: Harvard University Press.

Gaborieau, M. 1985. From Al-Beruni to Jinnah. Idiom, ritual and ideology of the Hindu–Muslim confrontation in South Asia. *Anthropology Today* **1**, 7–14.

Ganguly, D. 1982. Where there's lady of the night in every family. *Bangkok Post* 18th October.

Gazetteer of the Faridpur District. 1925. By O'Malley, L.S.S. Calcutta: C.I.E.

Godden, J. & Godden, R. 1972. *Shiva's pigeons. An experience of India*. London: Chatto Windus.

Golomb, L. 1985. *An anthropology of curing in multiethnic Thailand*. Urbana: University of Illinois Press.

Goffman, E. 1975. *Asylums*. Harmondsworth: Penguin Books.

Goffman, E. 1979. *Gender advertisments*. New York: Harper & Row.

Gorfain, P. 1986. Play and the problem of knowing in Hamlet: an excursion into interpretative anthropology. In *The anthropology of experience* (eds.) V.W. Turner & E.M. Bruner. Urbana: University of Illinois Press.

Greenough, P.R. 1983. Indulgence and abundance as Asian peasant values: a Bengali case in point. *The Journal of Asian Studies* **XLII**, 831–850.

Guhathakurta, M. 1988–1990. *Personal communication*.

Handelman, D. 1979. Is Naven ludic? *Social Analysis* **1**, 177–191.

Harris, G.G. 1989. Concepts of individual, self, and person in description and analysis. *American Anthropologist* **91**, 599–612.

Hastrup, K. 1978. The semantics of biology: virginity. In *Defining females* (ed.) S. Ardener. London: Croom Helm.

Hastrup, K. 1987. Fieldwork among friends: ethnographic exchange within the Northern civilization. In *Anthropology at home* (ed.) A. Cohen. London: Tavistock Publications.

Hatti, N. (n.d.). *Marriage among Havyak Brahmins and Namdhari Naiks*. Unpublished MS. Lund: Ekonomisk historiska institutionen, Lunds Universitet.

Hatti, N. & Ohlsson, R. 1983. *Age at marriage in India: a study of sirsi taluk, Karnataka, during the period 1961–1979* (Meddelande **31**). Lund: Ekonomisk historiska institutionen, Lunds universitet.

Hershman, P. 1974. Hair, sex and dirt. *Man* **9**, 274–298.

Herzfeld, M. 1987. *Anthropology through looking glass*. Cambridge: Cambridge University Press.

Hirschon, R. 1978. Open body/closed space: the transformation of female sexuality. In *Defining females* (ed.) S. Ardener. London: Croom Helm.

Hodder, I. 1982. *The present past. An introduction to anthropology for archeologists.* London: B.T. Batsford.

Hussain, M.B. 1988. Back to dark ages. *Vigil India* **9**, 8–14

Inden, R.B. 1976. *Marriage and rank in Bengali culture. A history of caste and clan in Middle period Bengal.* Berkeley: University of California Press.

Inden, R.B. & Nicholas, R.W. 1977. *Kinship in Bengali culture.* Chicago: Chicago University Press.

In praise of Krishna. Songs from the Bengali. 1967. Translated by E.C. Dimock, Jr. & D. Levertov. Chicago: University of Chicago Press.

Jackson, M. 1983a. Knowledge of the body. *Man* **18**, 327–345.

Jackson, M. 1983b. Thinking through the body: an essay on understanding metaphor. *Social Analysis* December, 127–149.

Jacobson-Widding, A. (ed.) 1983. *Identity: personal and socio-cultural. A symposium.* Uppsala Studies in Cultural Anthropology No. 5. Stockholm: Almqvist & Wiksell.

Jacobson-Widding, A. 1984. *African folk models and their appliction.* African Studies Programme, Department of Cultural Anthropology. Uppsala: Uppsala University.

Jensen, K.M. 1981. Method and field work in village level research: the Bangladesh case. *Asian Affairs* (Dhaka) **3**, 1–24.

Jensen, K.M. 1984/85. The basis of local level politics in Bangladesh. A case study from North Bengal. *Årskrift for etnografi.* Aarhus.

Kakar, S. 1978. *The inner world: a psycho-analytic study of childhood and society in India.* Delhi: Oxford University Press.

Kakar, S. 1984. *Shamans, mystics and doctors. A psychological inquiry into India and its healing traditions.* London: Unwin Paperback.

Kapferer, B. 1984. The ritual process and the problem of reflexivity in Sinhalese demon exorcism. In *Rite, drama festival, spectacle. Rehearsals toward a theory of cultural performance* (ed.) J.J. McAloon. Philadelphia: Institute for the Study of Human Issues.

Kapferer, B. 1986. Performance and the structuring of meaning and experience. In *Anthropology of Experience* (eds.) V.W. Turner & E.M. Bruner. Urbana: University of Illinois Press.

Karp, I. 1987. Laughter at marriage: subversion in performance. In *Transformations of African marriage* (eds.) D. Parkin & D. Nyamwaya. Manchester: University Press.

Keesing, R.M. 1975. *Kin groups and social structure.* New York: Holt, Rinehart and Winston.

Keyes, Ch. 1987. From death to birth. Ritual process and Buddhist meanings in Northern Thailand. *Folk* **29**, 181 –206.

Khan, Z.R. & Arafeen, H.K. 1988. Prostitution in Bangladeash. A study. *The Journal of Social Studies* **41**, 1–28.

Khare, R.S. 1975. Embedded affinity and consaguineal ethos: two properties of the northern kinship system. *Contributions to Indian Sociology* (n.s.) **9**, 245–261.

Khare, R.S. 1976. *The Hindu hearth and home: culinary systems old and new in North India.* New Delhi: Vikas Publishing House.

Khare, R.S. 1982. From *kanya* to *mata*: aspects of the cultural language of kinship in Northern India. In *Concepts of person. Kinship, caste and marriage in India.* (eds.) A'. Östör, L. Fruzzetti & S. Barnett. London: Harvard University Press.

Kirkpatrick, J. 1980. *The sociology of an Indian hospital ward.* Calcutta: South Asian Books.

Kolenda, P. 1982. Widowhood among "Untouchable" Chuhras. In *Concepts of person. Kinship, caste and marriage in India.* (eds.) A'. Östör, L. Fruzzetti & S. Barnett. London: Harvard University Press.

Kolenda, P. 1984. Woman as tribute, woman as flower: images of "woman" in weddings in north and south India. *American Ethnologist* **11**, 98–116.

Kondo, D. 1986. Dissolution and reconstitution of self: implications for anthropological epistemology. *Cultural Anthropology* **1**, 74–88.

Kotalová, J. 1984. *Personal and domestic hygiene in rural Bangladesh.* Stockholm: Swedish International Development Authority.

Kotalová, J. 1988 (1986). From anomaly to "acceptance"–the change in the perception of the identity of a female anthropologist. *Etnofor* **1**, 82–89 (*Antropologiska studier* nos. **38–39**, 56–60).

Lamaison, P. 1986. From rules to strategies: an interview with Pierre Bourdieu. *Cultural Anthropology* **1**, 110–120.

Lannoy, R. 1975. *The speaking tree. A study of Indian culture and society.* London: Oxford University Press.

Leach, E. 1982. *Social anthropology.* Glasgow: William Collins, Fontana Paperbacks.

Leaf, J.M. 1979. *Man, mind, and science. A history of anthropology.* New York: Columbia University Press.

Lévi-Strauss, C. 1967 (1963). *Structural anthropology.* Garden City: Anchor Book, Doubleday & Comp.

Lévi-Strauss, C. 1969. *The elementary structures of kinship.* Boston: Beacon Press.

Lewis, O. 1958. *Village life in northern India. Studies in a Delhi village.* Urbana.

Lindenbaum, S. 1965. *Infant care in rural East Pakistan.* Technical report. Dacca: Cholera Research Laboratory .

Lindenbaum, S. 1968. Woman and the left hand: social status and symbolism in East Pakistan. *Mankind* **6**, 537–543.

Lindenbaum, S. 1975. The value of women. In *Bengal in the 19th and 20th centuries* (ed.) J.R. McLane (South Asian Series, Occasional Paper **25**, 75–85). East Lansing: Michigan State University.

Lindenbaum, S. 1976. The 'last course': nutrition and anthropology in Asia. In *Nutrition and anthropology in action* (ed.) T.K. Fitzgerald. Assen: van Gorcum.

Lindenbaum, S. 1981. Implications for women of changing marriage transactions in Bangladesh. *Studies in Family Planning* **12**, 394–401.

Madan, T.N. 1972. Religious ideology in a plural society: the Muslims and Hindus of Kashmir. *Contributions to Indian Sociology* (n.s.), **6**, 106–141.

Majupuria, T.C. & Majupuria, I. 1978. *Sacred and useful plants and trees of Nepal.* Kathmandu: Sahayogi Prakashan.

Maloney, C., Aziz, K.M.A. & Sarkar, P. 1981. *Beliefs and fertility in Bangladesh.* Dacca: International Cholera Research Laboratory Bangladesh.

Maloney, C. 1985. Why does Bangladesh remain so poor? Part 1: The situation and efforts to change it. *University Field Staff International Reports* No. **29** (CM–1–85).

Marcus, G.E. & Fischer, M.M.J. 1986. *Anthropology as cultural critique. An experimental moment in the human sciences.* Chicago: University of Chicago Press.

Marglin, F.A. 1981. Kings and wives: the separation of status and royal power. *Contributions to Indian Sociology* (n.s.) **15**, 155–181.

Marriott, M. 1976. Hindu transactions: diversity without dualism. In *Transaction and meaning* (ed.) B. Kapferer. Philadelphia: Institute for the Study of Human Issues.

Mauss, M. 1950 (1934). Les techniques du corps. *Sociologie et Anthropologie.* Paris: Presses Universitaires de France.

Mauss, M. 1968 (1938). A category of the human spirit (a translation by L.Krader of "Une catégorie de l'esprit humain: La notion de personne, celle de 'moi'"). *Psychoanalytical Review* 55, 457–490.

Mauss, M. 1969 (1954). *The Gift. Forms and functions of exchange in archaic so-cieties*. London: Routledge & Kegan Paul.

McGilvray, D.B. 1980. Review of Inden & Nicholas "Kinship in Bengali cuture". *Man* **15**, 397–398.

Mead, G.H. 1934. *Mind, self, and society*. Chicago: University of Chicago Press.

Moore, H.L. 1986. *Space, text and gender. An anthropological study of Marakwet of Kenya*. Cambridge: Cambridge University Press.

Morgan, S.S. 1984. Borges's immortal: metaritual, metaliterature, metaperformance. In *Rite, drama, festival, spectacle. Rehearsals toward a theory of cultural perform-ance* (ed.) J.J. McAloon. Philadelphia: Institute for the Study of Human Issues.

Morsey, S. A. 1978. Sex differences and folk illness in an Egyptian village. In *Women in the Muslim world* (eds.) L. Beck & N. Keddie. Cambridge, Mass.: Harvard Uni-versity Press.

Murphy, Ch.P.H. 1986. Piety and honor: the meaning of Muslim feasts in Old Delhi. In *Food, society, and culture* (eds.) R.S. Khare & M.S.A. Rao. Durham: Carolina Ac-ademic Press.

Murshid, G. 1988. *Bengali–English–Bengali Dictionary*. London: Ruposhi Bangla.

Muslim, S. 1973–1975. *Sahih Muslim: being traditions of the sayings and doings of the Prophet*. Lahore.

Myerhoff, B.G. 1979. *Number our days*. New York.

Myerhoff, B.G. 1984. A death in due time: construction of self and culture in ritual drama. In *Rite, drama, festival, spectacle. Rehearsals toward a theory of cultural performance* (ed.) J.J. McAloon. Philadelphia: Institute for the Study of Human Is-sues.

News Letter 1987. Editor's Corner. (Research Center for Women Studies **8**, (Nos. 3 & 4, 1–14). Delhi.

Obeyesekere, G. 1976. The impact of Ayurvedic ideas on the culture and the individual in Sri Lanka. In *Asian medical systems* (ed.) Ch. Leslie. Berkeley: University of California Press.

Obeyesekere, G. 1981. *Medusa's hair: an essay on personal symbols and religious ex-perience*. Chicago: University of Chicago Press.

O'Flaherty, W. 1976. *The origins of evil in Hindu mythology*. Berkeley: University of California Press.

O'Hanlon, R. 1988. Recovering the subject. Subaltern studies and histories of resist-ance in colonial South Asia. *Modern Asian Studies* **22**, 189–224.

Östör, A'., Fruzzetti L. & Barnett S. (eds.). 1982. *Concepts of person. Kinship, caste and marriage in India*. London: Harvard University Press.

Parkin, D. 1982. Introduction. In *Semantic anthropology*. ASA Monograph **22** (ed.) D. Parkin. London: Academic Press.

Parkin, D. 1984. Political language. *Annual Review of Anthropology* **13**, 345–365.

Parkin, D. 1988. *Advanced theory in anthropology*. Lectures given at Department of Sociology and Anthropology at School of Oriental and African Studies, London.

Pitt-Rivers, J.A. 1977. *The fate of Shechem, or the politics of sex: essays in the anthro-pology of the Mediterranean*. Cambridge: Cambridge University Press.

Pitt-Rivers, J.A. 1979 (1973). The kith and the kin. In *The character of kinship* (ed.) J. Goody. Cambridge: Cambridge University Press.

Prindle, C. 1988. Occupation and orthopraxy in Bengali rank. In *Shariat and ambiguity in South Asian Islam* (ed.) K.P. Ewing. Berkeley: University of California Press.

Ramanuyan, A.K. 1989. Is there an Indian way of thinking? An informal essay. *Contri-butions to Indian Sociology* (n.s.) **23**, 41–58.

Rao, A.S. 1988. Rajastan sati: sad truths. *Vigil India*. February, 8–14.

Reynolds, H.B. 1983. The auspicious married woman. In *The powers of Tamil women* (ed.) S.S. Wadley. Syracuse: Maxwell School of Citizenship and Public Affairs.

Rhodes, L.A. 1989. Review article *"Paglami*: ethnopsychiatric knowledge in Bengal" by D.P. Bhattacharayya. 1986. Syracuse, New York: Syracuse University Press. *The Journal of Asian Studies* **48**, 194–195.

Ricoeur, P. 1971. The model of the text: meaningful action considered as a text. *Social Research* **11**, 529–562.

Rizvi, N. 1979. *Rural and urban food behavior in Bangladesh. An anthropological perspective to the problem of malnutrition*. PhD thesis. Los Angeles: University of California.

Roland, A. 1988. *In search of self in India and Japan. Toward a cross-cultural psychology*. Princeton: Princeton University Press.

Rolt, F. 1991. *On the brink in Bengal*. London: John Murray.

Rosaldo, R. 1983. Grief and a headhunter's rage: on the cultural force of emotions. In *Text, play, and story: the construction and reconstruction of self and society*. 1983 Proceedings of the American Ethnological Society (eds.) E.M. Bruner & S. Plattner. Washington, D.C.: American Ethnological Society.

Roy, M. 1975. *Bengali women*. Chicago: University of Chicago Press.

Ruzicka, L.T. & Chowdhury, A.K.M. 1978. Vital events, migration and marriages–1976. In *Demographic surveillance system–Matlab*. Dhaka: Cholera Research Laboratory.

Schaffer, T. 1986. *Profile of women in Bangladesh*. Dhaka: US Agency for International Development.

Schneider, D.M. 1980. *American kinship: a cultural account*. Chicago: University of Chicago Press.

Schwartzman, H.B. 1978. *Transformations. The anthropology of children's play*. New York: Plenum.

Sen, S. 1971. *An etymological dictionary of Bengali c. 1000–1800 A.D.* Calcutta: Eastern Publishers.

Selwyn, T. 1979. Images of reproduction: an analysis of a Hindu marriage ceremony. *Man* **14**, 684 –698.

Selwyn, T. 1981. Adharma. *Contributions to Indian Sociology* (n.s.) **15**, 381–400.

Sharma, U. 1978. Women and their affines: the veil as a symbol of separation. *Man* **13**, 13 –33.

Sharma U. 1986. *Women's work, class and the urban household. A study of Shimla, North India*. London: Tavistock Publications.

Shurreef, J. 1973 (1863). *Qanoon-e-Islam, customs of the Mussalmans of India*. Lahore: Al Irshad.

Singer, M. 1984. *Man's glassy essence: explorations in semiotic anthropology.* Bloomington: Indiana University Press.

Solshenitsyn, A. 1969. *Cancer ward*. New York: Dial Press.

Staff appraisal report Bangladesh. Fourth population and health project. 1991. Document of The World Bank. Report No. 9400–BD.

Stein, D.K. 1978. Women to burn: suttee as a normative institution. *Signs* **4**, 253–268.

Steinmeaz, H. 1977. *Bombay handbook*. Bombay: American Women's Association.

Strathern, A. 1979. *We are all of one father here': models of descent in New Guinea Highlands societies*. (The Queen's University Papers in Social Anthropology, ed. J. Blacking. **4**, 141–5). Belfast.

Tambiah, S.J. 1973. Dowry and bridewealth and the property rights of women in South Asia. In *Bridewealth and dowry* (eds.) J.R. Goody & S.J. Tambiah. Cambridge: Cambridge University Press.

Tambiah, S.J. 1974. From varna to caste through mixed unions. In *The Character of kinship* (ed.) J. Goody. Cambridge: Cambridge University Press.

Tapper, R. & Tapper, N. 1986. "Eat this, it'll do you a power of good": food and commensality among Durrani Pashtuns. *American Ethnologist* **13**, 62–79.

Tapper, R. & Tapper, N. 1987. The birth of the Prophet: ritual and gender in a Turkish Islam. *Man* **22**, 69–92.

Tapper, N. 1988. *Romantic love and illicit sex: the Middle Eastern case*. A paper presented at the departmental seminar, Department of Sociology and Anthropology, School of Oriental and African Studies, London.

Tham, A. 1989. Personal communication.

Thompson, C. 1983. Women, fertility and the worship of Gods in a Hindu village. In *Women's religious experience* (ed.) P. Holden. London: Croom Helm.

Toren, Ch. 1983. Children's perceptions of gender and hierarchy in Fiji. In *Acquiring culture: cross culture studied in child development* (eds.) G. Jahoda & I.M. Lewis. London: Croom Helm.

Thorp, J.P. 1982. The Muslim farmers of Bangladesh and Allah's creation of the world. *Asian Folklore Studies* **XLI**, 201–215.

Trevarthen, C. & Logotheti, K. 1989. Child in society, and society in children: the nature of basic trust. In *Societies at peace. Anthropological perspective* (eds.) S. Howell & R. Willis. London: Routledge.

Turner, V. 1967. *The forest of symbols. Aspects of Ndembu ritual*. Ithaca: Cornell University Press.

Turner, V. 1969. *The ritual process: structure and antistructure*. Harmondsworth: Penguin.

Turner, V. 1982. *From ritual to theatre. The human seriousness of play*. New York: Performing Arts Journal Publications.

Turner, V. 1984. Liminality and the performative genres. In *Rite, drama, festival, spectacle. Rehearsals toward a theory of cultural performance* (ed.) J.J. McAloon. Philadelphia: Institute for the Study of Human Issues.

Underwood, K.C. 1982. *The boundaries of intimacy: interactions among women in Madras, India* (The Kroeber Anthropological Society Nrs. **61 & 62**). Berkeley: University of California.

Upadhyaya, K.D. 1964–65. Indian botanical folklore. *Asian Folklore Studies* **23**, 15–34.

van der Veen, K.W. 1972. *I give thee my daughter: a study of marriage and hierarchy among the Anavil Brahmans of south Gujarat*. Assen: van Gorcum.

van Gennep, A. 1977 (1909). *The rites of passage*. London: Routledge and Kegan Paul.

van Schendel, W. 1981. *Peasant mobility. The odds of life in rural Bangladesh*. Assen: van Gorcum.

Vattimo, G. 1988. Hermeneutics as *koine. Theory Culture and Society* **5**, 402–403.

Vieille, P. 1978. Iranian women in family alliance and sexual politics. In *Women in the Muslim world* (eds.) L. Beck & N. Keddie. Cambridge, Mass.: Harvard University Press.

Vikasini 1988. Widow burning. **2**, 4–5.

Vygotsky, L. 1986 (1934). *Thought and language*. Cambridge, Mass.: The MIT Press.

Wadley, S. S. 1980. Introduction. In *The powers of Tamil women* (ed.) S.S. Wadley. Syracuse: Maxwell School of Citizenship and Public Affairs.

Walker, B. 1983 (1968). *Hindu world. An encyclopedic survey. Hinduism*. London: Allen Unwin.

Walraven, R. 1985. *Social stratification in a Bangladesh village. Report from a Minor Research Task within EIP*. Stockholm: University of Stockholm, Department of Social Anthropology.

Weekes, R.V. 1984. Introduction. In *Muslim peoples. A world ethnographic survey* (ed.) R.V. Weekes. Westport, Connecticut: Greenwood Press.

Weil, S. & Weil, M. 1987. Anthropology becomes home; home becomes anthropology. In *Anthropology at home*. ASA Monograph **25** (ed.) A. Cohen. London: Tavistock Publications.

Whyte, S.R. 1981. Men, women and the misfortune in Bunyole. *Man* **16**, 350–366.

Winslow, D. 1980. Rituals of first menstruation in Sri Lanka. *Man* **15**, 603–625.